A-level

POLITICS: POLITICAL IDEAS

SECOND EDITION

Adam Tomes and Simon Lemieux

Every effort has been made to trace all copyright holders, but if any have been inadvertently overlooked, the Publishers will be pleased to make the necessary arrangements at the first opportunity.

Although every effort has been made to ensure that website addresses are correct at time of going to press, Hodder Education cannot be held responsible for the content of any website mentioned in this book. It is sometimes possible to find a relocated web page by typing in the address of the home page for a website in the URL window of your browser.

Hachette UK's policy is to use papers that are natural, renewable and recyclable products and made from wood grown in well-managed forests and other controlled sources. The logging and manufacturing processes are expected to conform to the environment regulations of the country of origin.

Orders: please contact Hachette UK Distribution, Hely Hutchinson Centre, Milton Road, Didcot, Oxfordshire, OX11 7HH. Telephone: +44 (0)1235 827827. Email: education@hachette.co.uk. Lines are open from 9 a.m. to 5 p.m., Monday to Friday. You can also order through our website: www.hoddereducation.co.uk

ISBN: 978 1 3983 8550 4

© Adam Tomes and Simon Lemieux 2023

First published in 2023 by
Hodder Education,
An Hachette UK Company
Carmelite House
50 Victoria Embankment
London EC4Y 0DZ

www.hoddereducation.co.uk

Impression number   10 9 8 7 6 5 4 3 2

Year   2027 2026 2025 2024

All rights reserved. Apart from any use permitted under UK copyright law, no part of this publication may be reproduced or transmitted in any form or by any means, electronic or mechanical, including photocopying and recording, or held within any information storage and retrieval system, without permission in writing from the publisher or under licence from the Copyright Licensing Agency Limited. Further details of such licences (for reprographic reproduction) may be obtained from the Copyright Licensing Agency Limited, www.cla.co.uk

Typeset in India by Integra Software Services Pvt., Ltd.

Illustrations by Integra Software Services Pvt., Ltd.

Printed and bound by CPI Group (UK) Ltd, Croydon, CR0 4YY

A catalogue record for this title is available from the British Library.

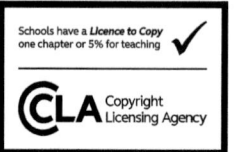

Get the most from this book

Everyone has to decide their own revision strategy, but it is essential to review your work, learn it and test your understanding. These Revision Notes will help you to do that in a planned way, topic by topic. Use this book as the cornerstone of your revision and don't hesitate to write in it – personalise your notes and check your progress by ticking off each section as you revise.

Tick to track your progress

Use the revision planner on pages 4 and 5 to plan your revision, topic by topic. Tick each box when you have:
+ revised and understood a topic
+ tested yourself
+ practised the exam questions and gone online to check your answers

You can also keep track of your revision by ticking off each topic heading in the book. You may find it helpful to add your own notes as you work through each topic.

Features to help you succeed

Exam tips
Expert tips are given throughout the book to help you polish your exam technique in order to maximise your chances in the exam.

Now test yourself
These short, knowledge-based questions provide the first step in testing your learning.

Key terms
Clear, concise definitions of essential key terms are provided where they first appear.

Making links
This feature identifies specific connections between topics and tells you how revising these will aid your exam answers.

Revision activities
These activities will help you to understand each topic in an interactive way.

Exam skills
These boxes highlight ways you can improve your exam technique, with examples.

Exam practice
Practice exam questions are provided for each topic. Use them to consolidate your revision and practise your exam skills.

Summaries
The summaries provide a quick-check bullet list for each topic.

Online
Go online to check your answers to the Now test yourself and Exam practice questions at www.hoddereducation.co.uk/myrevisionnotes

My Revision Notes: AQA A-level Politics: Political Ideas Second Edition

My revision planner

Introduction

Core ideologies

1 Liberalism
- 10 Origins of liberalism
- 10 Main beliefs of liberalism
- 11 Main strands of liberalism
- 19 Core ideas of liberalism
- 22 Agreement and tensions within liberalism

2 Conservatism
- 26 Origins of conservatism
- 28 Main beliefs of conservatism
- 28 Main strands of conservatism
- 34 Core ideas of conservatism
- 35 Agreement and tensions within conservatism

3 Socialism
- 41 Origins of socialism
- 41 Main beliefs of socialism
- 42 Historical materialism, class analysis and fundamental goals
- 45 The nature of socialism
- 47 Revisionist socialism
- 51 Core ideas of socialism
- 54 Tensions and agreements within socialism

Other ideologies

4 Nationalism
- 57 Origins of nationalism
- 58 Core concepts
- 59 Main strands of nationalism
- 68 Core ideas of nationalism
- 69 Key debates within nationalism

5 Feminism
- 72 Origins of feminism
- 72 Main waves of feminism
- 80 Core ideas of feminism
- 84 Key debates within feminism

6 Multiculturalism
- 87 Origins of multiculturalism
- 88 Debates around the nature of multiculturalism
- 91 Main strands of multiculturalism

Check your understanding and progress at www.hoddereducation.co.uk/myrevisionnotes

96 The critical view of multiculturalism
98 Core ideas of multiculturalism
100 Key debates within multiculturalism

7 Anarchism
103 Origins of anarchism
104 Main beliefs of anarchism
107 Main strands of anarchism
112 Core ideas of anarchism
115 Key debates within anarchism

8 Ecologism
118 Origins of ecologism
118 Main beliefs of ecologism
121 Main strands of ecologism
128 Core ideas of ecologism
131 Key debates within ecologism

134 Glossary

140 Index

Now test yourself answers and Exam practice answers at
www.hoddereducation.co.uk/myrevisionnotesdownloads

My Revision Notes: AQA A-level Politics: Political Ideas Second Edition

Countdown to my exams

6–8 weeks to go

- Start by looking at the specification. Make sure you know exactly what material you need to revise and the style of the examination. Use the revision planner on pp. 4 and 5 to familiarise yourself with the topics.
- Organise your notes, making sure you have covered everything on the specification. The revision planner will help you to group your notes into topics.
- Work out a realistic revision plan that will allow you time for relaxation. Set aside days and times for all the subjects that you need to study, and stick to your timetable.
- Set yourself sensible targets. Break your revision down into focused sessions of around 40 minutes, divided by breaks. These Revision Notes organise the basic facts into short, memorable sections to make revising easier.

REVISED

2–6 weeks to go

- Read through the relevant sections of this book and refer to the exam tips, summaries and key terms. Tick off the topics as you feel confident about them. Highlight those topics you find difficult and look at them again in detail.
- Test your understanding of each topic by working through the 'Now test yourself' questions and 'Revision activities' in the book. Look up the answers online at www.hoddereducation.co.uk/myrevisionnotesdownloads
- Make a note of any problem areas as you revise, and ask your teacher to go over these in class.
- Look at past papers. They are one of the best ways to revise and practise your exam skills. Write or prepare planned answers to the exam-style questions in the book. Check your answers online at www.hoddereducation.co.uk/myrevisionnotesdownloads.
- Try different revision methods. For example, you can make notes using mind maps, spider diagrams or flashcards.
- Track your progress using the revision planner and give yourself a reward when you have achieved your target.

REVISED

One week to go

- Try to fit in at least one more timed practice of an entire past paper and seek feedback from your teacher, comparing your work closely with the mark scheme.
- Check the revision planner to make sure you haven't missed out any topics. Brush up on any areas of difficulty by talking them over with a friend or getting help from your teacher.
- Attend any revision classes put on by your teacher. Remember, he or she is an expert at preparing people for examinations.

REVISED

The day before the examination

- Flick through these Revision Notes for useful reminders – for example, the exam tips and key terms.
- Check the time and place of your examination.
- Make sure you have everything you need – extra pens and pencils, tissues, a watch, bottled water.
- Allow some time to relax and have an early night to ensure you are fresh and alert for the examinations.

REVISED

Check your understanding and progress at www.hoddereducation.co.uk/myrevisionnotes

Introduction

Key things to know about studying AQA A-level Politics

This book covers all of Paper 3, Political Ideas. Paper 1, The Politics and Government of the UK, and Paper 2, The Government and Politics of the USA, and Comparative Politics, are covered in two other *My Revision Notes* books.

Remember that Paper 3 is worth a third of your A-level, so divide up your revision time evenly across all three papers.

As a student of A-level Politics, it is important that you know these five things about the examination:
+ the structure of the exam
+ the three assessment objectives
+ the command words used in Section A – explain, analyse, compare and evaluate (and what these terms mean)
+ the format of the extract-based essay question in Section B
+ the synoptic element for Section C

The structure of the exam

REVISED

Paper 3 on Political Ideas lasts for two hours. You are required to:
+ Answer **all three** Section A shorter-answer questions (total: 27 marks). There is one 9-marker on each of the three core political ideas – liberalism, conservatism and socialism – so all three must be revised.
+ Answer the Section B extract-based question (25 marks).
+ Answer the essay question on your optional ideology – nationalism, feminism, multiculturalism, anarchism or ecologism (25 marks). There is **no** choice of essay question, so you must revise your optional ideology thoroughly.

Assessment objectives

REVISED

Your answers will be marked by examiners who will look to see how well you have met the three assessment objectives. These are explained below:

Assessment objectives	Requirements
AO1: Knowledge and understanding	+ Identify/provide points related to the question. + Offer relevant examples referencing the key thinkers and the historical context in which they were writing. + Use relevant and appropriate political terminology from the thinkers, such as the 'harm principle' (John Stuart Mill, a key liberal thinker).
AO2: Analysis	+ Give a two-sided, balanced debate in the essay and the extract-based question. + Comment upon and explain any points made. + Identify tensions and different approaches within the same political idea, while noting that these are not contradictions so much as different ways of interpreting the same political idea.
AO3: Evaluation	+ Distinguish between strong and weak arguments, explicitly identifying which arguments/factors are most convincing and why. + Provide reasons for the judgements made. + Consider the issue of typicality and influence of the key thinkers on a particular political idea.

Command words in Section A

In Section A the question will start with the following words: *explain and analyse* three ways that liberals/conservatives/socialists view or define…

Explain means identify and describe a way, giving an example ideally based around a key thinker and then comment briefly on it: for example, quoting a key phrase or work, and explaining briefly the context of their opinion.

Analyse is a pretty open term; it involves taking your answer beyond simple explanation by examining the factor critically rather than just taking it at face value. What are the *implications* of this for other aspects of this political idea? For example, the view held by fundamentalist or revolutionary socialists such as Marx about capitalism meant that they argued for the common ownership of the means of production. Perhaps think of it as responding to the examiner's reaction of 'So what?' after you have explained or defined a way in which one thinker views a particular aspect of the political idea.

It often works well to approach the 9-mark questions chronologically and/or grouping thinkers by category. So, for liberalism, one paragraph could assess how classical liberals would approach the issue, followed by a second paragraph on how new liberals would view it, and a final paragraph focusing on feminist liberals. Note that you are not required to cite all key thinkers in your Section A answer, and probably lack the time to do so.

Don't include lots of examples of political events and party policies. The emphasis is very much on the ideas themselves, not whether or not they have been put into practice. This general principle also applies to Section B and Section C of the exam. This is different from the exam advice for Papers 1 and 2 where a range of relevant and often recent examples is required.

The extracts in Section B

As it is likely that the extracts will come from key thinkers themselves who hold contrasting views within a certain political idea (e.g. a classical liberal and a new liberal), the issue of reliability does not really arise because both thinkers will be accurately setting out their views. When dealing with provenance, therefore, focus on when and why they were writing, and their specific purpose. *Don't* provide generic comments about reliability, such as 'It is reliable as it was written by the author themselves.' Instead, it is much better to write something along the lines of 'Burke is offering a typical traditional conservative defence of the importance of established hierarchy but also duty in society.'

Ensure both extracts are analysed and compared in roughly equal detail. It can often work well to provide a brief overview of the key ideas/points in each extract in your introduction and to offer an initial judgement as to which extract is the more convincing. Short direct quotes from the extracts help to keep an answer focused, but you should avoid copying huge chunks of the extract. Use the extracts as 'springboards' to a wider discussion that they raise, but avoid writing a general essay on the question. The extracts must drive the answer.

Range and synopticity in Section C

It is really important that a wide range of key thinkers are included in your essay. While it is not essential that all thinkers are mentioned to gain top marks, you should include examples from all the main strands of the political idea. Thus, as a minimum, an essay on nationalism should make reference to a liberal nationalist (e.g. Rousseau) as well as a cultural nationalist (e.g. von Herder) and an anti-colonialist/pan-African thinker (e.g. Garvey). This will enable your answer to explore a wide range of views within the political idea. In addition, note that it is not required to include non-specified thinkers. While the examiner will give you credit when these are relevantly cited alongside set thinkers, it is certainly not expected even for top-level answers.

There must also be some brief synopticity in the essay – in other words, you need to reference material from other parts of the syllabus (i.e. Papers 1 and 2). But this should not be extensive and should occur almost automatically. For example, a discussion of the objectives of first-wave feminists would probably mention their campaign to secure the vote on an equal basis to men, which was finally achieved in 1928. This material is also covered in Paper 1 in the democracy and participation topic.

1 Liberalism

Liberalism is a political ideology with liberty and the individual (and their rights) at its core. It begins with the key question: when can governments or others intervene in the lives of others? The presumption is that humankind is free and unrestricted, unless there are solid and rational grounds for curtailing that freedom.

This chapter will explore the origins of liberalism, both classical and modern, and their key thinkers in relation to human nature, the state, society and the economy before looking at the similarities and differences between them.

Origins of liberalism

REVISED

+ The roots of liberalism can be found in the European Enlightenment of the seventeenth and eighteenth centuries.
+ Early liberalism argued that humans were born both free and morally equal and no one naturally has a right to rule over others. All laws and government must be **justified** and not accepted blindly or based purely on inherited tradition or custom. This directly attacked the natural form of government of the time, absolute monarchy.
+ It promoted a belief in reason, rather than faith, and advocated the importance of the individual and freedom.
+ Early liberalism was radical and potentially revolutionary, with its ideas central to the American Declaration of Independence of 1776 and the French Declaration of the Rights of Man and of the Citizen of 1789.
+ Liberalism has developed different variants. Classical or traditional liberalism dominated until the late nineteenth century and modern liberalism has dominated since that time.

Enlightenment An intellectual movement that opposed the medieval politics and philosophy of faith, superstition and religion.

Absolute monarchy When the monarch exercises arbitrary (unlimited) power over the people as God's representative on Earth. The concept of the 'divine right of kings' embodies this notion of royal absolutism.

> **Exam tip**
>
> When studying ideologies, it is often assumed that an idea is directly linked to the party of the same name (e.g. liberalism and the Liberal Democrats). However, liberal ideas can be found in a range of different parties including the Liberal Democrats, the Conservatives and Labour as well as both main parties in the USA.

Main beliefs of liberalism

REVISED

+ **Freedom and the individual**. Freedom is central to all liberals as it benefits the individual; however, there is debate among liberals about how to define freedom.
+ **Human nature**. Liberals have an optimistic view of human nature as rational and reasonable; however, classical liberals focus on humanity's natural qualities and the ability of the individual to satisfy their desires, whereas modern liberals focus on what the individual can become given the right conditions, such as a good education.
+ **The role of the state**. Classical liberals see a minimal role for the state, as it has the potential to restrict individual liberty. Modern liberals favour a more interventionist role for the state in order to ensure that everyone has the same life chances.
+ **Society**. Debates emerge in liberalism over how to protect a diverse and tolerant society, and over the nature of the relationship between society, freedom and the individual.

State A body that is sovereign within a defined territorial area, with a legitimate monopoly of the use of force.

Tolerant society A society that is willing to accept a wide range of moral values, lifestyles, faiths and beliefs.

+ **The economy.** One of the deepest debates among liberals is the role of the state in the economy. Classical liberals favour free-market capitalism to drive economic creativity and prosperity for all, whereas modern liberals favour state intervention in the economy to ensure that all can flourish. All liberals believe in the right to own private property, seeing it as an extension of individual freedom, but they disagree over how far others, such as the government through taxation, have some claims on that freedom.

> **Exam tip**
>
> Liberalism has evolved over time in reaction to events and other ideologies. It is worth keeping in mind how liberal ideas evolved in response to the emergence of modern, industrialised societies.

Main strands of liberalism

REVISED

Classical liberalism (late seventeenth to late nineteenth century)

Classical liberalism can be seen to have the following distinctive features:

+ **Radical politically.** Government by consent promoted the idea that government should represent and reflect the will of the people rather than be the master of the people. Note, though, that most early liberals rejected the concept of democracy. When talking about 'liberty for all', in reality they usually meant male owners of property. Furthermore, many eighteenth-century liberals did not extend the concept of liberty to enslaved people.
+ **Radical in gender terms (true for some classical liberals).** The optimistic view that all humans are rational was developed to include women by Mary Wollstonecraft in the eighteenth century.
+ **Egotistical individualism.** Humans are self-seeking, rational and independent, although this does involve practising restraint and some level of co-operation with others. Society is comprised of individuals rather than social groups.
+ **Negative freedom.** The belief in liberty leads classical liberals to define liberty in terms of absence of restraint, leaving the individual free to pursue their own view of the good life; the state can only legitimately intervene to prevent harm to others. John Locke, often seen as the founding father of liberalism, argued that humanity should embrace 'a State of perfect Freedom to order their Actions … as they think fit … without asking leave or depending on the Will of any other Man'.
+ **Night-watchman state.** The state must act only to protect 'the peace, safety and public good of the people', according to John Locke. It only has the right to impose its power on the basis of the harm principle in order to ensure the widest possible freedom. Any restrictions on liberty must be justified.
+ **Free-market capitalism.** Liberty and private property are intimately related. The market economy, based on property rights, can deliver prosperity for the individual and society provided there is free trade and competition. Unless people are free to make contracts, sell their labour, invest their incomes as they see fit and set up businesses, they are not really free. The state therefore must not interfere with free trade and competition by using subsidies, taxes or promoting monopolies. However, the state has a crucial role in ensuring that property is protected from theft and that contracts are enforced by an independent judiciary.

Egotistical individualism Humans naturally seek to advance their own happiness and interests. This selfish approach involves self-restraint and co-operation as the individual wants to have their rights respected, so in turn must respect the rights of others.

Negative freedom A concept of liberty or freedom that sees it as meaning an absence of constraint, described by the liberal thinker Isaiah Berlin as 'freedom from' rather than 'freedom to'.

Harm principle John Stuart Mill argued that the government can only rightfully extend its power over the individual to prevent actions or beliefs that bring harm to others. It cannot extend its power over the individual in relation to self-regarding actions to protect the individual's own good. For example, it is right to stop person A destroying the property of person B, but wrong to stop person A from destroying their own property.

1 Liberalism

> **Key thinker**
>
> ### John Locke (1632–1704)
>
> John Locke was a key thinker in classical liberalism, with his work, *Two Treatises of Government* (1690), attacking the idea that the monarchy has a natural right to rule over others and establishing a liberal justification for a minimal state.
>
> + Locke argued that humans are naturally free, equal and independent, and are not naturally under the **authority** of any other body or person.
> + He imagined life before the state – a **state of nature** – to understand why humankind created the state. Locke's state of nature is not a state of war but rather a state of peace.
> + Locke argued that in the state of nature humans are perfectly free. They are equal, with natural rights such as the right to property and bound by the law of nature where no one should harm another in their life, liberty or possessions.
> + In the state of nature, there would be clashes of interests between free individuals, which might limit individuals' ability to advance their own happiness. As rational beings, individuals would enter into a **social contract** to form the state so that it could act as a neutral umpire to resolve these clashes.
> + The state exists to protect and enhance natural rights. It only emerges because the people consent to create it.
> + The state reflects the consent of the people and that consent is ongoing. When the state breaks the contract by not protecting and enhancing natural rights, the people can withdraw their consent and replace the government.
> + The state is further limited by the principle of **constitutionalism**, with a clear separation of powers between the executive and legislature to prevent the abuse of power. The legislature should be the supreme power but is only a **fiduciary power**.
> + The state should represent directly the will of property-owning individuals.

> **Exam tip**
>
> It is worth comparing and contrasting the different attitudes of Locke and Hobbes to human nature and the state of nature to get a deeper understanding of both. Both embraced the concept of a social contract, but for Hobbes, human reason would lead humankind to settle upon a contract with a single supreme ruler.

> **Key thinker**
>
> ### Mary Wollstonecraft (1759–97)
>
> Mary Wollstonecraft was committed to extending liberal thinking, particularly in relation to gender equality in society, through her key work, *A Vindication of the Rights of Woman* (1792).
>
> + Wollstonecraft extended the optimistic view of human nature to both men and women. She pointed out how the existing state and society promoted the view that women were not rational because women had no **formal equality**. She commented that 'Virtue can only flourish among equals' and provocatively compared women to enslaved people.
> + Women should have formal equality: the right to property, as this right is crucial to freedom and **individualism**; the right to education, to allow reason to prosper; and the right to vote, to ensure that there really was government by consent.
> + Within marriage, women should be granted the right to divorce and protection against domestic violence. The right to property and employment meant that women would not need to marry out of financial necessity.
> + Wollstonecraft rejected the societal view that women are defined by their looks: 'Taught from infancy that beauty is woman's sceptre, the mind shapes itself to the body, and roaming round its gilt cage, only seeks to adorn its prison.'
> + By granting formal equality and giving women access to education, the state would increase society's resources of intellect, wisdom and morality to enable social and economic progress.

Authority The legitimate right to exercise power. For traditional conservatives, authority is placed in the natural elite, such as the monarchy and aristocracy, as they have the necessary wealth, status and power to govern for the benefit of others.

State of nature A concept used by political thinkers such as Locke and Hobbes to describe the hypothetical original characteristics of humankind and how people related to each other in a time before states and organised governments.

Social contract There is a contract between the individual and the government, where the individual agrees with the state to obey its laws and, in return, the state improves their life. The state is invalid *either* if there is no consent *or* if it fails to improve the individual's situation.

Constitutionalism The government must be legally limited in its powers by a constitution in order to protect freedom. This links in with the concept of the 'rule of law'.

Fiduciary power The state holds its power in trust and must act in the interests of and for the benefit of the people, otherwise the social contract is invalid.

Formal equality Equality under the law, as well as the principle that every individual is entitled to equal treatment in society.

Individualism The belief in the importance of the individual over the collective within political thought, which is central to liberalism, and also that the individual exists prior to society.

Check your understanding and progress at www.hoddereducation.co.uk/myrevisionnotes

- Wollstonecraft was also a key opponent of custom, **tradition** and practice that formed the basis for the **divine right of kings** and rule by the aristocracy. She argued these gave no basis for accepting laws or the government and were irrational, oppressive and ignorant.
- In its place, Wollstonecraft argued for **republicanism**, formal equality for all and a constitutional protection of individual rights.

Tradition A form of knowledge passed down through the generations as customs and habits. For their supporters, they provide security and stability in an uncertain world.

Divine right of kings The idea that a monarch is not subject to earthly authority but instead gains the right to rule directly from God.

Republicanism A republic is a political system without a monarch and emphasises citizens taking an active role in public and political life.

Making links

It is worth comparing Mary Wollstonecraft, who defended the revolution in France (1789), with the conservative thinker Edmund Burke's *Reflections on the Revolution in France* (1790) and his defence of custom, tradition and established practice.

Now test yourself
TESTED

1. According to Locke, when is it justified for the individual to seek to overthrow the government and replace it?
2. On what basis do classical liberals argue that the state should be limited?
3. Why can Wollstonecraft be seen as a radical for her time?

Key thinker

John Stuart Mill (1806–73)

John Stuart Mill provided the bridge between classical liberalism and modern liberalism by developing early liberal thinking on freedom and individualism. He is often described as a 'transitional liberal', embracing some aspects of classical liberalism, but also those of new liberalism. Among his key works are *On Liberty* (1859), *Utilitarianism* (1861) and *The Subjection of Women* (1869).

- Mill developed the concept of negative freedom, arguing that freedom was the absence of restraint as this leaves the individual free to pursue their own view of the good life.
- Governments should only make laws that restrict actions that harm others ('other-regarding actions'), not those that simply harm oneself ('self-regarding actions'). A modern example could be that laws against drink/drug driving (other regarding) are justified, but laws against alcoholism itself (self-regarding) are not.
- Mill saw liberty as more than a natural right. He saw it as the key to the ongoing development and learning of the individual, especially when they experience education. This focuses more on what the individual has the potential to become rather than on what they are now.
- Liberty is the driver of progress for the individual and allows them to achieve their **individuality**. This is best for the individual and also best for society because a 'diversity of character and culture' enables reasoned debate, discussion and argument to drive a society forward. Not surprisingly, as it can be an extension of individuality, Mill viewed eccentricity positively: 'The amount of eccentricity in a society has generally been proportional to the amount of genius, mental vigour, and moral courage it contained. That so few now dare to be eccentric marks the chief danger of the time' (*On Liberty*).
- In order to foster diversity, Mill argued that government and society should only be limited by the harm principle. In other words, government should not ban or restrict actions or lifestyles/religious beliefs that cause no harm to others. Mill attached great importance to education, criticising the **hedonism** of early liberal thinking. He distinguished between the lower pleasures (those of the body, such as eating and drinking) and the higher pleasures which involved the mind, such as doing a crossword or reading a high-brow novel: 'It is better to be a human being dissatisfied than a pig satisfied; better to be Socrates dissatisfied than a fool satisfied' (*Utilitarianism*).

Making links

If you are studying feminism as an optional political idea, Wollstonecraft is a good example of an early first-wave feminist, while fellow liberal feminist thinker, Betty Friedan, is better described as a second-wave feminist. You can use their arguments to inform your essay on feminism, but you must also refer to the set feminist thinkers.

Individuality Mill passionately believed in the uniqueness of each individual. Freedom was needed to allow them constantly to develop their distinctive talents, characteristics and knowledge.

Hedonism Happiness is the ultimate good and can be measured as pleasure and the absence of pain. This idea is based on the quantity of pleasure rather than the quality.

- The role of the state, via education, is to enable people constantly to improve their mind and so to increase their higher pleasures.
- Mill worried that Locke's principle of representative government could lead to 'tyranny of the majority' with the coming of universal suffrage, especially without a well-educated electorate. He feared the majority would infringe on the individualism of the minority by voting only for their own narrow-minded interests.
- Mill's solution was to promote representative democracy, with an educated electorate not making policy decisions themselves but instead choosing well-educated representatives to make decisions on their behalf. These representatives would aggregate all the demands of different individuals and parts of society to create broad, consensus decisions rather than strictly following the will of the majority.

> **Exam tip**
>
> John Stuart Mill's criticisms about the 'tyranny of the majority' work as a clear attack on direct democracy, especially the use of referendums in the UK and initiatives and propositions in the USA.

Is democracy compatible with liberalism?

Locke's view that government should only represent property-owning men and Mill's fears about democracy raise the debate about whether liberalism and democracy are compatible, as discussed in Table 1.1.

Table 1.1 Is democracy compatible with liberalism?

Yes	No
Democracy enhances individualism. Individuals use the vote rationally to shape the world. Exercise of the vote has an educational role for the individual.	Democracy may lead to the 'tyranny of the majority', especially where the people have not been educated. Universal suffrage should go hand in hand with universal education.
Democracy through regular, free and fair elections creates government by consent, a crucial principle of traditional liberalism.	Classical liberals wished to restrict the franchise to those with property and John Stuart Mill suggested giving more voting power to the educated, such as university graduates.
Democracy restricts the concentration of power by acting as a limit on the state – a belief that classical liberals support.	Representative democracy, rather than representative government or direct democracy, dilutes majority rule as the elected representatives make the decisions.

Modern (new/progressive) liberalism

Modern liberals question what is truly meant by liberty. This question was made particularly powerful by the rise of modern advanced societies and economies, where poverty appeared to restrict the individual's ability to develop, grow and pursue their own version of the good life.

Positive freedom

- Individualism was about the freedom not to allow self-seeking individuals to achieve their own pleasures, but to allow the individual to flourish and grow both morally and intellectually to achieve their own individuality – developmental individualism.
- Thomas Hill Green built on this to argue that in modern, capitalist societies, poverty and inequality should be tackled to 'maintain the conditions without which a free exercise of human faculties is impossible'.
- As a result, liberty needed to be redefined so it was no longer seen as absence of restraint but as positive freedom which would enable individuals so that they were free to achieve their individuality.
- This led to a revision of the role of the state, from the idea that it was a potential restriction on freedom to the idea that the state could promote freedom by protecting people from social injustice.

> **Revision activity**
>
> Define the following principles associated with classical liberalism:
> - egotistical individualism
> - negative freedom
> - harm principle
> - free-market capitalism

> **Developmental individualism** Focuses on personal growth and flourishing rather than just self-satisfaction, emphasising what the individual can become rather than what they are.
>
> **Positive freedom** Isaiah Berlin defined it as 'freedom to' rather than 'freedom from'. The individual is free to develop, flourish and pursue their own version of the good life.

Check your understanding and progress at www.hoddereducation.co.uk/myrevisionnotes

Enabling state

- The concept of positive freedom sees modern liberals redefine the role of the state so that it is justified to intervene to protect freedom and individualism. This involves an extension of the role of the state.
- The provision of a welfare state could be justified on the grounds that it provides equality of opportunity, so that all are free to flourish and develop. This would be funded by increased taxation and increased public spending.
- Based on the work of John Maynard Keynes, it was argued that the state needed to intervene in the economy to bring about full employment and economic growth, to ensure the necessary prosperity for all to be free to pursue their version of the good life.

Social liberalism

- Modern liberalism revises classical liberalism's position on toleration, which aims to safeguard it by granting formal equality to all.
- Modern liberals go further, arguing that society has discriminated against minorities. They therefore promote greater toleration and equality of opportunity, which is consistent with their view of positive freedom and the enabling state.
- There is a key role for state intervention to discriminate in favour of groups who have suffered historical discrimination to ensure that there really is a level playing field for all.
- Modern examples include support for same-sex marriage and the use of positive discrimination to promote real equality for women and minority ethnic groups.

Welfare state The provision of education, health, housing and social security (e.g. pensions and benefits) by the state.

Equality of opportunity The concept that all individuals have equal life chances, so inequalities generated by society must be tackled. If there is equality of opportunity, inequalities which result from differences in ability, creativity and hard work are acceptable.

Discrimination The differential treatment of groups or individuals, such as women, usually without any real justification for doing this based on the differences between them (e.g. between men and women).

Positive discrimination State intervention to give preferential treatment to particular groups in society to tackle historical discrimination and inequalities in society. Affirmative action in the USA is an example of positive discrimination.

Exam tip

Don't confuse the socialist idea of equality with modern liberalism. Foundational equality (the concept that all humans are born morally equal) and equality of opportunity can justify inequality based on the principle of meritocracy (the concept that social position and economic reward are based on talent and hard work) and the need to incentivise the individual.

Now test yourself

TESTED

4 Copy and complete the following table to show some of the tensions within liberalism.

Classical liberalism	Modern liberalism
Egotistical individualism	
Negative freedom	
Free-market capitalism	
Night-watchman state	

5 How can Mill be considered to be a bridge between classical and modern liberalism?

6 What is the difference between self-regarding actions and other-regarding actions?

My Revision Notes: AQA A-level Politics: Political Ideas Second Edition

Key thinker

Thomas Hill Green (1836–82)

Thomas Hill Green was an English thinker, Oxford academic and active member of the Liberal Party. He was influential in changing the approach of liberalism towards the state and developed clear arguments for positive freedom in his *Lectures on the Principles of Political Obligation* (1895). He was one of the major influences upon new or progressive liberalism and approached the notion of freedom in a far more communal rather than highly individualistic manner.

+ Central to Green's ideas is the concept of the 'common good', which constrains the individual rights so beloved of traditional liberals. This gives the state not just negative duties to refrain from interfering with the freedoms and opportunities of its citizens, but also positive duties to provide resources and opportunities for individual self-realisation.
+ Freedom therefore should not be understood in a purely negative sense, as 'freedom from'. It should also be understood in a positive sense – the freedom of the individual to rise above the narrow concerns of self-interest to contribute to the common good of society by making the very best of their own unique talents and ability – 'freedom to'.
+ Positive freedom can only be achieved by removing hereditary privilege in society and tackling poverty, but within a capitalist society. Unsurprisingly, Thomas Hill Green was active in educational reform, serving as an assistant commissioner on the Taunton Commission on Secondary Education in 1865–66, arguing for significant reforms to equalise opportunities for higher education. He was also a member of the Oxford School Board.
+ Green argued that the state had to take a more positive role by freeing the poor from ignorance, disease, poor-quality housing and exploitation in the workplace.

Key thinker

Betty Friedan (1921–2006)

Betty Friedan was an American liberal feminist thinker who approached modern liberalism in relation to true gender equality. Like other modern liberal thinkers, she argued that basic foundational equality, such as the right to vote, had not solved the problem of the power and wealth imbalance between the sexes. For genuine equality of opportunity between the genders, the state had to intervene further and attitudes towards gender in a liberal democracy needed to change.

+ In *The Feminine Mystique* (1963), Friedan argued that the traditional societal idea that women could find satisfaction exclusively in their roles as wife and mother left women feeling miserable and empty. She called this 'the problem that has no name'.
+ The idea that a woman who is a mother and a wife has no time for a career limits her development and potential. A key principle for Friedan and other second-wave feminists was that of choice. Women, like men, should be able to maximise the choices available to them.
+ Women could be liberated by working productively outside the home in a full-time career. Marriage, motherhood and a professional career, in her view, could all be sustained and balanced, but it would require a shift in society's attitudes and also more practical help by the state in areas such as childcare.
+ In her book, *The Second Stage* (1981), Friedan argued that there needed to be changes to public values, social institutions and leadership styles to allow all people to achieve personal fulfilment.
+ Friedan supported an activist women's movement to bring this about. She was a founder member of the National Organization for Women set up in 1966. This movement in many ways modelled itself on the black civil rights movement and the National Association for the Advancement of Colored People (NAACP).
+ This change would include the state not just granting formal equality but actively intervening to tackle gender inequality and ensure real equality of opportunity. This might include granting state benefits to single, divorced or widowed mothers so that they had equal opportunities to compete in the job marketplace. Friedan was also a strong supporter of women's access to birth control and of abortion rights.

Check your understanding and progress at www.hoddereducation.co.uk/myrevisionnotes

Key thinker

John Rawls (1921–2002)

John Rawls in *A Theory of Justice* (1971) further developed the idea of an enabling state based on the principle of justice as fairness and promoting a genuine equality of opportunity.

+ Rawls reaffirmed the liberal idea of **foundational equality**, arguing that everyone should have equal rights and basic liberties. He termed this the 'greatest equal liberty principle', arguing that 'Each person is to have an equal right to the most extensive total system of equal basic liberties compatible with a similar system of liberty for all.' This was his overriding principle, ensuring that basic liberties cannot be infringed upon.
+ Rawls then developed the idea of the 'original position', a thought experiment where people construct the society that they would like to live. In the construction, people would be under the 'veil of ignorance', so would have no idea what sort of person they would be in the new society in terms of their wealth.
+ In this context, the rational individual would choose a more socially and economically equal society, as avoiding poverty is a more powerful motivation than the desire for great wealth. Therefore, a larger enabling state with some wealth redistribution via taxation is consistent with the wider liberal goals of freedom and equality of opportunity.
+ This leads to the **difference principle**. Inequalities of wealth are legitimate as they incentivise people to work harder but only as long as they raise the income and wealth of the least well-off. This meant that 'Social and economic inequalities are to be arranged so that they are to the greatest benefit of the least advantaged.'
+ The final principle in Rawls' view of justice as fairness is the 'equal opportunity principle'. Here, he argued that inequalities should only exist if 'attached to offices and positions open to all under conditions of fair equality of opportunity'. As an example, this means that in Rawls' state, there could be scope for positive discrimination in university admissions, in favour of traditionally underrepresented groups held back by adverse educational opportunities or structural prejudice based on race or gender. In summary, Rawls would doubtless approve of contextual offers for university places!

Foundational equality All humans are born morally equal and so are deserving of equal natural rights, which are enshrined in law as legal and political rights.

Difference principle Economic inequality is permissible if there is equality of opportunity, and the inequalities in society are only justifiable if they are to the greatest benefit of the least well-off.

Exam tip

Classical liberals and neo-liberals would see the difference principle as a threat to freedom and the right to property, as it supports progressive taxation to redistribute wealth to the least well-off. This is a good example to use in an exam answer to distinguish between classical/neo-liberals and new/progressive liberals.

Key thinkers in context

John Locke

Locke was writing at a time when most of Europe was ruled by absolutist monarchies who rejected any notion of a contract between ruler and ruled. The Glorious Revolution, which peacefully removed James II from the English throne in favour of William and Mary, had just occurred (1688) when *Two Treatises* was published. This event embodied some of his key principles, including the belief in removing regimes that imperilled natural rights. Although broadly in favour of religious toleration, itself a radical idea in a time when most countries had a state church, in his *A Letter Concerning Toleration*, he excluded Roman Catholics. This reflects the view of that time that Catholicism was closely associated with royal absolutism and anti-liberal forces, as seen, for example, in France under Louis XIV, who believed in *'L'état c'est moi'* – in other words, the monarch *is* the state.

Mary Wollstonecraft

In the 1790s, when Wollstonecraft was writing, women lacked the most basic political rights, such as the right to vote, irrespective of their wealth or social class. Married women also had little by way of property rights. In addition, the French Revolution had just occurred, an event she supported.

John Stuart Mill

Mill was writing at the time Britain was beginning its journey towards a democratic state with the passage of the Second Reform Act (1867). This led him to be concerned about the implications for the politics of democracy if the newly enfranchised were not educated, and about the possibility of the 'tyranny of the majority'. Extension of the franchise also led him to argue for the inclusion of women in an expanded electorate.

Thomas Hill Green

By the second half of the nineteenth century, the Industrial Revolution had caused profound social and economic changes in Britain. Green was shocked at how largely unregulated, free-market capitalism and the small state beloved of classical liberals had failed to solve the problem of poverty. Self-help and basic foundational equality had not proved effective in creating a society where true equality of opportunity existed for individuals.

John Rawls

Rawls was writing in Cold War America, where the American Dream remained out of reach for many. Like Green, he wanted a capitalist society where the poorest were enabled and given true equality of opportunity by a more active and enlarged state. His arguments could also be seen as a response both to Soviet-style socialism and to New Right and neo-liberal views including those of his fellow Harvard academic Robert Nozick.

Betty Friedan

Despite the achievement of basic equality in terms of the vote, property ownership and access to education, at the time Friedan was writing in the 1960s many American women, especially housewives, felt unfulfilled. It was still largely accepted that married women should embrace motherhood and a primarily domestic role on becoming a wife. The 1960s was also an age of great social upheaval and protest across much of the Western world – seen, for example, in the civil rights and peace movements.

> **Now test yourself** TESTED
>
> How would:
> a) Green
> b) Rawls
> justify the state in increasing taxation and public spending to tackle the issues of poverty and inequality in society?

Revision activity

Define the following terms associated with modern liberalism:
+ enabling state
+ positive freedom
+ developmental individualism
+ equality of opportunity

Neo-liberalism (second half of the twentieth century to the present)

+ Neo-liberalism is essentially a reaction against the modern and progressive liberalism of thinkers such as Rawls, and the growth of state intervention and control.
+ It is primarily concerned with economic rather than social issues.
+ The most prominent neo-liberal thinker, F. A. Hayek, author of *The Road to Serfdom* (1944), sought to return liberalism to its classical roots. In 1978 he wrote that 'There can be no freedom of press if the instruments of printing are under government control, no freedom of assembly if the needed rooms are so controlled, no freedom of movement if the means of transport are a government monopoly.'
+ However, neo-liberalism has been most closely associated with political conservatives including Margaret Thatcher and Ronald Reagan.
+ Neo-liberalism is also seen as conservative because it is reactionary. It aims to roll back the welfare state and Keynesian economic management to return to the minimal state and free-market capitalism of the nineteenth century.

Key ideas of neo-liberalism

+ Neo-liberalism aimed to reapply the economic ideas of free-market capitalism and to campaign for a night-watchman state.
+ Private property and negative freedom are central to freedom and individualism. For example, as noted previously, Hayek argues that without private ownership of the press, there can be no freedom of the press.
+ The welfare state was the betrayal of individualism, replacing it with the collectivism favoured by socialism. It involves the state placing unjustifiable restrictions on individual liberty, such as high levels of taxation. The welfare state creates a dependency culture, leading to people relying on the state rather than helping themselves.
+ Free trade, free markets and globalisation are the best drivers of economic and social progress.

Collectivism The idea that the collective rather than the individual is the main economic, social and political unit.

Core ideas of liberalism

Freedom and the individual

+ Individualism is a key liberal assumption. The individual – rather than classes, races or nations – is the key basis for thinking about human nature, the state, society and the economy.
+ On the one hand, the individual is unique with their own talents and abilities while, on the other hand, everyone is morally equal on the basis that they are all individuals.
+ Locke argues that all individuals have natural rights to 'life, liberty and property'. As each individual is unique and equal, this places freedom as the core liberal value. Humans flourish and progress when they are given the widest possible freedom to make rational decisions, own property and establish their own beliefs, lifestyles and values.
+ This is best summed up by John Stuart Mill: 'Over himself, over his own body and mind, the individual is sovereign' (*On Liberty*).
+ Egotistical individualism is associated with classical liberals, who see the individual as self-seeking, self-reliant and independent, and view society as no more than a loose collection of individuals. It leads individuals to co-operate with others and show self-restraint regarding their own self-interest, living in a society of peace and harmony where their beliefs, values and lifestyle choices are respected.
+ Modern liberals have focused on developmental individualism by building on the ideas of John Stuart Mill. Thomas Hill Green argued that individuals are free when they rise above narrow self-interest to participate in a shared way of life and contribute to the common good by improving themselves.

> **Exam tip**
>
> This part of the course expects you to have a broad understanding of the key ideas of political thinkers and how they have influenced each ideology's view of human nature, the state, society and the economy. In answering exam questions, you must refer to the key ideas of a range of political thinkers.

Human nature

+ Liberalism's optimistic view of human nature emerged from the Enlightenment and opposed the religious view that humankind is imperfect and flawed, found in the concept of original sin.
+ Locke argued that humans are naturally free, equal and independent, and are not naturally under the authority of any other body or person. This means there is no need for a mighty state or authority figure, as in Hobbes's *Leviathan* (1651), to protect people from themselves.
+ Locke's idea that individuals should be given the widest possible freedom to act according to their will is based on their possession of reason.
+ Humans are rational and tolerant, able to understand the views of others and respect their life, liberty and possessions. Disputes and disagreements are settled through rational discussion and challenges can be overcome using reason.
+ The ability of the individual to pursue their own self-interest rationally produces individual happiness as well as social progress.
+ Wollstonecraft applied liberal views about human nature and potential to women, a position also taken by Mill.
+ Over time, liberal thinkers began to view this approach as being too optimistic and simplistic. It was felt that the egotistical element of human nature led to inequality, so the state needs to step in to promote equality of opportunity.
+ Both Green and Friedan argued that the state needs to intervene to tackle inequality, allowing individuals really to be free and secure their own happiness.
+ Friedan saw that human nature, left unchecked by the state, had produced gender inequality, stopping women from achieving individual happiness.

- Green argued that human nature was not just self-interested but rather had a social dimension as individuals can only grow and flourish in a society where everyone can grow and flourish.
- Rawls argued that human nature has the capacity for toleration and mutual respect, alongside a desire to improve the living standards of the poorest in society and thereby reduce wealth inequality.

The state

Although individualism and capitalism are core concepts in liberalism's view of the world, liberals argue that these principles are best supported by a certain type of state. How that state came about, what it aims to achieve and its structure and role are crucial to understanding liberalism and tensions within liberalism.

- The state is a human construction, built to ensure that the natural rights and laws of natural society are safeguarded so that individuals can flourish. Locke clearly made this point when he wrote 'where there is no law, there is no freedom' (*Second Treatise on Civil Government*).
- Based on the social contract theory, the individual consents to the state while the state protects natural rights, allowing the individual to flourish. It is only rational for the individual to consent to the state while it protects those rights better than in the state of nature. When the state fails to do so, it is rational for the individual to withdraw consent and replace the government. At the time and subsequently, therefore, liberals approved of the American Revolution, though they were more divided over the French Revolution.
- Government by consent is government from below. Through free, fair and regular elections, this consent can be given voluntarily by the people.
- Locke argues that the state must be limited to stop the emergence of a tyrannical government that could remove natural rights. The state can be limited by constitutionalism and fragmented government.
- Modern liberals have supported universal suffrage while being concerned about the 'tyranny of the majority' and so have strongly emphasised constitutionalism to strengthen limits on government.
- Mill developed Locke's ideas, arguing that the government must only intervene where it is necessary to protect the liberties and freedoms of the individual. The state should tolerate all actions and ideas unless they violate the harm principle.
- The state, in order to promote individualism, should be a meritocracy, allowing individuals to rise to the top as the result of their hard work and talents rather than through the hereditary principle or the artificial privilege of the aristocracy.
- As all are born morally equal, all should receive equal opportunities to flourish and achieve happiness, and success or failure is then solely down to the individual.
- Modern liberals are more positive about the state's ability to improve people's lives and see an expanded role of the state in helping people to help themselves.
- Green argued that the removal of poverty – via education, public housing and public healthcare – was essential to enable individuals to achieve their full potential.
- The role of the state was taken further by Rawls to include increased taxation and public spending to ensure that there was social justice and equality of opportunity for all.
- The power of the government must not be arbitrary or concentrated in the hands of one person. Liberalism has promoted limited government as the ideal structure for the state, as shown in Table 1.2.

Toleration The virtue of not using one's power to interfere with another's opinion or action over something morally important and where you morally disapprove of that opinion or action.

Meritocracy Social position and economic reward are based on talent and hard work. Where there is equality of opportunity, there is an incentive to work hard and realise your talent, ensuring everyone gets what they deserve and that society is led by the most talented.

Table 1.2 The features of limited government

Constitutionalism	The written constitution formalises the contract between the government and the people. It clearly lays out the rules and procedures which the government must act by and enshrines the natural rights of the citizens.
Fragmented government	This ensures the dispersal of power rather than its concentration in the hands of one person. This is achieved by a separation of power between the executive, the legislature and the judiciary and within the legislature through bicameralism (two Houses). Powers are shared between the institutions, creating a system of checks and balances. A further dispersal of power can be achieved by federalism, where power is shared between central and regional governments, each with their own distinct areas of jurisdiction.
Formal equality	All individuals are entitled to the same legal rights (all are equal before the law) and the same political rights (the right to vote). These rights are laid out in a Bill of Rights, allowing the judiciary to protect the rights of citizens against the decisions of the elected government.
Rule of law	Law is crucial to protecting natural rights and establishes the rules that everyone must obey. It applies to everyone equally, irrespective of whether they are an ordinary citizen or in the government and irrespective of their identity (gender, race, religion or class). The law's main purpose is to protect liberty.

Society

+ The optimistic view of human nature underpins the liberal view of society.
+ Locke argued that, in the state of nature, there would be a natural society as there are natural rights such as life, liberty and possessions, and natural law which states that no one should harm another's natural rights.
+ Natural society is built on the principle of individualism. As natural society is one of peace, the state should behave as a neutral umpire, safeguarding the natural law and natural rights found in natural society.
+ Wollstonecraft was critical of society for its failure to recognise the rights of women. She argued that women should be given access to education to develop their powers of reason and formal equality, so society would benefit from the talents of women.
+ Mill argued that the main aim of society is to promote individualism as humans are by nature freedom-seeking and this is based upon the principle of foundational equality.
+ Society should be tolerant and diverse, respecting the individual's right to hold their own beliefs and values as long as they do not restrict the rights of others.
+ For Locke, in *A Letter Concerning Toleration* (1689), this involved religious toleration as religion was a private matter and so should be left to the individual.
+ Mill took this further, seeing toleration and diversity as key ingredients of a vibrant, progressive society. Competition, a free market of sorts, between ideas will sharpen and refine good ideas while exposing the weakness of bad ideas.
+ From the late twentieth century, liberals have championed the rights of minority groups that have been discriminated against by society based on gender, sexual orientation, race or religion.
+ Friedan argued that the state had to take a more proactive role, including positive discrimination due to historical discrimination, to ensure that there was real equality of opportunity for women in the present.

The economy

+ Liberalism's central belief in the right to property, established by Locke, underpins its approach to the economy.
+ The free market, based on private property, incentivises the individual to make rational choices about making contracts, buying and selling labour, how to save, invest or spend their money, and raising capital and starting businesses. This is the embodiment of freedom, so liberals support capitalism.

> **Exam tip**
>
> The classical liberal theory of the economy is clearly laid out by Adam Smith in his pivotal work, *The Wealth of Nations* (1776). Although he is not a set liberal thinker, referencing Smith could enhance an exam answer dealing with liberals and the economy.

- The government should be limited to ensuring that property is secure and contracts are honoured to allow for free trade and competition – a free market.
- The 'invisible hand' of the market is automatic, guiding individuals to make rational choices. Where products are scarce, people will pay more and investment is made to increase production; where products are abundant, people will pay less and investment is moved to other areas.
- This optimistic view sees the market guiding individuals to economic success, creating wealth for all individuals and for all nations.
- Modern liberals such as Green saw free-market capitalism as creating social and economic obstacles to individuals achieving their full potential.
- This led modern liberals to endorse Keynesian theory, based on John Maynard Keynes' *General Theory of Employment, Interest and Money* (1936).
- Feminist liberals have argued that women should be given full and equal access to employment opportunities to enable them to contribute fully to a free-market economy. Later writers, such as Friedan, argued for more state involvement to bring this about, including anti-discrimination measures.

> **Exam tip**
>
> It could be worth referencing briefly, in an exam answer, how the modern liberal approach to the economy and freedom can be seen in a range of twentieth-century government policy programmes. These include, in the USA, President Roosevelt's New Deal and President Johnson's Great Society, as well as the policies of the Labour and Conservative parties in the UK between 1945 and 1979.

> **Now test yourself** TESTED
>
> 8 Copy and complete the following table with the key views of both classical and modern liberals.
>
> | | Classical liberalism | Modern liberalism |
> |---|---|---|
> | Freedom and the individual | | |
> | Human nature | | |
> | The state | | |
> | Society | | |
> | The economy | | |

> **Revision activity**
>
> To what extent are the UK and the US constitutions informed by liberal principles?

Agreement and tensions within liberalism

REVISED

Human nature

Areas of agreement
- An optimistic view of human nature and progress. Liberals view individuals as morally equal, independent and rational, desiring to pursue their own version of the good life.
- Individualism needs to be protected and promoted, and there should be toleration of different values, beliefs and versions of the good life.

Areas of tension
- Classical liberals (in line with neo-liberals) see these qualities as innate for individuals and that individuals develop best when left free to pursue their own happiness.
- Modern liberals build on Mill's view that rationalism needs to be developed and individualism is more of a reflection of what humans can become, especially via education, than simply what they are.
- Green saw human nature as having a clear social dimension, arguing that freedom is achieved by working towards the common good. This provides the basis for the state to enable individuals to help themselves by providing not just formal equality but equality of opportunity.
- Feminist and modern liberals apply the same levels of rationality to both men and women. Early liberals such as Locke were less concerned with gender equality. Locke even referred to men as 'the abler and the stronger' in his *Second Treatise*.

> **Exam tip**
>
> As you draw comparisons and links between classical and modern liberalism, look to show how modern liberalism has built upon the ideas of the earlier classical liberals. This is especially important when analysing their approaches to freedom and the individual.

The state

Areas of agreement
+ The state's role is to promote, protect and uphold individual freedoms, and thus enable individual flourishing of talents and enterprise.
+ All liberals argue that the state should be limited by constitutionalism, the fragmentation of power, formal equality for citizens and the rule of law.

Areas of tension
+ Classical liberals argued that the state should have a night-watchman role, justified by the concept of negative freedom, with intervention justified only to prevent actions that are harmful to others. This will leave the individual free to follow their own version of the good life.
+ Modern liberals make the case for an enabling state, where intervention should be far greater in order to enable people to be free to pursue their own individuality, in line with the concept of positive freedom.
+ Classical liberals such as Locke favoured a representative government that only reflected the interests of property-owning individuals.
+ Modern liberals favour representative democracy, with universal suffrage and strong constitutional limits, but are concerned that democracy may lead to a 'tyranny of the majority'. They view education as crucial to the wise use of the ballot.

Society

Areas of agreement
+ Society could exist without the state. In this 'state of nature', natural rights and laws would also be present. This reflects liberalism's belief in humankind being innately a social creature.
+ All liberals stress individualism and freedom in society, and that society should be arranged to allow the individual to flourish and achieve their own self-fulfilment.

Areas of tension
+ Classical liberals stressed that natural society existed before the state and was one of peace (Locke); individuals are self-seeking and independent but constrained by their rational nature, which leads them to respect the rights of others so that their own rights are respected in turn.
+ Modern liberals see modern industrial societies, based around free-market capitalism, as restricting the ability of individuals to be free (Green). This leads to a support for social justice, where poverty and inequality, as well as any discrimination based on identity, are tackled by the state, to ensure positive freedom.
+ Neo-liberals hark back to negative freedom, arguing that the enabling state has unjustly reduced liberty and created a dependency culture which limits individualism by taking away people's self-reliance.

The economy

Areas of agreement
+ Emerging from Locke's natural laws, all liberals emphasise the right to own property and advocate an economy based on private property as the best route to creating wealth.
+ Property is seen as essential to freedom and protecting the individual from the state.

Areas of tension

+ Classical liberals and neo-liberals adopt the view that the state's only role is to protect property and enforce contracts, and that the market should be left to guide rational individuals.
+ Free trade, without subsidies, taxes or regulations, will provide the most efficient outcomes and drive economic creativity and prosperity for all.
+ Modern liberals argue that the state is justified in intervening in the economy, using the tools of taxation and public spending, in order to manage capitalism so that it delivers full employment for all.
+ Furthermore, modern liberals would argue that full employment provides the necessary wealth to reduce poverty, so that everyone can be free to choose their own version of the good life. The means of production should be left in the hands of private companies as a safeguard of personal liberty.

> **Revision activity**
>
> Create a set of flashcards for all the key terms in this chapter.

> **Now test yourself** — TESTED
>
> 9 Copy and complete the following table with the main ideas of the key thinkers.
>
> | Thinker | Human nature | The state | Society | The economy |
> |---|---|---|---|---|
> | John Locke | | | | |
> | Mary Wollstonecraft | | | | |
> | John Stuart Mill | | | | |
> | Thomas Hill Green | | | | |
> | John Rawls | | | | |
> | Betty Friedan | | | | |

> **Exam skills**
>
> Here is a sample paragraph answering the 9-mark Section A question: 'Explain and analyse three ways that liberal thinkers have viewed human nature.'
>
> > Feminist liberals also share an optimistic view of human nature along with other liberals. However, they believe that women and men are equally rational and capable of reason and deserve equal rights such as the vote and fairness in the workplace. They tend to write against the background of seeing society as patriarchal and sexist, and want radical changes. Some argue that women are unfulfilled, 'the problem that has no name'.
>
> This is a weak and short paragraph that would struggle to get much above Level 1. Why?
> + First, it is very vague and general – no key thinkers or their works are identified. The opening sentence should directly reference Wollstonecraft and Frieden, and perhaps their key works.
> + Secondly, a distinction could be made between first-wave liberal feminists, who were arguing for basic social and political rights, and later writers such as Frieden, who argued that women's talents and potential were still going to waste in post-war Western society. The phrase 'fairness in the workplace' is also rather unclear – 'advocated for an end to workplace discrimination in terms of pay and promotion' would read better.
> + Finally, the whole paragraph needs a more consistent focus on human nature and how liberal feminists regard it. The last sentence needs to link lack of fulfilment with human nature.

Check your understanding and progress at www.hoddereducation.co.uk/myrevisionnotes

Exam practice

1. Explain and analyse three ways that the concept of human nature is significant to liberal thinkers. [9]

2. Explain and analyse three ways that liberal thinkers have viewed the role of the state in the economy. [9]

Read the extracts below and answer Question 3 that follows.

> It is true, governments cannot be supported without great expense, and it is right that everyone who enjoys his share of the protection should pay out of his wealth his proportion for the maintenance of it. But still it must be with his own consent, i.e. the consent of the majority, giving it either by themselves, or their representatives chosen by them: for if anyone shall claim a power to lay and levy taxes on the people, by his own authority, and without such consent of the people, he thereby invades the fundamental law of property, and subverts the end of government.
>
> Source: adapted from John Locke, *Two Treatises of Government*
>
> Rights have been allowed to landlords, incompatible with the true principle on which rights of property rest. The right to freedom in unlimited acquisition of wealth, does not imply the right of anyone to do as he likes with those gifts of nature, without which there would be nothing to spend labour upon. Land is just as much an original natural material necessary to productive industry, as are air, light, and water, but while the latter from the nature of the case cannot be appropriated, the earth can be and has been. The only justification for this seizure, as for any other, is that it contributes on the whole to social well-being; that land taken by individuals becomes more beneficial to society as a whole, including those who are not owners of the soil, than if it were held in common. The justification disappears if these conditions are not observed.
>
> Source: adapted from Thomas Hill Green, *Lectures on the Principles of Political Obligation*

3. Analyse, evaluate and compare the arguments being made in the above extracts over liberalism's approach to private property. In your answer, you should refer to the thinkers you have studied. [25]

Summary

You should now have an understanding of:
+ the difference between egotistical and developmental individualism
+ the distinction between positive and negative freedom
+ the contributions of the six key thinkers (Locke, Wollstonecraft, Mill, Green, Rawls and Friedan) to the development of liberalism
+ the relationship between liberalism and democracy
+ the tensions and agreements within liberalism over human nature, the state, society and the economy
+ the extent to which modern liberalism has built on classical liberal principles

2 Conservatism

Conservatism is a political approach that is generally suspicious of radical change and promotes change only to conserve. Conservatism has three aspects: an attitude to society, an idea about government and a political practice. All three are informed by a broad scepticism towards liberal and socialist ideas of human nature. This chapter will look at the origins, the key debates and the different schools/thinkers of conservatism before looking at areas of tension and agreement within it.

Origins of conservatism

- Conservatism began to crystallise as an idea in the late eighteenth century as a response to the French Revolution. The initial aim of the revolution (1789–99) was to replace the monarchy and aristocracy with a written constitution and representative government based on the Enlightenment ideals of rationalism and individualism.
- Conservatism focused on the value of custom, tradition and continuity rather than the abstract philosophical ideals of liberalism. It did not believe that a perfect society based on reason could be achieved. Rather, attempts to create a utopian society based on abstract principles, such as liberty and equality, would result in suffering and failure. Therefore, early conservatism was profoundly anti-revolutionary.
- As conservatism opposed revolution, it promoted the idea of change to conserve. As Edmund Burke argues in his *Reflections on the Revolution in France* (1790), 'A state without the means of some change is without the means of its conservation.'
- Conservatism was a philosophy of imperfection, seeing human nature as flawed and limited in its grasp of the world, in contrast to the optimistic view of liberals and socialists. This sceptical view of human nature finds its roots in the writings of Thomas Hobbes.
- Conservatism emphasised organic society over individualism, with society dependent on bonds of trust and affection between Burke's 'little platoons' (local communities and small societal groups like families, churches, schools and universities).
- The state needed to be strong to provide order, peace and stability, seen as vital to society and freedom. Conservatives emphasised hierarchy and authority over equality and democracy.
- Conservatism has developed different variants. Traditional conservatism dominated from the French Revolution to the late nineteenth century before developing into one-nation conservatism. Since the mid-twentieth century, New Right thinking has pushed conservatism in a more neo-liberal direction.

Organic society Society is a natural, complex body like a tree. It develops and grows slowly, needs constant nurturing and pruning to ensure its health, and should not be uprooted and replaced with something new through radical change/revolution.

Hierarchy Human nature and society are naturally divided by wealth, status and power. For conservatives, there is a natural ruling class with the necessary wealth and authority to govern, while the masses should naturally obey the elite that is governing in their best interest.

Change to conserve
Most conservatives oppose radical social change as they view society as an organic, complex whole. Long-established institutions and practices, such as the monarchy and parliamentary sovereignty, reflect the accumulated wisdom of the past and so are tried and tested. Change should be incremental, building on what works in order to conserve what is valuable.

Exam tip
When discussing freedom and conservative thought, in a 9-marker or extract question, remember that traditional conservatives believed that peace and security were necessary conditions before freedoms could be enjoyed. For example, to take a classroom scenario, students are not free to learn or indeed enjoy the company of their fellow students, if there is no underlying discipline and order in the school/college.

> **Exam tip**
>
> When analysing the historical context of Hobbes's ideas, explain how he viewed the English Civil Wars as resulting from power being divided between the monarch, Lords and Commons. Instead, to preserve peace and order, he argued that power must be placed in one supreme authority. Hobbes also believed that religious toleration led to disputes and quarrels between competing groups. He therefore argued for a single state-run church.

> **Key thinker**
>
> **Thomas Hobbes (1588–1679)**
>
> Thomas Hobbes, in his work *Leviathan* (1651), was the first philosopher in the English-speaking world to outline a modern justification for the state. His work was written in response to the English Civil Wars (1642–51) and the anarchy that he associated with that period.
>
> **Human nature**
> - For Hobbes, political philosophy starts with the study of human nature.
> - His view of human nature is perhaps the most gloomy and cynical. He sees humans as endlessly restless in their pursuit of power in order to satisfy their immediate desires and any potential future desires.
> - This desire for power is both selfish and competitive, and is evidence of Hobbes's emphasis on the individual.
> - Humans are also roughly equal in strength and ability, so must be always fearful of others as the 'weakest has strength enough to kill the strongest'.
>
> **State of nature/natural law**
> - In Hobbes's state of nature, resources are scarce. Therefore, given humans' desire for power and that they are roughly equal, there will be a 'war … of every man against every man' and 'notions of right and wrong, justice and injustice, have no place'.
> - Hobbes famously argued that life in the state of nature will be 'solitary, poor, nasty, brutish and short'.
> - However, the first natural law is that man should seek peace as far as he can and then, if not, use war.
> - As humans are rational, it is reasonable to assume that the people, for self-preservation, will rise above the state of nature. They will achieve this by agreeing a social contract between themselves and a powerful ruler.
>
> **Power of the sovereign**
> - The social contract between the people establishes a sovereign, with absolute power to provide order, security and stability, which will lead to the emergence of society.
> - The key for Hobbes was that sovereign power was placed in one supreme authority which is not limited by the legal rights of other bodies.
> - His preferred form of government was monarchy. However, it is clear that his arguments can apply to all forms of government where there is one absolute authority.
> - The social contract is made between the people, not between the people and the sovereign. When the contract is completed, the power of the people is at an end as the sovereign has all power and the people only have the rights that the sovereign chooses to give them.

> **Exam tip**
>
> In your answers, be careful not to exaggerate Hobbes's pessimistic view of human nature. He did believe that humans were rational enough to surrender, voluntarily, their individual rights to a supreme power, which would thus derive its authority and legitimacy ultimately from the people.

> **Revision activity**
>
> How does Hobbes's state of nature differ from that of Locke (see p. 12)?

> **Exam tip**
>
> It is inaccurate to see Hobbes as a purely conservative thinker. He predates the birth of conservatism and served as an inspiration to both conservatives and liberals. His pessimistic view of human nature is shared by conservatives. However, Anthony Quinton, in his book *The Politics of Imperfection* (1978), did not count Hobbes as a conservative due to his rationalism, individualism and absolutism.

2 Conservatism

Main beliefs of conservatism

REVISED

In order to get a full understanding of conservatism, you need to be aware of the following aspects of conservatism:
+ conservatism as an ideology – the extent to which conservatism is actually a political ideology, and the divisions within conservatism between traditional conservatism and the New Right
+ government, the free market and the individual – conservatism's common key themes
+ human nature, the state, society and the economy – the extent to which conservatives agree and disagree in their attitudes to these four key areas

Conservatism as an ideology

+ Some political theorists have argued that conservatism is politically incoherent due to the inbuilt tensions between one-nation conservativism and the New Right.
+ Others have argued that it is a jumbled collection of beliefs, attitudes and ideas that are, in the words of Michael Oakeshott, 'more psychology than ideology'. Critics argue that this jumble of ideas amounts to no more than a defence of property, privilege and inequality in order to prevent power passing into the hands of what Burke describes as the 'swinish multitudes'.
+ Conservatism emerged as a response to the French Revolution, attacking it as an attempt to 'change and pervert the natural order of things'. This was a criticism Burke originally made about the seventeenth-century English radical group called the Levellers who, he went on to argue, 'load the edifice of society by setting up in the air what the solidity of the structure requires to be on the ground' (*Reflections on the Revolution in France*).
+ Conservatism lacks an end goal. It has no view of the type of society or economy it is working towards, and so lacks any concrete idea of progress or development.
+ Conservatism is pragmatic and flexible in its approach to politics, and can therefore be seen as having a lack of clear underlying principles.
+ This flexibility is used to allow conservatism to develop and adapt in order to preserve inequality and privilege. This can be seen in conservatism's gradual acceptance of democracy over time in order to preserve hierarchy and authority.
+ Conservatives support change, but the type of gradual change and the traditions that they support leave them open to the charge that they are simply concerned with preserving inequality and privilege. For example, why do conservatives support the traditions of monarchy but not labour-movement traditions like trade unionism?
+ These criticisms of conservatism have been challenged, with conservative thinkers from the traditional and New Right traditions putting forward their views of a coherent, principled view of conservatism that is much more ideological in nature.

> **Exam tip**
>
> In exam answers, where relevant, explain that the British Conservative Party does not just follow the principles of traditional conservatism. The 2022 'mini budget' announced under short-lived prime minister Liz Truss reflected the classical liberal ideals of individualism and free-market capitalism, with lower taxes for the richest and a belief in 'trickle-down' economics. Similar views can also be seen in 1980s Thatcherism.

> **Exam tip**
>
> In an exam answer, as an example of pragmatism you could cite the Conservative Prime Minister Rishi Sunak's raising of many taxes in 2022 due to the need to balance public finances, even though, ideologically, the Conservative Party favours lower taxes.

Main strands of conservatism

REVISED

Traditional conservatism (from the French Revolution to the late nineteenth century)

Traditional conservatism can be seen to have the following distinctive features:
+ **Hierarchy**. Human nature and society are naturally divided by wealth, status and power.
+ **Paternalism**. The ruling elite have a sense of obligation and duty to the many. Government should act like a 'father' to its 'children', the people. This involves governing in their best interests, remembering that the

government often has a clearer view of those best interests than the people. The people should show deference to their leaders.
+ **Order.** The government provides clear rules, discipline and guidance to ensure that society is ordered, peaceful and stable. This will create the responsible citizen and ensure that freedom benefits everyone and is not abused.
+ **Freedom.** Traditional conservatism is about freedom and the limits to freedom provided by institutions and attitudes that allow everyone to enjoy that freedom responsibly. These limits allow everyone to understand that their good behaviour, trust and care for others will be reciprocated by others, partly through fear of breaking the law.
+ **Social attitudes**. Traditional conservatism upholds that there are proven moral values that have provided stability and certainty. These values include traditional marriage and conventional family life with traditional gender roles. Individual freedoms will need to be limited to protect these attitudes and values, to ensure society is cohesive and stable and works for all.
+ **'Little platoons'.** Society is a collection of little platoons, not individuals. Each community provides the sense of security, order and stability that an individual desires. The little platoons provide the first link in the chain to 'a love of our country and to mankind', according to Burke. A powerful, centralised state, remote from these 'little platoons', would be damaging to society.
+ **Change to conserve.** Change and reform must be gradual and respect the accumulated wisdom of tradition.
+ Empiricism. The traditional conservative approach to political problems is to focus on *what works* (tradition, customs and attitudes) rather than what theory and abstract principles *say will work*. This means conservatism is pragmatic and flexible in its approach to tackling political problems.

> **Empiricism** Politics should be based on what works most effectively, not on abstract principles or ideas. This idea emerges from the politics of imperfection, as human are limited in what they are able to know and understand about the world.

> **Now test yourself** TESTED
> 1 Explain the ways in which conservatism can be considered not to be a coherent ideology.
> 2 Explain the ways in which conservatism can be seen as a ruling-class ideology.

> **Key thinker**
>
> **Edmund Burke (1729–97)**
> Edmund Burke is often regarded as the father of conservatism, with his key text being a passionate opposition to the French Revolution, *Reflections on the Revolution in France* (1790). Burke was a Whig MP and his thinking was based on the Whig principle of opposition to absolute, arbitrary power.
>
> **American and French revolutions**
> + Burke was a supporter of the American Revolution, which ended in 1783, but was fundamentally opposed to the French Revolution.
> + Burke supported the American Revolution as its aim was to protect the ancient rights and privileges of the people, which existed before the monarch in London began to tax them without authority. It was 'change to conserve'.
> + In contrast, the French Revolution was based on abstract theory and idealism born out of frustration with the French power structure and the resultant poverty of the majority of the population. It aimed to destroy the collective wisdom of the ages by throwing out existing institutions, customs and traditions to create a new society based on 'philosophical abstractions' rather than empiricism.

> **Exam tip**
>
> To show a deeper understanding, you can illustrate the differences between liberalism and traditional conservatism, which has opposed unrestrained individualism on the grounds that it will undermine the natural bonds of affection and trust that hold society together.

Human nature

- Burke had a broadly sceptical view of human nature. He saw the individual as foolish but the species as wise.
- He argued that humans could not rely on individual reason (rationalism) but could rely on tradition and custom, which was the 'general bank and capital of nations and ages'.
- Burke also opposed the idea of a social contract as suggested by Hobbes.
- He argued that the only contract that existed was between 'the dead, the living and the yet to be born'. The present must nurture and protect past tradition and custom to pass it on to future generations.
- The French Revolution was a destruction of that contract as it destroyed existing institutions, practices and customs, and so removed the inheritance of those yet to be born.

Society

- Burke was highly critical of individualism, defending the importance of the 'we' over the 'I'. 'Little platoons' are the places where traditions and customs are formed, which are the bank of knowledge developed from trial and error in dealing with political problems.
- In this sense, society is organic as it develops naturally. Traditions and customs change slowly based on practical knowledge and evidence, not theory.
- Burke also attacked the French Revolution's emphasis on equality, arguing that hierarchy was natural in organic societies.

One-nation conservatism (from the late nineteenth century to the late twentieth century)

Threat of disorder

One-nation conservatism emerged from the threat to the order of state and society from socialism, class conflict and the effects of free-market capitalism that emerged from classical liberalism. One-nation conservatism updates traditional conservatism's ideas to deal with this threat.

One nation

Conservatism should emphasise and focus on the bonds of affection and trust that hold society together as part of a nation. All classes and groups in society are part of one nation because society is organic, where damage or distress to one element will damage the whole. This is summed up in Benjamin Disraeli's phrase 'the palace is not safe when the cottage is not happy'.

Change to conserve

Disraeli was particularly concerned with the ravaging effects on society of an unchecked free market. He accepted the rise of big cities and the spirit of commercialism as inevitable, so did not want reactionary policies to head back to a previous time. He wanted instead to tackle the worst consequences of the market to conserve society, as he saw reform as an inoculation against revolution.

Paternalism

There is a clear bond between groups, so it is clear that the wealthy have a responsibility to the less well-off. This would involve the state intervening in the free-market economy and society in order to ensure social stability.

> **Exam tip**
>
> One-nation conservatism is most closely associated with Benjamin Disraeli, leader of the Conservative Party and prime minister in 1868 and between 1874 and 1880. Examples of one-nation conservatism in action include the Employers and Workmen Act (1875), which allowed workers to sue employers if they broke contracts, and the Public Health Act (1875), which sought to combat filthy urban living conditions and diseases such as cholera. Conservative statements under Boris Johnson and Rishi Sunak concerning 'levelling up', redirecting more public spending to the north of England and away from the south, could be viewed in a similar light.

> **Exam tip**
>
> You can illustrate the flexibility of conservatism, driven by the idea of 'change to conserve', using the example of Disraeli as the first prime minister who viewed one role of the state as providing essential public services. It can also be seen in Conservative leaders adapting further in the twentieth and twenty-first centuries, supporting increased taxation and extensive public spending on welfare to ensure social stability.

Check your understanding and progress at www.hoddereducation.co.uk/myrevisionnotes

> **Key thinker**
>
> **Michael Oakeshott (1901–90)**
> Michael Oakeshott updated the conservative approach to human nature and the conservative view on gradual reform, in particular, in his collection *Rationalism in Politics and Other Essays* (1962).
> + Oakeshott saw humans as fragile and fallible, unable to understand the world because it is too complex for human reason to grasp.
> + He was highly critical of the politics of 'rationalism', which is the idea of remaking society based on the abstract ideas and principles of political philosophers.
> + Abstract ideas will always fail as they are not based on concrete experience. Worse, the remaking of society can do untold damage to traditions which are based on hundreds of years of practical experience.
> + Humans and societies prefer instead 'the familiar to the unknown … the actual to the possible', so a pragmatic and empirical approach to problems works best.
> + Oakeshott rejected the 'politics of faith', with its faith in the ability of the government to improve the condition of mankind or even to perfect mankind. In its place, he proposed the 'politics of scepticism', as the government's attempts to perfect mankind are dangerous for human liberty and dignity.
> + The idea of perfection is absurd and there should be scepticism about the ability of the government, staffed by officials – who are human like us – to use their power justly and efficiently. Instead, the government's role should be limited to preserving public order.
> + Conservatism is a 'disposition' not an ideology, and although conservatives are disposed towards limited government, it should not be on the basis of some abstract ideal.
> + Oakeshott argued that 'In political activity, then, men sail a boundless and bottomless sea; there is neither harbour for shelter nor floor for anchorage, neither starting-place nor appointed destination. The enterprise is to keep afloat on an even keel.'

The New Right (from the mid-twentieth century to the present)

Origins
+ It could be said that the conservatism of Hobbes and Burke emerged from reactions to the horrors of the English Civil Wars and the French Revolution. The New Right, in contrast, can be traced back to the rise of authoritarian regimes in the twentieth century such as Nazi Germany and, perhaps even more so, Stalin's Soviet Union.
+ Alongside this, the New Right is also a response to the growth of the state in Western democracies after the Second World War, and the development of the welfare state and increased taxation.

Small state
+ The New Right is partly inspired by Ayn Rand's idea of the 'morality of rational self-interest' (*The Virtue of Selfishness*).
+ For rational self-interest to be the key principle of society, the state needs to be rolled back.
+ For example, the state should be limited to providing armed forces, a police force and a court system in order to ensure that property is respected and contracts are enforced.
+ The New Right opposes public spending on welfare as it is both unjust, according to Robert Nozick, and creates a dependency culture. Why should individuals bother to work if the state is going to provide for them in any case?

Free-market capitalism
+ The New Right believes that market forces are the best method for the distribution and management of society's resources.
+ Therefore, deep cuts in taxation, privatisation, deregulation and tight restrictions on government spending are needed to return to free-market capitalism. Everyone should be free to follow all the opportunities they can in the marketplace, with minimal levels of taxation and regulation, in order to create greater prosperity for all.
+ Echoes of this can be found in what is often termed 'trickle-down economics', where it is argued that cutting taxes for the richest will trickle down the economy to benefit everyone.

> **Exam tip**
>
> You can use Oakeshott's views as an attack both on left-wing social planning, which oversaw the growth of government control over an increasing range of human activities, and on neo-liberalism (see below). Oakeshott comments that 'A plan to resist all planning may be better than its opposite, but it belongs to the same style of politics.'

Society

Socially, the New Right is divided between neo-conservatives, who wish to return to a society built on authority, national identity and traditional morality, and neo-liberals, who advocate a society built on individual choice:

+ Neo-conservatives are anti-permissive and would extend the role of the state to promote traditional family values, like traditional marriage, and to protect national security and defence. Neo-conservatives, for example, fear the impact of immigration on social cohesion and national identity.
+ For neo-liberals, individual choice is not just about economics but also about morality. Therefore, the state should not intervene in areas of private morality. The state should be stripped back to the minimum to minimise tax and spending. Neo-liberals are relaxed about immigration as it is natural for a free market to have the free movement of people/labour.
+ Although there are clear tensions within the New Right, neo-conservatism and neo-liberalism can work in a complementary fashion, as shown in Table 2.1.

Anti-permissive A rejection of permissiveness, which is the liberal belief that people should make their own moral choices (e.g. about abortion, marriage and relationships), stemming from the 1960s. The state should impose social order and public morality by promoting traditional values and tough law and order policies.

Table 2.1 Tensions within the New Right

Neo-conservatism	Neo-liberalism	Areas of agreement
The state should be strengthened in terms of law and order, promoting traditional values and patriotism.	Roll back the frontiers of the state – spending cuts, privatisation and deregulation.	Free-market economics creates tension as inequality may flourish, increasing the need for law and order and the protection of private property. A strong, but limited, state.
Restrict individual liberties to promote law and order and national security – increased police power, longer prison sentences. The state should direct the moral life of society, (e.g. Thatcher's Clause 28, banning the teaching within schools of the acceptability of homosexuality).	Advance individual liberty through the reduction of tax and the reduction of the welfare state. The state has no role in intervening in areas of private morality.	The smaller state means those in need will need support and guidance from society in the forms of 'little platoons' to promote the bonds of affection and trust between individuals and communities.
Increase spending to promote the country abroad and for defence and national security.	Minimise government spending in all areas where possible, but accept the need for government funding of defence and justice.	Reduce funding in other areas like welfare to concentrate money on law and order, promoting the country and national security.

Exam tip

When writing about how the New Right's conservative and liberal elements appear contradictory, comment that they are also complementary. It is important to recognise that the New Right has important continuities with traditional conservatism.

Key thinker

Ayn Rand (1905–82)

Ayn Rand was one of the most controversial, if maverick, thinkers of the New Right, offering a stark and radical challenge to the ideas of statism and collectivism through her novels, like *Atlas Shrugged* (1957), and her works of philosophy, including *The Virtue of Selfishness* (1964).

+ Rand was born in Russia but escaped to the USA as a young adult, having witnessed first-hand the 1917 Russian Revolution and the creation of a one-party communist state. Her family were prosperous members of the upper-middle class who lost their property and wealth during the upheavals. This in large part explains Rand's hostility to socialism and the big state, and her championing of private wealth and individual freedom.
+ Rand offered a new concept of rational and ethical egoism; an ethics of rational selfishness which is the basis of a new morality and can be seen as a form of radical individualism. She describes her philosophy as objectivism.

Statism A political system where the state has a large degree of control over social and economic affairs.

Objectivism Rand's philosophy based on the principles of reason, self-interest and capitalism, which she claims will deliver freedom, justice, progress and human happiness. It is set against statism or collectivism, where people's life and work belong to the state, which she argues leads to 'slavery, brute force, stagnant terror and sacrificial furnaces'.

Check your understanding and progress at www.hoddereducation.co.uk/myrevisionnotes

- In 1962 she argued '[Man] must exist for his own sake, neither sacrificing himself to others nor sacrificing others to himself. The pursuit of his own rational self-interest and of his own happiness is the highest moral purpose of his life.'
- Selfishness does not mean doing as you please; rather it means humans must pursue their own happiness as the highest moral aim and prosper by treating others as individuals. This supports the idea of **atomism**, where there is no such thing as society, only a collection of individuals pursuing their own happiness.
- Following reason means rejecting emotions, faith and any other forms of authority in order to think for yourself.
- The ideal social system is free-market capitalism, which involves 'a separation of state and economics'. This system protects the rights of the individual to use their own mind, act on their own judgement, work for their values and keep the product of their labour.
- Her view is meritocratic not hierarchical; the most talented individuals start businesses, invent new technologies and create ideas and art through their own talents and trade with other rational egoists to reach their goals.
- The state's role is vital but strictly limited to acting as a policeman, protecting the rights of each individual against criminals and foreign invaders.

Atomism The concept that society, if indeed it exists, is a collection of individuals pursuing their own individual lives and being responsible for themselves. Collective identities, like class, are meaningless.

> **Exam tip**
>
> You can highlight the tensions within conservatism by showing how Rand's radical individualism breaks with the traditional conservative view of human imperfection and the importance of tradition. Her atheism and opposition to any role for the state in social morality are also a source of conflict with traditional conservatism.

> **Exam tip**
>
> Be careful not to confuse Rand's ideas with those of anarchists. Rand and the New Right did not reject the state as a concept, but argued that it must be strictly limited in its power and intrusion into the lives of individuals.

Key thinker

Robert Nozick (1938–2002)

Writing in the 1970s, Robert Nozick has become one of the key thinkers of the New Right. His work *Anarchy, State and Utopia* (1974) can be seen as an attack on socialism and wealth redistribution of any kind.

- Nozick broke from the Hobbesian tradition and has a far more optimistic view of human nature.
- All individuals have self-ownership; they are the owners of their own body, mind and abilities.
- He saw individuals as having their own ends and projects to which they rationally devote themselves. Individuals have rights that existed before any social contract or state and 'there are things no person or group may do to them (without violating their rights)'.
- As individuals are so central, liberty is the fundamental value. This means individuals should be free from any form of legally enforced obligations in either the social or the economic sphere.
- Any attempt to achieve social justice via the redistribution of wealth and progressive taxation is an assault on liberty, as 'taxation of earnings is on par with forced labour'.
- The individual should be able to keep the fruits of their labour, as they have been earned in a free market through their hard work and talents.
- Nozick proposed the 'Wilt Chamberlain' argument, based on a famous basketball player. Chamberlain was in demand, so included in his contract that 25 cents from each spectator went to him. One million people attended games he played throughout the season, earning him $250,000, much more than everyone else. According to Nozick, this payment is just and he should keep it all, as he earned it through his own labour and the contract was freely entered into by all parties.
- A minimalist state could be justified if it is strictly limited to the protection of person, property and contract. This is a concession to the conservative view that the state does need to be strong but limited, to provide the necessary order for liberty to flourish.
- Nozick's positive view of human nature led him to conclude that 'there are only individual people, different individual people, with their own individual lives' who are dignified and rational in pursuit of their own goals rather than brutishly competitive atoms.
- The minimal state is just but inspiring. It allows for the emergence and peaceful co-existence of voluntarily formed communities, with their own morals, values and ideals. As long as individuals are free to contract in or out of these communities, it allows them to fully explore and live their own lives.

> **Exam tip**
>
> When analysing the ideas on human nature of conservative thinkers such as Rand and Nozick, comment on how they believed the success of talented individuals creates the moral space and material conditions for the less talented to thrive too. This reflects a more positive view of human nature and its potential than is normally associated with conservatism.

> **Exam tip**
>
> You can show a deeper understanding by showing that *Anarchy, State and Utopia* is a direct attack on Rawls' principle of distributive justice, arguing that progressive taxation and redistribution of wealth make the individual a slave to the collectivist goals of the state.

2 Conservatism

> **Exam tip**
> You can use the Wilt Chamberlain argument to illustrate Nozick's justification of inequalities in wealth resulting from freely exchanged contracts.

> **Now test yourself**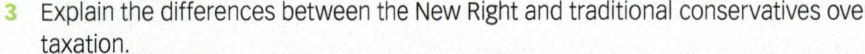
> 3 Explain the differences between the New Right and traditional conservatives over taxation.
> 4 Outline the links between traditional conservatives' view of human nature and their attitude to tradition and order.
> 5 Explain why Burke supported the American Revolution but not the French Revolution.

> **Revision activity**
> Compare and contrast the approaches of Rawls (see p. 17) and Nozick to justice and inequality.

Key thinkers in context

Thomas Hobbes
The English Civil Wars of the 1640s, convinced Hobbes of the need for a strong and powerful state that would prioritise peace and order over individual rights.

Edmund Burke
The French Revolution in the late eighteenth century made Burke hostile to violent revolution and states based on abstract ideas. Instead, he valued the notion of a 'natural' and organic state.

Michael Oakeshott
The experience both of the Second World War and the post-war welfare state led Oakeshott to emphasise the importance of pragmatism by governments. He also rejected the ideas of utopian societies, both left and right wing.

Ayn Rand
Growing up during the Russian Revolution gave Rand an intense hatred of socialism and collectivism. Her subsequent experiences in the USA and the growth of the federal government there led her to fear a similar restriction on individual freedom in the USA as well.

Robert Nozick
Writing in a similar period to Rand, Nozick too emphasised individual freedom and rejected the higher taxes that an expanded post-war state required from its citizens. He was writing, in part, to challenge the new liberal ideas of his Harvard contemporary John Rawls.

Core ideas of conservatism

Government, free-market capitalism and the individual

Government
Conservatives agree that government is necessary to provide order, security and stability. The government should be limited in size but should be committed to preserving and protecting the nation-state. However, there is disagreement among conservatives about how far the government can play a role in the economy and society, and in people's choices, morality and private lives.

Free-market capitalism
+ The free market, built on the principle of private property and capitalism, is central to a thriving economy that can provide wealth for all.
+ One-nation conservatives would argue, based on the principle of paternalism, that the wealthy have a duty to the less wealthy. Inequality plus large influxes of cheap imports and immigrant labour threatens stability, so a more interventionist role for the state in the economy is needed.
+ Neo-liberals would minimise the role of the state in the economy to create the conditions for individuals to help themselves and have their hard work and creativity fully rewarded.

Check your understanding and progress at www.hoddereducation.co.uk/myrevisionnotes

> **Exam tip**
>
> Conservative scepticism about the free market and globalisation is concerned with the fear that they will increase inequality and threaten the order in society. You can use this in your answers to explain conservatism's historic support for protectionist policies (taxes on imports) and the mixed economy.

The individual

+ Conservatives support the view that freedom and choice for the individual are important. However, conservatives also argue that the state needs to provide stability and order for freedom and choice to exist, so they support strong law and order measures.
+ Traditional conservatives support a more interventionist state to protect the organic society, whereas neo-liberals tend to see society in atomistic terms, so placing far greater value on the individual and a small state.

Agreement and tensions within conservatism

Human nature

Areas of agreement

+ Most conservatives, with the exception of New Right thinkers, have a pessimistic view of human nature – conservatism has been described as a 'philosophy of imperfection'. They stress the fallibility and weakness of human nature.
+ This leads conservatives to argue that the idea of a perfect society is unachievable and dangerous. The liberal idea of a society built on rational individuals is not based in true human nature, whereas the socialist idea that society can perfect humanity is deeply misplaced as human nature is fixed and constant.

Areas of tension

Hobbes

+ Hobbes held a largely cynical view of human nature, seeing humans as selfish, fearful of others and driven by a 'desire of power after power, that ceaseth only in death' (*Leviathan*).
+ However, for Hobbes human nature is rational, placing his views in this respect closer to liberalism and later neo-liberalism than to traditional conservatism.

Burke

+ Like Hobbes, Burke was sceptical about human nature. He agreed with Hobbes that human nature is neither flawless nor could be perfected.
+ However, Burke did not see human nature as individualistic, selfish and brutal like Hobbes. Burke viewed humans as flawed but capable of goodness and affection to others if their actions are informed by custom and tradition. Humans naturally seek the bonds of trust with others in 'little platoons'.

Oakeshott

+ Oakeshott built on Burke's view, seeing human nature as 'fragile and fallible' with an instinctive preference for the known over the unknown. Where humans have security and their lives are shaped by custom and traditional morality, humanity can be both 'benign and benevolent'.
+ This focus on imperfection highlights human fallibility rather than human potential, the gap between human dreams and reality, and so underpins opposition to the utopian visions of radical movements and ideas. This is the 'politics of scepticism' over the 'politics of faith'.

Rand and Nozick
- Rand and Nozick broke from the philosophy of imperfection. Their view of human nature was more positive, seeing humans as rational individuals who are dignified, not brutal, in pursuit of their own goals.
- As such, the New Right leaves individuals to make their own choices in the social and economic sphere, as this will lead to an inspiring and fulfilling future of human achievement.

The state

Area of agreement
The central purpose of the state for all conservatives is to provide national security and law and order.

Areas of tension
- Hobbes argued that the people come together in a social contract to create a sovereign. This sovereign has absolute power in order to ensure the necessary order and stability to allow society and freedom to thrive.
- Burke argued that there was no social contract in Hobbesian terms, only a contract between the dead, the living and the yet to be born. The state is natural and organic and emerges gradually in response to human needs.
- Traditional conservatives see an active role for the state in protecting and promoting the interests of all its citizens.
- Burke argued that hierarchy was natural and that the state and ruling class should act with a sense of public service, not self-interest, and have a sense of duty towards the less well-off in society.
- Traditional conservatives see the state as paternalist and argue that moderate social reform and intervention can be justified to benefit the less fortunate.
- Burke was opposed to vast, centralised and remote state structures, instead favouring local communities where the natural bonds of trust, duty and loyalty can emerge.
- Oakeshott believed that the state should be guided by pragmatism.
- For New Right thinkers, the state should be small; it should exist for the purposes of national security, enforcing contracts, and maintaining law and order.
- For Nozick, distributive justice, in the form of taxation and the welfare state, was unjust as it legalised the theft of wealth, in the form of taxation, to benefit those who have done nothing to contribute towards its creation. In 1974, he famously compared taxation on earnings to 'forced labour'.

> **Exam tip**
>
> It is not enough to explain the differences and similarities between the different strands within conservatism. You should evaluate the significance of both the similarities and differences to show your judgement.

> **Exam tip**
>
> Some students assume that the New Right opposes the modern welfare state as it is both inefficient and incompetent, creating a dependency culture that limits individualism. While this is correct, better answers would state that, even if the state were effective and efficient, Nozick would still argue that it is unjust as it makes slaves of the citizens of that state.

Society

Traditional forms of conservatism
- Traditional conservatism has a paternalistic view of society. Society is natural, organic and living, with individuals bound together by common ties, obligations and responsibilities, much like a family.
- Tradition, custom and continuity are crucial parts of society as they form the basis of the common ties. Any attempt to radically overhaul traditional institutions, customs and practices risks doing untold and lasting damage to society.
- Shared values and morals also provide these common ties, hence the conservative support for long-established Judeo-Christian moral values, not least in the areas of the family and marriage.
- Hobbes argued that society could only exist when stability, authority and order were present. This requires obedience and loyalty to the sovereign.
- Burke held an organic view of society, with a natural hierarchy where those with the natural talents to govern use the power of government responsibly in the best interests of all of society.

- Burke favoured a society built around the 'little platoons', which established the common ties of affection and built up the wisdom of custom and tradition over time.
- Oakeshott emphasised the importance of the known, the tried and tested, as he was sceptical about human progress. Change should be modest, rooted in the past and most of all realistic, rather than based on some fanciful, optimistic view of human nature.

The New Right
- Rand and Nozick directly challenged the organic view of society, instead seeing it as atomistic, with individuals rationally pursuing their own ends. They share a much more positive view of human progress.
- Society has no right to place obligations or restrictions on the individual, such as traditions, customs and shared values and morals. The individual should be free to make their own rational choices, in both the economic and social spheres. Rand, for example, while admitting she personally found homosexuality 'disgusting', did not believe it should be banned or restricted by the state. She also opposed racial segregation, which was then a feature in much of America's Deep South.

> **Exam tip**
>
> In 1987, Margaret Thatcher wrote, 'There is no such thing as society. There are individual men and women and there are families.' Although this appears to endorse the New Right view, it is worth pointing out that Thatcher was neo-conservative in her approach, extending the role of the state in promoting 'Victorian values' when it came to social issues such as gay rights and gambling.

The economy

Areas of agreement

Private property
- Conservatives agree that private property is good and its ownership constitutes a fundamental human right.
- It provides the individual with security and safety in an ever-changing world.
- It provides the basis for respecting the property rights of others, as we wish our property to be respected. So, property is vital for order.
- Property has been seen as an expression of the individual, as individuals see themselves in the property that they own.
- The economy should be based on private property and, although there is disagreement about the role of the state in the economy, conservatives agree that excessive restrictions on private property will limit individual freedom, creativity and hard work.

Capitalism
- Capitalism is the most efficient and effective means of creating wealth. It also links directly to conservatives' view of human nature as selfish, since people will work harder if they know they will get to keep the fruits of their labour.
- Wealth inequality is natural and a reflection of the different talents, hard work and effort of individuals in society.
- The desire to impose wealth equality on society is immoral as it is not rooted in the natural justice idea that people should benefit from their own hard work.

Areas of tension
- Hobbes argued that a powerful sovereign, able to impose order and stability, is essential to the working of the economy.
- Burke focused on the importance of property rights and the importance of the state in protecting property rights. He believed that markets should be left to operate free from government interference.
- Burke argued that 'to provide for us in our necessities is not in the power of government' but rather was the paternalistic responsibility of the natural elites. The alleviation of poverty should be achieved by private charity.

- Traditional conservatives, taking a pragmatic approach, have supported protectionism, the mixed economy and welfarism in order to protect against the threat to one nation from unregulated capitalism.
- Oakeshott saw private property as a form of security and power. It should be as widely spread as possible in society in order to protect liberty.
- The New Right are the staunchest defenders of the free market. The free market, unencumbered by the state, will reward the rational individual for their hard work and creativity, leading to the benefits of trickle-down economics.
- For Nozick, the welfare state was like forced labour. Individuals are forced to pay taxes to create financial resources for the state to give to those who have contributed nothing towards those resources.

> **Exam tip**
>
> You can illustrate that faith in the market has its roots in Burke, who argued that 'the moment that government appears at market, the principles of the market will be subverted'.

Now test yourself

TESTED

6. Explain how conservatives justify private property.
7. Explain the ways in which New Right thinking can be linked to classical liberalism.
8. Describe why traditional conservatives may be cautious in their support for free-market capitalism and globalisation.
9. Copy and complete the following table with the key views of both traditional conservatives and the New Right.

Traditional conservatism	New Right
Pragmatism	Principle
Hierarchy	
Organic society	
Change to conserve	
Mixed economy and protectionism	
Welfare for social stability	

> **Revision activity**
>
> Distinguish between:
> a) traditional conservatism and the New Right
> b) neo-liberalism and neo-conservatism

Key differences between traditional conservatism and the New Right conservatism

Key differences between traditional and New Right conservatism are summarised in Table 2.2.

Table 2.2 Tensions between traditional conservatism and the New Right

	Traditional conservatism	The New Right
Human nature	The politics of imperfection dominates the understanding of human nature. From this view emerges the need for order, stability and tradition. This also underpins a generally sceptical approach to politics, based on pragmatism not abstract principles.	A more optimistic view of human nature, based on the rationalism of the individual. The minimal state, with a free market, will provide the basis for individuals to flourish. This leads to a strongly ideological approach based on the principles of the small state and the free market, creating a positive view of progress; the 'politics of faith' over the 'politics of scepticism'.
The state	The state, dominated by a natural ruling class, should govern in the interests of the governed. A pragmatic approach to the role of the state, which should take an active role to ensure the social stability of 'one nation'.	The rolling back of the state to a small, but strong state that provides security, law and order. This is just, maximises freedom and will reverse the dependency culture. Opposition to the idea of a natural hierarchy, arguing instead for meritocracy where the most talented should lead.
Society	Society is organic, based on 'little platoons'. Tradition, custom and practice are important to provide continuity in a changing world. These traditions should be nurtured in line with the principle of 'change to conserve'.	Society is a collection of individuals, each rationally pursuing their own ends. Society should be meritocratic not hierarchical, allowing the most talented to thrive and lead. Tradition, custom and practice should be challenged and changed if they stand in the way of individual freedom or the free market.

| The economy | The free market, based on the principle of private property, is the best creator of wealth. However, it can create tensions and divisions, so moderate reform, regulation and intervention may be necessary to conserve one nation and protect against radical ideas like socialism. | The free market should be unregulated as it generates the most wealth, productivity and freedom for all. It will allow innovation and the best ideas to drive the economy. This will create generalised wealth and raise the standard of living for all by reducing the cost of goods and services while increasing productivity and wages. |

Now test yourself

TESTED

10 Explain the difference between the New Right and traditional conservatives in their attitude to progress.

11 Copy and complete the following table with the main ideas of the key thinkers.

Thinker	Human nature	The state	Society	The economy
Thomas Hobbes				
Edmund Burke				
Michael Oakeshott				
Ayn Rand				
Robert Nozick				

Revision activity

Create a set of flashcards for all the key terms in this chapter.

Exam skills

Here is a sample paragraph answering the following 9-mark Section A question: 'Explain and analyse three ways that conservative thinkers have viewed private property.'

> New Right thinkers from the post-war era such as Nozick and Rand believe that the rights of individuals to private property are virtually sacrosanct. For example, in her novel *Atlas Shrugged*, Rand had as her hero the inventor John Galt who created his own community, Galt's Gulch, in response to the collectivist state which posed a growing threat to private wealth. Both thinkers believed that as all property and wealth was generated by individuals' own efforts, they should, in a free capitalist country, be allowed to keep their wealth. It should not be taken away by the state to spend on welfare programmes that benefited the lazy and less creative/hardworking. Nozick once referred to taxation as 'forced labour'. Their views are significant as they not only contrast with paternalist one-nation conservatism, but also help explain why they opposed the creation of a large and active state, partly in response to the rise of the Soviet Union but also the rise of the welfare state in the West which required higher taxes.

This is a strong paragraph as the student directly identifies the approach of the New Right towards property. Both key thinkers are identified and there is supporting own knowledge about their ideas (e.g. the reference to Galt's Gulch and the quote from Nozick). There is also awareness of the context in which they were writing, and analysis of the significance of their views (e.g. how they viewed the state).

Exam practice

1. Explain and analyse three ways that conservatism can be considered as the politics of imperfection. [9]

2. Explain and analyse three ways that conservative thinkers have viewed the state. [9]

Read the extract below and answer question 3 that follows.

> Working after the pattern of nature, we receive, we hold, we pass on our government and our privileges, in the same manner in which we enjoy and pass on our property and our lives. The institutions of politics, the goods of fortune, the gifts of providence are handed down to us, and from us. Our political system is placed in symmetry with the order of the world, and with the way of existence decreed to a permanent body composed of transitory or temporary parts; where, by wisdom, moulding together the great mysterious incorporation of the human race, the whole, at one time, is never old, or middle-aged, or young, but, in a condition of unchangeable constancy, moves on through the varied tenor of perpetual decay, fall, renovation, and progression. Thus, by preserving the method of nature in the conduct of the state, in what we improve, we are never wholly new.
>
> Source: adapted from Edmund Burke, *Reflections on the French Revolution*
>
> Nozick's political ideas differ in many ways from those often labelled as 'conservative' by academics and students. For example, the traditional hallmarks of conservative political thought include a high regard for custom, trust of longstanding traditions, and scepticism of ideological revolutions. Conservative political thinkers also usually argue that authority is crucial because it enables stability and order in human societies. However, none of these qualities can really be seen in Nozick's view of the state. His political philosophy does not directly refer to custom or tradition at all. In fact, if the outcome of consenting citizens leads to radical breaks with customs and traditional culture, that is a valid judgement on the old culture. In Nozick's view, there would be nothing wrong or problematic about such an outcome.
>
> Source: secondary material created by the authors for this book, 2023

3. Analyse, evaluate and compare the arguments being made in the above extracts over conservatism's views on the state. In your answer, you should refer to the thinkers you have studied. [25]

Summary

You should now have an understanding of:
+ whether conservatism is a coherent political idea
+ core conservative ideas and values concerning government, the free market and the individual
+ the contributions of the five key thinkers (Hobbes, Burke, Oakeshott, Rand and Nozick) to the development of conservatism
+ the beliefs of conservatism in relation to human nature, the state, society and the economy
+ the key differences between traditional conservatism and the New Right

Check your understanding and progress at www.hoddereducation.co.uk/myrevisionnotes

3 Socialism

Socialism is a broad outlook on the human condition that has historically been defined by its opposition to capitalism. The central idea of socialism is equality, especially social equality, which is seen as a prerequisite of freedom and a society built on collective action. This chapter will explore the origins of socialism, the different schools of thought and then summarise the areas of tension and agreement.

> **Social equality** An equal distribution of wealth, income and status within society. However, within socialism there is disagreement about how far this equality should extend.
>
> **Collective action** Working together in order to achieve mutual benefit, as co-operation is both more effective than, and morally superior to, individual competition.

Origins of socialism

REVISED

+ Socialism developed in the nineteenth century from the interaction between the Enlightenment (see p. 10) and emerging issues such as the rich–poor divide created by the Industrial Revolution and modern capitalism.
+ The term 'socialism' was first brought into use by the utopian socialists Charles Fourier and Robert Owen.
+ Fourier and Owen both aimed to apply the ideals of the Enlightenment to the problem that wealth and power were becoming increasingly unequal in society between the few and the many.
+ Robert Owen's idea was that human nature was malleable; our characters 'are made for us, not by us'. Owen argued that the conditions of capitalism were creating lives of vice, misery and conduct that were unworthy of rational beings. Hence, socialism of all varieties assumes that social engineering is both possible and desirable.
+ Owen was convinced that if he provided the right environment, he could produce co-operative, dutiful, public-spirited characters.
+ Karl Marx was critical of Owen's socialism, seeing it as utopian because it put forward an ideal without understanding the actual conditions that made it impossible.
+ Karl Marx and Friedrich Engels offered a scientific socialism that shows how socialism *would* inevitably replace capitalism rather simply why it *should* replace capitalism.

> **Utopian socialists** Those who adhere to the blueprint for an ideal, future socialist society, or Utopia, to illustrate how life will be better under socialism.
>
> **Scientific socialism** A scientific analysis of the economic development of society that reveals the division of society into distinct classes locked into struggle with each other. This struggle is the motor of history, meaning it is inevitable that socialism will replace capitalism.

> **Exam tip**
>
> One example of social engineering to use in the exam is Owen's model community in New Lanark in the early nineteenth century, with its communal facilities, education and welfare alongside satisfying work with good wages and good conditions. Owen described New Lanark as 'the most important experiment for the happiness of the human race that has yet been instituted in any part of the world'.

Main beliefs of socialism

REVISED

The main issue in defining socialism, as with all ideologies, is how to show what unites socialists while at the same time illustrating the critical differences which separate them. Socialism offers a criticism of the existing world we live in, an alternative to that world and a theory of change.

- **Egalitarianism**. Socialism favours equality of some sort – people should be treated the same, get the same, or be treated as equals in some respect. Most socialists have viewed capitalism as an unequal economic system that concentrates wealth in the hands of the few, and condemns the many to poverty and powerlessness. This creates totally unacceptable differences in life chances in deeply divided societies.
- **Collectivism**. The individualism of conservatism and liberalism produces competition not co-operation and inequality not fairness. Society is enhanced by collective action, as working together is both morally superior and economically more successful than individual action. True humanity flows from being part of a genuine community which will replace the isolation and marginalisation people experience under capitalism.
- **Change**. Socialism is a challenge and a response to the presumed negative effects of capitalism and wants change to the distribution of resources in favour of the many not the few. There are clear tensions here between the revolutionary road and the parliamentary road to socialism.
- **An alternative society**. Socialism favours a society built on the principles of freedom, equality and community, although the different strands of socialism have differing understandings of these terms and how to value them.
- **Common humanity**. Socialists believe in the changing nature of humanity over time, as human nature is shaped by society rather than being fixed. However, there is common humanity in that humans have the need to be, are, or can become social beings desiring freedom, equality and community.

> **Exam tip**
>
> Socialists are critical of the way freedom is defined in other political ideologies. It is not enough to say freedom means the absence of restraint, as free markets create poverty and those in poverty cannot be completely free. Socialists might ask: what is the point of the freedom to eat in any restaurant you choose, if you can't pay the bill? In the exam, this can be used when discussing views on, and the significance of, freedom and capitalism.

Historical materialism, class analysis and fundamental goals

REVISED

Marxism

The aim of Marxism is to explain the world in which you live and what is wrong with society. Marx's view of historical change, of how societies rise and fall, and how this dynamic is driven by social class is called historical materialism. The dynamic that drives history is the struggle between contending groups within society. Marx argued that 'Men make their own history, but they do not make it as they please; they do not make it under self-selected circumstances, but under circumstances existing already, given and transmitted from the past' (*The Eighteenth Brumaire of Louis Bonaparte*, 1852).

- The contending groups, or classes, in society are created by the relations between those who own the means of production and those who do not.
- Towards the end of feudal societies, international trade created the move from production by crafts people, often in their homes, to steam-powered machinery and industrial production in larger factories.
- The bourgeoisie – the owners of this new means of production – accumulated huge wealth and overthrew the existing feudal class relations between landowners and peasants, which no longer reflected the material conditions of society.
- The rise of capitalism presented for the first time the chance for humans to live free from oppression and from poverty through its revolutionary technological changes and ability to create wealth.
- At the same time, it created a large proletariat, who had to sell their labour to survive, and concentrated wealth in the hands of the bourgeoisie. In creating the proletariat, famously seen by Marx as the 'gravediggers' of capitalism, the capitalist system is the precondition for socialism.

> **Historical materialism** Marx's view of historical change is based on the idea that changes in the way humans work together to produce things then change the way society is organised and the attitude of people in that society.
>
> **Bourgeoisie** The Marxist term for the class that owns the means of production in capitalism.
>
> **Proletariat** The Marxist term for the class in capitalism that has to sell its labour to the bourgeoisie in order to survive, as it has no ownership over the means of production.

Class analysis

For Marxists, the contradictions between the classes, created by the means of production, are essential to understanding the world:
+ In capitalism, the bourgeoisie (ruling class) owns the means of production. They exploit the proletariat (the working class) who are forced to sell their labour to survive.
+ Under capitalism, workers are alienated from their labour as they work to produce commodities, which are owned by the capitalists and sold for profit, rather than producing what is needed or useful. The workers can see that the more wealth they produce, the poorer they become as labour becomes a commodity to be purchased at the lowest possible price.
+ At the same time, capitalism is driven by internal contradictions as the desire for profit drives down wages and living standards for the workers, while increasing the accumulation of wealth in the hands of the few. This makes capitalism increasingly unstable and prone to deeper and deeper economic crises.
+ Alienation, exploitation and the deepening crises of capitalism create a class consciousness, as the worker is forced to face 'with sober senses his real conditions of life, and his relations with his kind' (*The Communist Manifesto*, 1848).
+ Class consciousness drives the working classes to rise up and overthrow the existing society and state, and replace them with socialism.

Fundamental goals

+ The class relationship to the means of production and the distribution of wealth are the basis for the legal, political and social structure of society. This structure expresses, enforces and consolidates the class relationships. Therefore, the state is not neutral but 'a committee for managing the common affairs of the whole bourgeoisie' (*The Commmunist Manifesto*, 1848).
+ As such, the socialist revolution must overthrow the state, society and the existing economic system based on private property.
+ The dictatorship of the proletariat will be a short-term strategy to collectivise all property into common ownership for the good of all.
+ Marx and Engels realised that this would meet strong opposition, so the dictatorship of the proletariat would need to defeat the opposing forces (counter-revolutionaries) through force in something like a civil war.
+ The common ownership of property would lead to the end of class and class conflict. With exploitation a thing of the past, there would be no need for struggles over political power.
+ There is no need for a workers' state once the class struggle has ended and there will be true democracy as all will be free.
+ The state will wither away as society transforms from socialism to communism.
+ Marxism argues that wealth is increasingly located in fewer and fewer hands. It is worth exploring whether more wealth is concentrated in fewer hands in the UK, the USA and globally to see if this analysis stands up.
+ It is also worth asking: has capitalism really created its own gravediggers? Marxist revolutions have not occurred as Marx predicted they would. Has capitalism made the proletariat poorer or raised living standards in the UK and USA?

Communism A classless society, with no state and the common ownership of wealth. Production would be for necessary consumption and use, and to satisfy need rather than profit, freeing humans' creative energies and allowing full freedom for all.

Exam tip
Marxism seeks to explain why capitalism is inevitably shaken by the boom and bust cycle and all the chaos for workers that this entails. In the exam, you could point to the global financial crash of 2008 and the global recession of 2020 as recent examples of increasing instability from a Marxist perspective.

Class consciousness
Workers first become conscious of sharing common complaints against capitalism (a class 'in itself') and then develop an awareness of themselves as forming a social class, the proletariat (a class 'for itself'), opposed to the bourgeoisie.

Dictatorship of the proletariat
The transitional phase from capitalism to communism, where the workers' state protects the gains of the revolution and replaces private ownership with common ownership.

Common ownership
The means of production are placed in the hands of the workers, so that they can control their working lives and the economy as a whole.

Revision activity
Describe what is meant by class consciousness and outline how it comes about.

Key thinkers

Karl Marx (1818–83) and Friedrich Engels (1820–95)

Marx and Engels are regarded as the key thinkers of socialism, with *The Communist Manifesto* (1848) and *Das Kapital* (1867) providing a powerful analysis and critique of capitalism and a guide to political action.

+ Their key idea was that 'the history of all hitherto existing society is the history of class struggles'. It was the history of conflict between oppressed and oppressor that ends in the revolutionary remaking of society along communist lines.
+ Capitalism has split society into 'two great hostile camps, into two classes directly facing each other – bourgeoisie and proletariat'.
+ The ideological superstructure – society's values, culture and the political institutions of the state – is a reflection of the material base (see Figure 3.1). It therefore reinforces the interests of whoever controls the means of production.

Reinforces and legitimises the base

IDEOLOGICAL SUPERSTRUCURE
Law, religion, politics and ideology, media, education, the arts, culture

MATERIAL BASE
Means of production: technology, raw materials, land, factories, etc.
Relations of production: the bourgeoisie and the proletariat

Shapes the ideological superstructure

Figure 3.1 The base and superstructure

+ This means that the state, law, religion, the media, education, the arts and culture reflect the values and ideals of the ruling class; in capitalism, these are the values and ideals of the bourgeoisie. The ideological superstructure creates a false consciousness among the proletariat, who are led to believe there is no alternative to the world as it is.
+ Marx and Engels therefore concluded that a communist society cannot be created using the bourgeois state, so revolution is necessary.
+ Socialism is inevitable as it is driven by historical materialism and it must be delivered from below by the working classes.
+ The revolution must be followed by a dictatorship of the proletariat to bring all private property into common ownership and defend the gains of the revolution against the dispossessed bourgeoisie.
+ The dictatorship of the proletariat is a transition to the abolition of all classes and to a classless society, where the state will wither away. Society will be ordered on the principle 'from each according to his ability, to each according to his needs' (*Critique of the Gotha Programme*, 1875).

Exam tip

It is worth linking your discussion of socialism to recent historical examples. The collapse of communism in the Soviet Union and eastern Europe at the end of the twentieth century led many to claim that socialism was now dead and that there is no alternative to capitalism – a view strongly endorsed by Anthony Giddens. Yet others argued that that the Soviet Union and eastern Europe never reflected the ideas of Marx and Engels.

Marx and Engels also argued that capitalism would conquer the whole earth for its markets, seemingly identifying the forces of globalisation in the modern world. The spread of the market has triggered new global, anti-capitalist and anti-globalisation movements, with some suggesting that the global market has made a new global proletariat, largely based in the global South, which will be the agent of change from capitalism to socialism.

Check your understanding and progress at www.hoddereducation.co.uk/myrevisionnotes

The nature of socialism

How should a socialist society come about?

The first major debate within socialism is about the path to socialism: can it be achieved through evolution or does it require revolution? Table 3.1 reflects the two main views.

Table 3.1 Revolution or evolution?

Revolutionary socialism	<ul><li>Marx and Engels argued that socialism will be achieved by revolution from below, as the few will never willingly surrender their power and wealth. Socialism will come about through a class-based revolution and workers must be prepared to use force to defeat a violent counter-revolution by the few.</li><li>Liberal democracy, which is dictatorship by the few, will be replaced by the dictatorship of the proletariat, which is the democracy of the masses.</li><li>The dictatorship of the proletariat will abolish private ownership of the means of production and replace it with common ownership.</li><li>This will lead to the abolition of all classes and a classless society, which leads to communism and the withering away of the state.</li></ul>
Evolutionary/reformist socialism	<ul><li>In **evolutionary/reformist socialism**, there is a parliamentary road to socialism, so democratic politics rather than class struggle is the motor for change.</li><li>**Democratic socialists** like Beatrice Webb believe in the 'inevitability of gradualism', where a political democracy will naturally lead to the common ownership of the means of production and thus to a socialist society.</li><li>Universal suffrage (votes for all) enable the working class, whose lives are uniformly miserable within capitalism, to vote together in their class interest for socialist parties.</li><li>Socialism can then be achieved by working within the existing state through education and gradual, piecemeal reforms delivered in a legal and peaceful way.</li><li>In the end, socialism would come about due to all classes recognising its ethical superiority, so a working-class revolution is not needed or desirable.</li></ul>

Evolutionary/reformist socialism Socialism delivered by the ballot box and legal, piecemeal reforms. It rejects the revolutionary road to socialism.

Democratic socialists Those who believe that socialism should be pursued by democratic means, where the electorate is persuaded of the moral superiority of socialism in a state with representative institutions.

Exam tip

Rosa Luxemburg's *Reform or Revolution* (1900) can be used to illustrate the Marxist criticisms of evolutionary socialism. She argued that socialism cannot be delivered by working within the state, as the state is controlled by and represents the interests of the ruling class. The parliamentary road is not a different path to the same end, socialism; rather it involves surrendering to capitalism.

Key thinker

Rosa Luxemburg (1871–1919)

Rosa Luxemburg was a Polish-born socialist who developed the Marxist view of revolution and was a key critic of reformism.
+ Luxemburg's work, *The Mass Strike, the Political Party and the Trade Unions* (1906) built on the Marxist view that the emancipation of the working class can only be achieved by the working class, arguing that the mass strike is the strategy for revolution.
+ The mass strike is 'a historical phenomenon which, at a given moment, results from social conditions with historical inevitability'. When the antagonism between the bourgeoisie and proletariat is at its greatest, the mass strike will appear to be 'spontaneous' and overthrow the very conditions that made it possible.
+ The mass strike will:
  + bring the proletariat together as a mass, giving them a sense of their common interests and their power, overcoming the atomisation of workers under capitalism.

- educate the workers in organisations, so that they can develop an ability to organise society themselves in the interests of the many.
- bring the proletariat together so that they can undermine and overthrow the state.
+ In *Reform or Revolution* (1900), Luxemburg attacked the idea that socialism could be achieved by reform, arguing that those who argued for legislative reform 'do not choose a more tranquil, calmer and slower road to the same goal, but a different goal'.
+ The legislative reform route fails to recognise that:
  - the state represents and is controlled by the ruling class.
  - reformism will not mean socialism but accommodating capitalism.
  - socialists value reforms not only for their benefits to workers but because the process of fighting for reform generates the organisation and strength to take on capitalism as a whole.
  - it abandons the historical materialism of scientific socialism.

Key thinker

Beatrice Webb (1858–1943)

Beatrice Webb was a key thinker in reformist socialism who underpinned democratic socialism. She was instrumental in establishing the Fabian Society, aligning it with the Labour Party, and in drafting Clause IV of the Labour constitution of 1918 which focused on 'the common ownership of the means of production, distribution and exchange'.

+ Through painstaking research, Webb identified that 'crippling poverty and demeaning inequality' are the by-products of the social structures of capitalism, not individual actions or failings. Therefore, poverty cannot be tackled through paternalism or charity. It can only be tackled by moving from capitalism to socialism.
+ Capitalism was a 'corrupting force' for human nature, making humans unnaturally selfish and greedy.
+ Webb's *Minority Report of the Poor Law Commission* (1909) argued for a 'national minimum of civilised life'.
+ The nationalisation programme, the health service and the welfare state of the Attlee government of 1945–51 can be seen as rooted in Webb's ideas of the national minimum standard of civilised life.
+ Webb argued for the 'inevitability of gradualism':
  + Webb rejected the Marxist idea that the class struggle would bring about socialism through revolution.
  + In its place, Webb argued that socialism was still inevitable, but it would be delivered gradually through piecemeal, social and political reform by the state.
  + The process was inevitable as, in the age of universal suffrage, the working classes would realise they were being exploited under capitalism and would vote for socialist parties.
  + Socialist governments would gradually reform capitalism and take the means of production into public ownership. This reform would produce a socialist society and shape human nature to be more co-operative, altruistic and fraternal.
  + As the benefits of socialism become clear to all – because it is ethically superior to capitalism – the transformation from capitalism to socialism will become permanent.

Making links

Clause IV of the 1918 constitution of the Labour Party proposes common ownership but in practice this meant that the Labour Party supported nationalisation to bring key industries into public ownership under the control of the state, *not* common ownership under the control of workers. Be careful to state that nationalisation took place under Clement Attlee and prior to the emergence of social democracy. It is also worth noting that Clause IV was amended in 1995, under the leadership of Tony Blair, to remove the commitment to nationalisation in favour of 'a community in which power, wealth and opportunity are in the hands of the many not the few'.

Exam tip

It is worth noting in the exam that evolutionary socialists, social democrats and the 'third way' all accept the parliamentary road to socialism, in contrast to the revolutionary socialism of Marx, Engels and Luxemburg.

To what extent is socialism compatible with capitalism?

+ The Marxist tradition (fundamental socialism) is entirely hostile to capitalism, where the means of production are under private ownership. Capitalism's thirst for profit can only be satisfied by driving down the wages of the workers, leading to exploitation and misery.
+ Capitalism's tendency towards worsening economic crises throws workers on the unemployment scrapheap, creating further misery.
+ Marx and Engels, as well as Luxemburg, argued that private property and the market must be abolished and replaced by common ownership and co-operation.

Check your understanding and progress at www.hoddereducation.co.uk/myrevisionnotes

- Once common ownership has been established, there will be a classless society and the state will wither away, creating a true democracy that will allow humans to be free to develop their fraternal and co-operative nature.
- Revisionist socialists (see p. 47) argue that capitalism is incredibly efficient at producing economic growth and raising living standards. Capitalism should be harnessed and humanised to achieve socialist ends.
- Social democrats, like Anthony Crosland (see p. 48), argue that progressive taxation, high levels of spending on public services and universal welfare could be used to distribute rewards, status and privileges fairly to minimise social resentment between classes, to create equal opportunities for all and to secure justice between individuals. They do not see the issue of ownership as important.
- Advocates of the third way, like Anthony Giddens (see p. 49), argue that the increased tax revenues produced by the free market could be invested in infrastructure and public services, especially education, to create equality of opportunity.

Social democrats Those who believe in philosophical and practical attempts to blend democracy, capitalism and social justice. Social democracy is a form of revisionist socialism as it looks to depart from earlier socialist theories to present a different interpretation of socialism. Social justice is fairness in the distribution of assets, wealth and advantages within society, involving a commitment to equality through redistribution via the state. Examples include progressive taxation on the wealthy and the provision of universal welfare.

Exam tip
Common ownership should not be confused with public ownership, which is the ownership of the means of production by the state. Under public ownership, the workers are *not* the masters of their work.

Now test yourself
1. Outline the key difference between revolutionary socialism and evolutionary socialism.
2. Outline the reasons why Luxemburg believed that evolutionary socialism was like 'proposing to change the sea of capitalist bitterness into a sea of socialist sweetness, by progressively pouring into it bottles of social reformist lemonade'?
3. On what basis have Marxist thinkers argued that the collapse of capitalism is inevitable?
4. What is the difference between common ownership and public ownership?

Revision activity
Define utopian socialism, social democracy and democratic socialism.

Revisionist socialism

Revisionist socialism is a reinterpretation of socialism to take account of changes in the world in order to update it. It is associated with humanising rather than abolishing capitalism.

Social democracy
- The harsh world of capitalism had been transformed by the reforms of the post-war Labour government under Clement Attlee (1945–51) through nationalisation, the creation of the welfare state and Keynesian economics.
- The Marxist theory of the misery of the working classes and deeper economic crises had been disproved by growing economic output and higher living standards.
- The power of the business-owning class had been reduced by the increased power of government and the rise of the trade unions.
- Managers, not business owners, were now running industry, so it was better to focus on the control/regulation of capitalism rather than public ownership. Managers are a new class in society, weakening Marx's idea of two competing classes under capitalism.
- The mixed economy – public ownership of key industries and services (e.g. rail, water and electricity) but most other industries under private ownership – had been economically successful and reduced inequality.

Keynesian economics The use of taxation and spending policies to create full employment and continuous economic growth.

- Modern socialism was about social justice: this involved improving welfare and social equality through progressive taxation and the redistribution of wealth to rectify the inequalities produced by the market.
- Modern socialism was about social equality – tackling poverty and reducing inequality. In social democracy it did not go as far as complete equality, as 'extra responsibility and exceptional talent require and deserve a differential reward', in the words of Anthony Crosland (*The Future of Socialism*, 1956).
- In Crosland's eyes, social democracy would 'weaken the existing deep-seated class stratification with its consistent feelings of envy and inferiority, and its barriers to uninhibited mingling between the classes'.

> **Key thinker**
>
> **Anthony Crosland (1918–77)**
>
> Anthony Crosland's *The Future of Socialism* (1956) is arguably the most important revisionist work of the postwar era and its aim was to bring social democracy up to date for the time.
> - Crosland was a revisionist, arguing that socialism had 'no precise, descriptive meaning' and was really a set of values, not a fixed programme. He argued that social equality was the fundamental aim, *not* ownership of the means of production.
> - He argued that 'Marx has little to offer the contemporary socialist' and that the Marxist idea of imminent capitalist collapse had been disproven by events.
> - Crosland was extremely optimistic about economic growth and stated that 'I no longer regard questions of growth and efficiency as being, on a long view, of primary importance to socialism.'
> - Capitalism was becoming more managerial and technocratic, less focused on profit and more willing to accept systems of regulation imposed by states.
> - The Keynesian economic approach could be used to control the economy to keep delivering growth and to ensure full employment without the need for more public ownership. Crosland therefore rejected nationalisation as a main aim of the Labour Party.
> - The ability of managed capitalism to produce continuous growth could be harnessed by progressively taxing and redistributing wealth via the welfare state and public services to promote social equality and tackle poverty – capitalism with a human face.
> - Crosland emphasised the ending of segregation and selection in school education to provide comprehensive education for all. This would help break down the barriers between classes, minimising class distinctions and providing all pupils with equality of opportunity.
> - Ultimately, Crosland emphasised quality of life issues and breaking down class barriers, so that everyone could be free to achieve happiness and flourishing lives.

> **Exam tip**
>
> When writing about the significance of equality, it is possible to offer a definition of the term, but it would be wrong to assume that all socialists agree about what 'equality' means. Marxists promote equality based on the principle 'from each according to his ability, to each according to his needs' and argue that equality cannot exist under capitalism. In contrast, social democrats see it in terms of tackling poverty and reducing the inequality between classes within capitalism. Social democracy has tended to view some level of social equality as a prerequisite of equality of opportunity.

> **Exam tip**
>
> Crosland's optimistic view of the case for social democracy was built on the ideals of continuous growth and higher living standards, with an effective state that cared for people, strong trade unions protecting workers' rights and socially conscious managers running businesses. It is worth noting in the exam that this view became problematic in the 1970s as the UK suffered from stagflation – high inflation and stagnant economic growth – and in the face of the rise of Thatcherism in the 1980s. This helps explain why Labour reinvented itself in the 1990s using the ideas of the third way.

The third way

- The third way is associated with the thinking of Anthony Giddens and the practice of the Labour Party under Tony Blair.
- The third way accepts that the managed capitalism of Keynesian economics is dead and has been replaced by the free market of

neo-liberalism (see p. 18). It aims to balance this with social democracy's commitment to community and equality of opportunity.
- Drawing on the socialist ideals of co-operative human nature, the third way is willing to accept free-market economics (see p. 32) but not the ideas of an atomistic society (see p. 37). It proposes the widest possible freedoms, but tied to responsibilities to the wider community.
- The emphasis on community, and the ties that bind everyone together, tends to downplay the importance of class divisions and inequality. The focus is on consensus and social harmony, not class conflict.
- The third way rejects the emphasis on social equality, instead focusing on social justice by providing equality of opportunity. People are given access to education and welfare is targeted at those who are socially excluded (e.g. the poorest) so they can access the opportunities in society.
- This is a clear emphasis on the redistribution of possibilities, with tax and benefit changes targeted at helping the poorest, although it is recognised that a meritocratic society may be very unequal in terms of the level of outcome.
- The role of the state is not social engineering through redistribution, in the way that Crosland proposed. The social investment state should concentrate on investing in economic infrastructure and human resources, to make the state more competitive in the global market.
- Education in particular is seen as key, as it creates a skilled and knowledgeable workforce that can compete in the modern, globalised economy, driving economic growth and allowing the individual to realise their full potential.
- Economic growth is crucial to the third way as it provides the tax base to enable social investment in areas like education, transport infrastructure and technology infrastructure.

> **Exam tip**
>
> It is worth noting in the exam that the 1997 Labour manifesto claimed, 'The old left would have sought state control of industry. The Conservative right is content to leave all to the market. We reject both approaches.'

> **Exam tip**
>
> The third way accepts that there is no alternative to free-market capitalism and rejects a class-based analysis of society. In the exam, this can be used to raise questions about how compatible the third way is with the rest of socialism in its view on the economy and the significance of capitalism.

> **Key thinker**
>
> **Anthony Giddens (1938–)**
>
> Giddens' main ideas included the rejection of the traditional conception of socialism and his favouring of the 'third way' in politics.
> - In his book, *Beyond Left and Right* (1994), Giddens states that 'Old Conservatism, at least in its more principled forms, is, as has been aptly said, the "other God that failed" alongside Communism and radical socialism.'
> - The third way is a response to the changing world, where globalisation has transformed modern economies and the role of government; rather than the big state of social democracy, there should be an intelligent, social investment state. The capacity for government to manage the economy is therefore much reduced, leaving government with two clear roles:
>   - to make the workforce more competitive by building their skills and knowledge through education and training.
>   - to build the necessary infrastructure – transport, schools and hospitals – in order to maximise trade and investment.
> - Giddens argued for a combination of right-wing economic and left-wing social policies:
>   - In his book, *The Third Way: The Renewal of Social Democracy* (1998), he argued that socialism had to accept that neo-liberalism was here to stay and was crucial as it promoted growth, entrepreneurship, enterprise and wealth creation.
> - He argued that neo-liberalism had empowered the individual economically, bringing greater freedom, but had also undermined traditional communities. So, neo-liberalism needs to be married to the principles of community and equality of opportunity from social democracy.
> - The principle of community can be delivered through devolving power to Scotland, Wales, regional assemblies and directly elected mayors, who represent the various communities. It is also evident in the drive for social inclusion and idea of rights coming with responsibilities.
> - He focused on equality of opportunity, recognising that it is denied to many and that this can be corrected by targeted, efficient public spending. With this targeted spending comes individual responsibility – local schools will be improved, but parents have a responsibility to make sure their child attends and will face consequences if they don't.
> - Work is the path out of poverty, so work needs to be made worthwhile as it will give people a sense of dignity and worth. The state has the responsibility to train and educate workers, but individuals have a responsibility to take those jobs.

> **Exam tip**
>
> It is worth noting that Giddens argues that the nation-state is too big for small problems and too small for big ones – and so he was a supporter of the decentralisation of power through the process of devolution.

> **Exam tip**
>
> Good illustrations to use of the third way in practice are the policies of Tony Blair. These included cutting class sizes, bringing down NHS waiting lists, introducing the minimum wage, devolution, no rises in income tax, getting 250,000 under-25-year-olds off benefits and into work, and reforming the welfare system to make work pay.

> **Exam tip**
>
> It is worth noting in the exam that Giddens argued that New Labour was not a continuation of Thatcherism; the third way recognises the virtues of markets but does not worship them. The third way should be concerned with social justice – to improve the position of the poor, especially children in poverty, and to ensure large-scale investment in public services to create a redistribution of possibilities.

Now test yourself   TESTED

5 What are the key differences between social democracy and Marxism in their attitude to capitalism?
6 How do social democracy and the third way differ in their views of the role of the state?
7 Copy and complete the following table to show the differences between social democracy and the third way.

Social democracy	Third way
The politics of class	
Relative social equality	
The state's role as social engineer	
Redistributive welfare	
Keynesian economics	

> **Revision activity**
>
> Create a spider diagram detailing the key ideas of Marx and Engels, Luxemburg, Webb, Crosland and Giddens.

Key thinkers in context

Karl Marx and Friedrich Engels

Marx and Engels believed that communism was both the ideal society and inevitable. The revolutions of 1848 across Europe provided the inspiration for Marx and Engels to develop their theory of both how and why communism must come about.

Rosa Luxemburg

Luxembourg was a militant activist and one of the most original thinkers in the history of Marxism. She was an uncompromising critic of the parliamentary road to socialism at the turn of the nineteenth century, which had been put forward by Edouard Bernstein of the German Social Democratic Party (SPD). She applauded the success of the Russian Revolution of 1917, but warned that a revolution led by a party, not guided by the masses, would run the risk of crushing the freedoms that socialism promised to deliver.

Beatrice Webb

Webb's studies in the East End of London revealed to her the misery of the general population created by landlords and capitalists at the end of the nineteenth century. Without some socialism, Webb believed a national minimum of civilised life could not be achieved and she argued for an evolutionary rather than revolutionary road to socialism.

Anthony Crosland

Crosland published his key work, *The Future of Socialism*, to revise the aims of socialism in light of the economic and societal changes since Marx and Engels were writing, and, in particular, the transformation of society in the UK by the Attlee government of 1945–51.

Anthony Giddens

Giddens' work during the 1990s looked to reform social democracy in light of the perceived failures of Keynesian economics, the collapse of eastern European communism, the rise of globalisation and the disappearance of the traditional working class.

Check your understanding and progress at www.hoddereducation.co.uk/myrevisionnotes

Core ideas of socialism

REVISED

Human nature

Areas of agreement
- Socialism has tended to favour the view that humans are social beings, naturally fraternal, co-operative and communal, seeking solidarity rather than competition.
- The most important view of human nature held by socialists is that it is flexible, multifaceted and shaped by social circumstances.
- Humans change as their circumstances change, but they also create new and different social relations and adapt to them. So, if humans can create capitalism, they can create socialism.
- Socialism holds an optimistic view of what human nature can become given the right social relations.

Areas of tension
- Marx and Engels argued that human nature is not fixed and cannot be understood independently of society. Human essence is 'the ensemble of social relations'.
- The only consistent feature for Marx and Engels is the need to labour to satisfy human needs. Marx and Engels saw capitalism turning labour into forced labour, to create profit not to satisfy needs. This alienates the worker, preventing them from living satisfying lives, engaging in fulfilling work and relating to others.
- By bringing the means of production into common ownership, labour will be socialised, creating the right social conditions to foster co-operation, fraternity and solidarity.
- Luxemburg was optimistic about human nature, arguing that the 'intellectual, cultural growth of the proletariat' would be achieved through the mass strike and the struggle against capitalism.
- The political consciousness of the working classes would be developed 'in the fight and by the fight', leading to revolution from below.
- Gradualist thinkers like Webb believed that poverty and inequality were a 'corrupting force' that fostered greed and selfishness. Through the gradual reform of the state to promote common ownership, socialism could guide human nature back to its co-operative essence.
- Revisionist thinkers such as Crosland saw inequality and class distinctions as creating feelings of envy, inferiority and resentment. Social equality would create greater co-operation and community by reducing the effects of class distinctions.
- For Giddens, human nature should be seen positively, with the free market empowering the individual economically and giving them freedom, but he reinforced the importance of community and the sense of responsibility towards others.

> **Fraternity** The uniting of all humanity in bonds of affection on the basis of common humanity.

Exam tip
One key criticism levelled at socialism is that its view of human nature is utopian – socialism is impossible to achieve as humans are naturally selfish, greedy and competitive. This is based on the view that human nature has fixed traits and is not flexible. In the exam, it is worth considering whether this criticism of socialism's view of human nature undermines its prescriptions for the state, society and the economy. Or is it the case that capitalism breeds selfishness even if you want to put others first – the worker who wants to do the best for their family must constantly struggle against others for a better job or higher pay?

The state

Areas of agreement
+ Socialists have tended to favour the state as the key tool to drive political, economic and social change.
+ The right kind of state can improve society by promoting equality, co-operation and community. However, there is clear disagreement about what is the right kind of state.

Areas of tension

Revolutionary socialism
+ According to Marx and Engels, the state is merely a committee for the ruling classes. It will promote and defend the existing economic relations and ideology, which benefit the ruling classes. As such, the state cannot be captured and reformed; it must be overthrown and replaced by a dictatorship of the proletariat.
+ Once the dictatorship of the proletariat has fought off the backlash from the ruling classes and taken the means of production into common ownership, class divides will disappear and the state will wither away.
+ According to Luxemburg, the mass strike and the struggle for economic reforms, such as the eight-hour working day, will bring workers into direct conflict with the ideological, political and economic power of the state, creating a class consciousness.
+ She argued that the state and the economic powers that the state protects must be overthrown from below by the working class and not by a minority in the name of the working class.
+ The revolution must replace bourgeois democracy with unlimited democracy, based on 'the most active, unlimited participation of the mass of the people'.

Evolutionary socialism
+ According to Webb, the state could be harnessed by socialism through parliamentary democracy and the ethical superiority of its ideas.
+ The state could gradually and peacefully be expanded to bring the economy into common ownership and subject it to planning controls. The state could then steer society towards socialism.

Social democracy
+ Social democracy sees the state playing a key role in managing the economy, using Keynesian economics to control growth and maintain full employment.
+ According to Crosland, progressive taxation and redistributive welfare could be used to promote social equality and equality of opportunity.

The third way
+ According to Giddens, the modern state needs to be an intelligent state and a social investment state, reforming to work better through devolving power, investing in infrastructure and education to promote equality of opportunity.
+ Social exclusion should be tackled through targeted public spending to promote work as the route out of poverty.

Society

Areas of agreement
+ Socialists see human nature and individuals as the product of the society in which they live. In particular, the nature of economic relations and the distribution of wealth have a key impact on society and human nature.
+ Socialists have traditionally focused on how class and inequality play a significant role in shaping an individual's prospects.

> **Exam tip**
>
> In 1918, Luxemburg wrote a pamphlet on the Russian Revolution, which supported the revolution but was critical of its tactics. She argued that only unlimited democracy could ensure that the dictatorship of the proletariat was the rule of the working class, not the dictatorship of a handful of politicians. This can be used to illustrate that there are divisions among revolutionary socialists about how to achieve socialism.

+ Society needs to be reconfigured in line with a concept of justice to provide greater equality, although there is considerable debate as to what type of equality.

Areas of tension

Revolutionary socialism

+ Marx and Engels saw society as constructed by relations to the means of production and distribution of wealth, creating clear class divisions between the few and the many. The concept of equality under capitalism is meaningless.
+ Society is dominated by the ideas of the ruling class, such as racism, sexism and patriotism, which are used to divide workers among themselves.
+ This 'muck of ages' must be overthrown to create a classless society based not on the principle of 'to each according to what he does' but rather 'from each according to his ability, to each according to his needs'.
+ Luxemburg saw capitalist society as a society of exploitation that could not be reformed by piecemeal changes to improved conditions. Such reforms are merely a renegotiation of the terms of exploitation and will be quickly overturned when those in power regroup.
+ She argued that by participating in strikes, workers would be able to break their ties to the dominant ideas of society and develop the ability to organise society for themselves.

Evolutionary socialism

+ Webb studied poverty in Lancashire and the east end of London, concluding that it could not be accounted for by individual behaviour or moral weakness, or tackled by private charity. Poverty was structural and so society needed a structural response to tackle it.
+ She argued that society should focus on a 'national minimum' – a minimum level of wages and quality of life below which no one should be allowed to fall.

Social democracy

+ Crosland argued that society should focus on minimising inequality and class divides, not eradicating them as Marx and Engels had argued.
+ This could be achieved by progressive taxation, the redistribution of wealth, universal welfare and comprehensive education.

The third way

+ Giddens focused on the importance of community to balance out the negative effects of free-market capitalism.
+ Society should be ordered around the values of community, focusing on individual responsibility to others, social cohesion and social inclusion, rather than on class divides and conflicts.

> **Exam tip**
>
> In the exam, when discussing socialist views of society and the significance of class, it can be noted that the third way seems to stand alone from other strands of socialism in its rejection of a class-based analysis of society.

The economy

Areas of agreement

+ Socialism's focus on class and equality means that socialists agree that the economy must work in the interests of all of society.
+ Socialists agree that private property and capitalism are problematic, but disagree over whether private property and capitalism are compatible with socialism.

Areas of tension

+ For Marx and Engels, capitalism and private property are 'naked, shameless, direct, brutal exploitation' and form the consciousness of the working class, who become the 'gravediggers' of capitalism.

- The revolution will replace capitalism with the common ownership of the means of production, making conflict, poverty and oppression things of the past.
- Communism will abolish private property, alienation and wage slavery, leading to worker emancipation and, by extension, universal emancipation, so all are free 'to hunt in the morning, fish in the afternoon, rear cattle in the evening, criticise after dinner' (Marx and Engels, *German Ideology*, 1846).
- Webb believed that the parliamentary road to socialism would permeate the state with the ideas of socialism, leading to the state gradually taking the economy into common ownership. The state could ensure that there was 'a national minimum' for all in relation to wages and quality of life.
- Crosland felt that there was no need for further public ownership, following the nationalisations carried out under the Attlee government of 1945–51. The state should adopt a Keynesian approach to generate full employment and sufficient growth to create the tax base necessary to deliver greater social equality.
- Giddens valued the dynamism and entrepreneurship generated by a free market, based on deregulation, private not public ownership and low taxes. The taxes generated could be spent on infrastructure, education and social inclusion to create greater equality of opportunity.

> **Revision activity**
>
> Make a spider diagram with key quotes from the five thinkers and your own explanation of the importance of each quote underneath.

Now test yourself

TESTED

8. Is the third way really a variant of socialism?
9. Why was Luxemburg critical of the tactics of the Russian Revolution?
10. Explain Webb's theory of the inevitability of gradualism.
11. Copy and complete the following table with the key views of both Marxism and social democracy.

Marxism	Social democracy

Tensions and agreements within socialism

REVISED

Revolutionary socialism

- Revolution is both inevitable and vital. This involves overthrowing the existing state, society and economic relations. The defence of the revolution against the backlash from the ruling classes will probably involve the use of force.
- Liberal democracy is a 'swindle' used by the ruling class to stop workers developing class consciousness. The ruling class also uses its ideological dominance to promote patriotism and prejudices, like sexism, to divide workers among themselves.
- The state and society are an expression of class relations, enforcing the ideas of the ruling class, and so must be overthrown.
- Capitalism and private property will be overthrown and replaced by common ownership.
- Equality means the end of inequality in terms of status, wealth and income. Society is ordered by the principle 'from each according to his ability, to each according to his needs'. This will create a true democracy and the state will wither away as society will be classless.
- Class is a key analytical tool for understanding society. The objective is the classless society.

Social democracy and the third way

+ Socialism can be delivered via the ballot box and piecemeal, legal reforms. This process takes place gradually and peacefully within democracy (the 'inevitability of gradualism').
+ With universal suffrage, socialist parties will be able to campaign and convince workers of the benefits of socialism. When voted into power, the gradual, peaceful change to socialism will convince everyone of its ethical superiority.
+ The state can be used to deliver reform, improving society.
+ Capitalism and private property are compatible with socialism but need to be harnessed for socialist ends. Social democracy supports the mixed economy, Keynesian economics and redistributive welfare. The third way supports the free market of neo-liberalism blended with a sense of community and social justice.
+ Social democracy emphasises relative social equality, which involves tackling poverty and limiting inequality. Without some level of social equality, equality of opportunity is not possible. The third way places its emphasis on equality of opportunity, but this is underpinned by targeted welfare and public spending to generate social inclusion.
+ Social democracy still views class as important and wishes to minimise class divisions within society. The third way dismisses the emphasis on class, focusing more on community and social inclusion.

> **Revision activity**
>
> Create a set of flashcards for all the key terms in this chapter.

> **Now test yourself** TESTED
>
> 12 Explain the difference between the Marxists' and social democracy's attitude to equality.
> 13 Explain the difference between the attitudes of social democracy and the third way to equality.
> 14 Copy and complete the table below with the main ideas of the key thinkers.
>
> | Thinker | Human nature | The state | Society | The economy |
> |---|---|---|---|---|
> | Marx and Engels | | | | |
> | Rosa Luxemburg | | | | |
> | Beatrice Webb | | | | |
> | Anthony Crosland | | | | |
> | Anthony Giddens | | | | |

> **Exam skills**
>
> Marx and Engels believed that there could be no equality in a capitalist society; the real content of the proletarian demand for equality is the abolition of classes. This can only occur via the destruction of capitalism and private property to create common ownership where production is based on the objective of meeting human needs. This can be summed up in Marx's principle of communist society as 'From each according to his abilities, to each according to his needs'. This stands in contrast to revisionist forms of social democracy and the thinking of Anthony Crosland, who rejected the Marxist analysis. For Crosland, equality could be achieved under capitalism and the bourgeois state based on the rising living standards of the working classes since the war. The effective and caring state could manage capitalism to ensure continuous economic growth, and through progressive taxation and the redistribution of wealth could minimise class divisions and deliver social equality. These differing views of equality help to explain why Marx and Engels argued that only a revolutionary path was available rather than the parliamentary road of social democracy.

The sample paragraph above answers the following Section A 9-marker question: 'Explain and analyse three ways that socialist thinkers have viewed equality.'
This is a strong paragraph as the student directly identifies the approach of Marxism and social democracy towards equality. Two key thinkers are identified and there is supporting own knowledge about their ideas (e.g. the quote from Marx about the communist society and the views of Crosland). There is also awareness of the context in which Crosland was writing, and analysis of the significance of their views (e.g. how their view of equality shapes their view of how to change society).

Exam practice

1. Explain and analyse three ways that socialist thinkers have viewed human nature. [9]

2. Explain and analyse three ways that socialist thinkers have viewed capitalism. [9]

Read the extract below and answer question 3 that follows.

> The history of all hitherto existing society is the history of class struggles … in a word, oppressor and oppressed, stood in constant opposition to one another, carried on an uninterrupted, now hidden, now open fight, a fight that each time ended, either in a revolutionary reconstitution of society at large, or in the common ruin of the contending classes.
>
> The modern bourgeois society that has sprouted from the ruins of feudal society has not done away with class antagonisms. It has but established new classes, new conditions of oppression, new forms of struggle in place of the old ones.
>
> Our epoch, the epoch of the bourgeoisie, possesses, however, this distinct feature: it has simplified class antagonisms. Society as a whole is more and more splitting up into two great hostile camps, into two great classes directly facing each other – bourgeoisie and proletariat.
>
> Source: adapted from Karl Marx and Friedrich Engels, *The Communist Manifesto* (1848)
>
> According to Tony Crosland, 'Marx has little or nothing to offer the contemporary socialist, either in respect of practical policy or of the correct analysis of our society, or even of the right conceptual tools or framework.' It was not capitalism that was the enemy but the massive inequalities in the distribution of resources and life chances. He argued that 'In Britain, equality of opportunity and social mobility … are not enough. They need to be combined with measures … to equalise the distribution of rewards and privileges so as to diminish the degree of class stratification, the injustices of large inequalities.'
>
> Source: secondary material quoting from Anthony Crosland, *The Future of Socialism* (1956)

3. Analyse, evaluate and compare the arguments being made in the above extracts over socialism's views on society. In your answer, you should refer to the thinkers you have studied. [25]

Summary

You should now have an understanding of:
+ debates about the nature of socialism
+ core socialist views and values concerning Marxism, class analysis and the fundamental goals of socialism
+ differing views and tensions within and between revolutionary socialism and social democracy
+ the contributions of the six key thinkers (Marx and Engels, Webb, Luxemburg, Crosland and Giddens) to socialism in the areas of human nature, the state, society and the economy

Check your understanding and progress at www.hoddereducation.co.uk/myrevisionnotes

4 Nationalism

Nationalism has an overriding concern with the nation, aiming to place the nation at the centre of its ideas and promote its wellbeing. The main goals of nationalism are national autonomy, national unity and national identity.

> **National autonomy** The right to self-government.
>
> **National identity** Individuals identify with the distinctive heritage and culture of their community, recognising it as distinct from other nations.

Origins of nationalism

- Nationalism has its roots in the French Revolution, 1789–99. The ideas of Jean-Jacques Rousseau were particularly influential to many of the French revolutionaries.
- Before the revolution there were empires, kingdoms and realms where identity was about allegiance to a particular ruler or monarch. People were seen as 'subjects' of the realm who owed obedience to their ruler. Nationalism, by contrast, ushered in the notion of citizenship.
- The French Revolution was carried out in the name of the French nation and for French citizens.
- Nationalism played a key role in redrawing the European map during the nineteenth century, spreading across Europe to form nation-states such as Italy and Germany.
- As the century wore on, nationalism became an increasingly popular movement and the concept was adopted by conservative and reactionary politicians.
- In the twentieth century, nationalism spread across the globe in two main ways. First, there was the rise of an aggressive racist nationalism in the form of fascism, epitomised by Hitler's Germany but also mirrored elsewhere. Secondly, there was the emergence of a postcolonial black nationalism, not least in Africa and the West Indies, as a direct reaction to the imperialist practices of the European nations. In this case, nationalism was strongly allied with struggles for independence from declining imperial powers such as Britain and France.

> **Exam tip**
>
> Rousseau predated nationalism, so he is often seen as an Enlightenment thinker rather than a nationalist thinker. However, since his works have been referenced by 'proper' nationalist thinkers from across the spectrum, he certainly merits mention in nationalism essays.

> **Imperialist** Relating to the extension of power through conquest, to establish political and economic control over another country.

Key thinker

Jean-Jacques Rousseau (1712–78)

Rousseau is regarded as the inspiration for the emergence of nationalism, especially liberal nationalism, with *The Social Contract* (1762) seen as his most influential work.

- Rousseau viewed the nation as a people, who as a collection of individuals voluntarily choose to establish their own governing authority through a social contract. This is done without any distinction based on wealth, religion or birth.
- The bond among the members of this community is purely the agreement to obey the political authority that they have created for themselves.
- Popular sovereignty for Rousseau was detailed in the idea of the people's general will, where there is 'only one will which is directed towards their common preservation and general wellbeing'. The general will entailed a form of radical democracy, where the legislative powers reside directly with the people and not in representative assemblies.

> **General will** Human society is a collective individual and the general will comes from all and applies to all. This ensures liberty and equality while also helping to develop a sense of fraternity.

- Rousseau's opposition to representative assemblies comes from his idea that the state rests upon the active participation of its citizens, without which the state will crumble and die, and this forms the basis of civic nationalism.
- Rousseau argued that a viable political system requires social cohesion, so there is the need to build a 'civic profession of faith' based on the values and ideas that make people good citizens.
- Civic nationalism can be achieved through education, such as people studying the literature of their own country 'to shape the soul of citizens in a national pattern', and this can be strengthened by mass culture including sports, games and ceremonies.
- Rousseau was writing at a time when France was ruled by an absolute monarchy. His ideas were influential among many leaders of the French Revolution. His legacy can be seen in some aspects of the modern French state – for example, the emphasis on the state being secular and the banning of all religious symbols in civic buildings or workplaces.

Exam tip
You can use the French Revolution of 1789–99 as a key expression of Rousseau's ideas – in Article VI of the Declaration of the Rights of Man and of the Citizen (1789), which stated that 'the law is the expression of the general will', and in the revolution's motto 'liberty, equality and fraternity'.

Core concepts

REVISED

The nation
- According to Anthony D. Smith in his book *Nationalism: Theory, Ideology, History* (2010), a nation is 'a named human community [e.g. the French people] residing in a perceived homeland [e.g. France], and having common myths and a shared history, a distinct public culture, and common laws and customs for all members'.
- There is debate about what constitutes a nation and the history of nations. For some, nations are the products of the nineteenth century, in that they were invented by nationalism to create the necessary social cohesion for the effective working of the state. Benedict Anderson argued in 1983 that nations are 'imagined communities'. Others such as Anthony D. Smith have argued that modern nations are linked to *ethnies*, which long predate the state.

Ethnies Historical entities bound by shared beliefs and commitments, shared memories and the perception that their culture is different from and distinctive to others.

The nation-state
The nation-state is a geographical area where the cultural boundaries of the nation match up with the political boundaries of the state and the people have the ability to govern themselves. The issue with the concept of the nation-state is that it is an 'ideal':
- Most modern nation-states contain elements of different nations and cultures. For example, Belgium is a state where the members claim both a cultural identity (e.g. Flemish or Walloon) and a national identity. The same observation can be made about Northern Ireland, where the unionist and nationalist communities have competing and opposing identities, one focused on maintaining ties with the rest of the United Kingdom, the other on unification with southern Ireland.
- Some nations do not have a state. For example, Kurdish people are the largest nation (over 30 million people) without a state, spread across Iraq, Syria, Turkey and Iran.
- Some states do not have a nation with a sense of common ties that bind. For example, Iraq is a nation without a state as it has no distinct public culture.

Exam tip
Although it is important to be able to provide clear definitions of the nation, the state and the nation-state, it is important also to realise that these terms are highly contested and complex.

Making links
The example of Northern Ireland links with the Paper 1 devolution topic and the problems of establishing devolved government there.

Main strands of nationalism

REVISED

+ Nationalism is probably the most diverse of all the political ideas. There is agreement within nationalism that nations have the right to autonomy to govern themselves.
+ Nationalism requires national unity and identity, although there is disagreement about where this comes from and how it can be strengthened.
+ One of the first key divisions among nationalists is the idea of state nationalism as against minority nationalism:
  + **State nationalism**. This is where the state, in order to realise its political values, must be based on a homogeneous national culture. In this sense, nationalism is the process of creating, reinforcing or developing the shared culture needed for the state to function effectively. This can be seen through the national flag (e.g. the tricolour of France), the national anthem (e.g. the French 'La Marseillaise'), oaths of allegiance (as in the USA), national assemblies (e.g. the Houses of Parliament), processions (e.g. the Trooping of the Colour), national sporting achievements and failures, as well as national fêtes and events (e.g. royal weddings and coronations in the UK).
  + **Minority nationalism**. This emerges in opposition to state nationalism. Minority groups within states feel that their identity and culture is under threat from state nationalism and see that their culture warrants the need of a state to protect it. For example, the SNP in Scotland seeks to separate from the UK to create an independent Scottish nation-state, while the Conservatives, Labour and Liberal Democrats all emphasise the unity of the UK. Another example is the movement for independence in Catalonia to create a Catalan state separate from Spain to protect their identity and language, while the Spanish government emphasises Spanish identity.

> **Culture** The values, beliefs and customs that are passed down the generations through learning.

> **Making links**
> There are links here with the Paper 1 topic 'UK political parties' and the policies of the nationalist parties in the UK, such as the SNP and Plaid Cymru, and those of their pro-union opponents, such as Labour and the Conservatives. Their contrasting views about national identity and sovereignty highlight how nationalism can influence modern political parties.

> **Exam tip**
> Identify where the tensions within nationalism lie and the extent to which each of these tensions weakens the notion that nationalism is a single doctrine.

Liberal nationalism

Liberal nationalism is the earliest type of nationalism, dating back to the French Revolution of 1789–99. It aimed to liberate people from royal absolutism and end oppression within a society.

+ Liberal nationalism is founded on the liberal principle that morally equal, rational individuals should be sovereign over their own mind and body and have certain guaranteed, natural rights.
+ It sees nations as individuals on the international stage. These are morally equal entities that should be sovereign and autonomous, and they have certain basic rights, the most important of which is self-determination.

Self-determination

Self-determination arises from the meeting of the idea of the nation and the idea of popular sovereignty. Self-determination is based on the idea of political nationalism:

+ The goal of nationalism is the formation of the nation-state.
+ This can be achieved through unification or through the achievement of independence in order to free the nation from domination and oppression, by either a foreign power or an absolute monarchy.

> **Popular sovereignty** No law or rule can be legitimate unless it comes directly (direct democracy) or indirectly (representative democracy) from the consent of the individuals concerned.

> **Political nationalism** Where the nation is the natural political community and has the right to govern itself.

My Revision Notes: AQA A-level Politics: Political Ideas Second Edition

- The ultimate goal of liberal nationalism is the creation of a world of independent, equal nation-states.
- As the nation-state practises self-government, the government must be based on democracy where there is consent by the people. The act of consent is the expression of the individual's rationality, so the nation-state is also rational.

> **Now test yourself** TESTED
>
> 1. Why are nations and states frequently confused?
> 2. Are nations an invention of nationalism or do they predate the emergence of modern nations?
> 3. Explain what is meant by the term self-determination.

Liberal internationalism

A world of independent nation-states will create a world order of balance and harmony:

- This idea is built on the principle that nation-states would respect the sovereignty of other states in return for having their own independence recognised and respected.
- This can be achieved by the growing interdependence between states through free trade, which promotes mutual understanding and co-operation, and ensures the costs of war make conflict unlikely.
- International organisations, such as the United Nations, will create forums where nation-states can resolve issues through rational debate and discussion.
- Democratic nation-states will not declare war on each other, as going to war requires the consent of the people and it is they who have to fight and will bear the costs.
- Cosmopolitan ideals will develop, where individuals feel a moral and ethical connection to all others irrespective of their nationhood, believing they are entitled to basic rights and freedoms.

Sovereignty The principle of unrestricted power.

Civic nationalism

Nationalism is developed out of shared political values and allegiances:

- This type of nationalism is open and voluntary: if you choose to sign up to the values of the nation-state, you are welcomed, and this is not restricted by any identity-related criteria (gender, ethnicity, religion, language, sexual orientation or culture).
- This type of nationalism is inclusive as members see themselves as part of a community of citizens, unified by a commitment to shared political ideals.
- It is the basis of a peaceful, dynamic and diverse society that will drive social and economic progress.

The state can play a key role in building the shared national culture, so the state can realise its political values such as democracy or economic welfare.

Exam tip

You could use the words of Massimo d'Azeglio (1798–1866) following the Italian Risorgimento (the successful movement to unify Italy): 'We have made Italy: now we must make Italians' to illustrate this idea.

> **Case study**
>
> **The USA's motto 'E pluribus unum' ('Out of many, one')**
>
> Civic nationalism is essential to creating a healthy US society.
>
> It is inclusive: new arrivals can learn the language, sign up to the social contract and learn to understand the culture without having to abandon their own traditions, languages or identities. This creates a 'melting pot' society where it is possible to be an Irish American, Italian American or black American, for example. This also opposes the extreme individualism associated with the conservative Ayn Rand (see p. 32) and her followers, by giving citizens a sense of collective unity and identity.
>
> Civic nationalism creates a sense of 'us' and 'we', where US citizens identify with all Americans. This allows for policies to share resources within society.

'Melting pot' A diverse society becoming more homogeneous as the diverse elements 'melt together' into a unified whole with a common culture.

Check your understanding and progress at www.hoddereducation.co.uk/myrevisionnotes

> **Key thinker**
>
> **Giuseppe Mazzini (1805–72)**
>
> Mazzini was a political thinker and activist who formed the movement 'Young Italy', which wanted the unification of Italy and the removal of foreign influence and monarchical power from the country.
> + The main aim of Young Italy was 'reconstituting Italy as one independent sovereign nation of free men and equals'.
> + At the same time, Mazzini was committed to republicanism. This had two key aspects that place him as a liberal nationalist:
>   + All nations should be free and equal – 'theoretically every nation is destined, by the law of God and humanity, to form a free and equal community of brothers'.
> + A republic 'is the only form of government that ensures this future', stressing Mazzini's belief in the need for representative democracy.
> + However, in contrast to liberal nationalists, Mazzini saw the nation as more than a rational concept that linked the nation to a territory and the right to self-determination. His idea of 'thought and action' argues that the unification of Italy was a moral and not a rational mission.
> + Mazzini saw the nation as more than just territory; it was about 'the sentiment of love, the sense of fellowship which binds together all the sons of that territory'. This gives a romantic aspect to his nationalism.

Conservative nationalism

Unity and order

Conservatives were initially suspicious of the arrival of nationalism as it appeared to pit the nation against traditional forms of authority, such as the Church and the monarchy. However, conservative nationalists saw that the idea had the potential to increase unity and order:

+ **Nation-state.** Once the nation and the state had been brought together in the nation-state, conservatives saw that nationalism could be a force for protecting the state against radicals and socialists who were promoting revolution, especially in older states like the UK and France.
+ **Organic.** The nation is organic and emerges from the conservative view of the imperfection of human nature. Nationalism encourages a deep connection to the nation because nations emerge naturally from people in their desire for security, drawing together with others who share their attitudes, values, practices and appearances.
+ **Order.** Nationalism could be used to protect and enhance the existing social order and traditional institutions, creating the security and stability that people need.
+ **One nation.** The unity and identity of the nation is of overriding importance. Symbols, values, myths, memories and traditions should be used to nurture a romantic connection to the nation to combat divisions like age, gender, class and wealth.
+ **Romantic nationalism.** This stresses the importance of a shared culture, language and history over rationalism as the foundation of the nation, based on the writing of the philosophers Johann Gottlieb Fichte and Johann Gottfried von Herder.

Rights of the nation

Instead of the rights of self-determination of all nations, conservative nationalism is about the rights of *one* particular nation. This can be seen in two ways:

+ It sought to preserve the identity and unity of the nation by preserving the status quo against change or returning society back to the 'golden age' of the nation, based on a romanticised view of the past.
+ It follows that a particular nation-state should promote its own economic and political interests at the expense of other nations.

> **Exam tip**
>
> Bismarck's unification of Germany in 1870–71 is a good example to use of conservative nationalism in the nineteenth century, involving the forging of a powerful new nation-state but led largely by its traditional ruling class. In Germany's case this was the Kaiser (emperor) and the royal family, alongside landed aristocrats and wealthy industrialists.

Exclusive nationalism

Exclusive nationalism is about the importance of a shared culture, language and history, resulting in opposition to large-scale immigration, which is seen as a threat to the national identity:

+ Strong and stable societies are based on shared values and a common culture. There is opposition to multiculturalism.
+ Newcomers have to accept the common culture to become part of the nation. This can be seen, for example, with citizenship tests and citizenship ceremonies, which require a pledge of loyalty to the state.
+ Immigration, especially from societies where there are practices, values or religions that are seen to be in conflict with the majority culture, should be restricted.

> **Multiculturalism** State-led policies to balance diversity and unity by creating political unity through recognising the rights of different cultural groups to respect and recognition.

Opposition to supranationalism

+ Supranationalism is when regional or international bodies have the power or influence to impose their will on nation-states.
+ National institutions (such as parliaments) and laws and currency (as symbols of cultural unity) should not be weakened by supranational bodies.
+ Opposition to the EU and the euro was strong among Eurosceptics in the Conservative Party. It was crucial to the rise of UKIP in the UK, and to its campaign to secure the withdrawal of the UK from the EU. Since Brexit, some of this hostility to supranationalism has moved on to opposing the UK's continued involvement with the European Court of Human Rights (ECHR), and demands instead for a British Bill of Rights.
+ The idea that the EU can move to an 'ever-closer union' is seen as absurd due to the cultural, linguistic and national diversity of Europe.

> **Making links**
>
> This links to the Paper 1 topics of both the EU and UK political parties. The EU is a classic example of a supranational institution, and this type of nationalism is especially influential in the Conservative and smaller Eurosceptic parties, including UKIP and Reform UK.

Case study

President Trump's 'America First' and 'Make America Great Again'

Some commentators perceive former President Trump's slogans to be examples of conservative nationalism. His main ideas to put 'America First' and 'Make American Great Again' included:

+ to return the USA to its perceived 'golden age' so that it can be 'great again' by pushing back against multiculturalism and globalisation
+ protectionist economic policies, such as for steel and aluminium, to return the USA to its golden era as a manufacturing country
+ withdrawal from or remaking of international bodies or treaties where they do not further US interests, such as the Transatlantic Trade and Investment Partnership (TTIP) and the Paris Climate Change Agreement
+ tough policies on immigration to preserve the unity and identity of the American nation, such as the unrealised plans to build a full border wall with Mexico
+ opposition to NFL players protesting during the American national anthem before games, seeing their actions as unpatriotic

Despite losing the 2020 presidential election, Trump's ideas and policies retain much support within the Republican Party.

Key thinker

Johann Gottfried von Herder (1744–1803)

The German critic and philosopher von Herder developed the concept of a romantic nationalism or organic nationalism, where the state's legitimacy lies in the distinct national spirit and culture of each nation.

+ Von Herder was the first thinker to use the term 'nationalism', 'identifying it with a strong attachment to one's own nation that spills over into prejudice against other nations' (Herder, *Philosophical Writings*, ed. by Michael Forster).
+ Von Herder was writing at a time when his own state, Prussia, was ruled by a dominant landed aristocracy and monarchy, where even middle-class intellectuals like himself were not allowed to be very active politically.
+ He argued that individuals find meaning and value in their national culture.
+ Each nation's culture is different, with its own unique character defined by its history and its relationship to its own natural environment. This can be seen through its language, literature, arts, folklore and law.

> **Protectionist economic policies** Shielding the domestic industries of a country by imposing taxes on imports.

Check your understanding and progress at www.hoddereducation.co.uk/myrevisionnotes

+ Von Herder encouraged all nations to explore their own linguistic, artistic and cultural spirit.
+ In this way, he sought to promote **cultural nationalism** rather than the political nationalism of liberal nationalism – 'an empire consisting of one nation is a family, a well-ordered household'.
+ He saw patriotism as a spiritual attachment to the nation, with the aim of energising and protecting the nation and its unique culture.
+ He opposed any form of authority which extends over more than one nation: 'an empire forcing together a hundred peoples and a hundred-twenty provinces is a monstrosity and no body of state'. Unlike many other forms of nationalism, however, von Herder's was one built upon peace; he believed that his idea of nations would guarantee that humankind would become peaceful and less aggressive.
+ This places von Herder against empires that cover multiple nations and against supranational communities. He was also against leaders who do not emerge from the ranks of the people.
+ Von Herder's influence can be seen in this 1882 definition of a nation by the French historian Ernest Renan: 'A nation for us is a soul, a spirit, a spiritual family … What constitutes a nation is not to speak the same language or to belong to the same ethnic group. It is to have done great things together in the past and wanting to do these again in the future.'

Cultural nationalism This focuses on protecting a nation's unique culture rather than on the importance of self-determination. The state is there to support the nation, not the nation to support the state.

Exam tip

Von Herder never argued that each cultural nation should have a state of its own, but many people (e.g. Bismarck) have subsequently used his arguments to make that case.

Now test yourself

TESTED

4 How does the motto of the USA reflect civic nationalism?
5 Why is Mazzini viewed as a liberal nationalist?
6 What is the difference between inclusive and exclusive nationalism? Give an example of a country that reflects each definition.
7 What is meant by supranationalism?

Anti-colonial and postcolonial nationalism

Anti-colonial and postcolonial nationalism has the following characteristics:

+ **Opposition to colonialism**. The imperialism of the European powers created a desire for national liberation and sense of nationhood among the peoples of Africa and Asia. The colonised peoples, based in artificial territories defined by colonial boundary makers, were given unity and identity through their opposition to and struggle against the colonial powers.
+ **Self-determination**. The European colonial powers brought with them the ideas of liberal nationalism, with many of the leaders of national liberation movements from Africa and Asia educated in the West. They applied the liberal idea of self-determination to their struggles.
+ **Under-development**. The national liberation movements identified the economic exploitation of colonialism and how it had exploited them and their natural resources. This gave the movement an economic perspective.
+ **Socialism**. As a result, national liberation movements blended the need for self-determination with the economic ideas of socialism (see Chapter 3).
+ **Nation building**. In postcolonialism, the aim of nationalism and the state was to build a national identity, a unity – in effect, build a nation. In this sense, nationalism preceded the nation.
+ **A new form of nationalism**. The struggle against colonialism led to a wide array of ideas that blended nationalism with non-Western ideas:
  + Tanzanian president Julius Nyerere's Ujamaa ('familyhood') advocated collectivised agriculture, nationalised banks and industries, and the self-reliance of the individual and the nation.
  + Ghanaian revolutionary and then president Kwame Nkrumah introduced the idea of the 'African personality': 'We are going to see that we create our own African personality and identity.'

My Revision Notes: AQA A-level Politics: Political Ideas Second Edition

Black nationalism

Black nationalism is a complex set of ideas based on the desire for the cultural, political and economic separation of African Americans from white American society that developed in the early twentieth century in the USA. It has two keys elements:

+ **Black pride**. A feeling of pride and unity in black identity, culture and achievements based on the sense that there is a common ancestry for all black Africans.
+ **Separation**. For some, this meant separate political, social and economic institutions for African Americans; for others, it meant a separate nation for African Americans with its own independent state in the USA or the return of all Africans to a free Africa.

Pan-Africanism and Marcus Garvey

Pan-Africanism is a movement, informed by the ideas of black nationalism, that wishes to unite all black Africans behind a consciousness of their unique political identity and common political destiny. There are three key elements:

+ **Diaspora**. All peoples across the world descended from Africans have a common ancestry, culture and identity. Much of this diaspora (scattered population) was created by the forcible removing of Africans from Africa in the slave trade.
+ **Colonialism**. Africans were divided within Africa by the imperial powers in order to make it easier for them to dominate the continent. This colonial domination was backed up by an ideological domination that saw Africans and African culture as backward.
+ **Freedom**. Freedom for Africa can only be achieved by the total liberation of the whole African continent, with all Africans needing to work together if they wish to escape colonialism and neo-colonialism.

> **Neo-colonialism**
> Where the state *appears* sovereign, but its economic and political policies are directed from outside by multinational companies and international organisations like the World Bank and Western countries like the USA.

Key thinker

Marcus Garvey (1887–1940)

Marcus Garvey was a Jamaican immigrant to the USA who was central to the creation of black nationalism and seen as an inspiration for anti-colonialism in Africa and pan-Africanism.

+ Garvey founded the Universal Negro Improvement Association (UNIA) in 1914 for 'the absolute purpose of bettering our [African Americans'] condition, industrially, commercially, socially, religiously and politically'.
+ He established the Negro Factories Corporation and the Black Star Line (a shipping/passenger company) so that African Americans could become self-reliant and separate from the white society and the economy.
+ Garvey placed a strong emphasis on black pride to give black people a sense of worthiness in their race and colour: 'Be Black, buy Black, think Black, and all else will take care of itself.'
+ He advocated African unity, arguing that all Africans across the globe share a common ancestry: 'Our union must know no clime, boundary, or nationality … let us hold together under all climes and in every country.'
+ He believed in Africa for Africans, as this would give all Africans 'national independence, an independence so strong as to enable us to rout others if they attempt to interfere with us'.
+ Garvey was an inspiration for future black movements and leaders in the USA, including Malcolm X and the Black Panthers.
+ He was a hugely influential figure in pan-Africanism and on African leaders in the struggle against colonialism. Ghana placed the Black Star in the centre of its national flag and its football team is nicknamed the 'Black Stars' in memory of Garvey's Black Star Line.

Making links

There are links to be made here between black and postcolonial nationalism and pressure groups campaigning for racial justice in both the UK and USA. The Black Lives Matter movement is one such example. Direct action such as the toppling in 2020 of the statue of Bristol enslaver (but also local philanthropist) Edward Colston was inspired by these sentiments. It also raises an interesting question of local civic nationalism. For many decades, Colston was remembered and portrayed primarily as a generous charitable benefactor to his city. Changing attitudes, greater awareness of racial justice issues and more widespread knowledge about his cruel actions as a trader of enslaved people have now led him to be vilified by many Bristol citizens.

Exam tip

You can use the words of Kwame Nkrumah about Ghanaian independence to show the influence of Marcus Garvey: 'Our independence is meaningless unless it is linked up with the total liberation of the African continent.'

Check your understanding and progress at www.hoddereducation.co.uk/myrevisionnotes

Expansionist nationalism

Darwinian and chauvinistic nationalism
Expansionist nationalists based their ideas on the assumption that international politics was a struggle based on Charles Darwin's idea of the 'survival of the fittest' (from his work, *On the Origin of Species*, 1859). The political, economic or military success of a nation-state was down to the superior qualities of that nation. Underpinning this view is the idea that some nations are superior to others: chauvinistic nationalism.

> **Chauvinistic nationalism** An irrational dedication to a particular group or community based on the idea that it is superior.
>
> **Militarism** The idea that a nation-state should keep a strong military capability and be prepared to use it aggressively to defend or promote national interests.

Imperialism and colonialism
+ During the nineteenth century, expansionist nationalism expressed itself as imperialism and colonialism, with the aim of establishing colonies to be exploited to serve the national interest of the imperial power.
+ This form of nationalism is one of militarism.
+ The struggle for empire against other nations created a sense of national unity and pride, and successful conquest appeared to prove the superiority of that particular nation – an idea often described as jingoism.
+ Imperialism ignores the principle of self-determination, with Europeans in the nineteenth century seeing the peoples of Africa and Asia as unable to govern themselves.
+ Imperialism was seen as part of an idealistic, moral campaign to deliver civilisation to the world by introducing good government, culture and religion to the less developed nations.

Pan-nationalism
This is the emergence of a chauvinist nationalism that sought to unite people of one culture or language or a related language under one state. For example, pan-Slavism emerged in the late nineteenth century into the early twentieth century:
+ Russians and the other Slavic peoples of eastern and south-eastern Europe are seen as one, with Russians as the natural leaders. Russia's full-scale invasion of Ukraine in 2022 could be seen as a modern manifestation of this, since Ukraine had been part of the former Soviet Union until the latter's break-up. Ukraine is also a Slavic nation.
+ The idea is that Slavic peoples are superior to western European nations, so pan-Slavism is both anti-liberal and anti-Western.

Integral nationalism
+ Chauvinist nationalism became more militant with the idea of integral nationalism, closely associated with the thinking of Charles Maurras.
+ Integral nationalism places the nation at the centre of the life of all its citizens.
+ It is anti-democratic, anti-individualistic and irrational, as all other loyalties or identities are absorbed into loyalty to the nation-state. This is a form of ethnic nationalism.
+ It promotes individual sacrifice for the benefit of the nation.
+ It tends to be highly militaristic and has a strong appeal to nations that feel isolated, powerless and under threat, or nations that have recently achieved statehood through conflict.

> **Ethnic nationalism** Nationalism driven by the idea that there is a loyalty to a distinctive population, territorial area or cultural group where the group is believed (rightly or not) to have common ancestors.

Fascism and aggressive nationalism
+ This is the most extreme and radical form of expansionist nationalism.
+ Nazism in Germany crystallised around the ideas of the 'Aryan race' and '*Ein Volk, Ein Reich, Ein Führer*' ('One people, one nation, one leader'), as well as *Lebensraum* ('living space').
+ Fascism involves placing the political state above the nation, with the nation serving the state – in the words of Mussolini (the Italian fascist dictator from the 1920s until the Second World War), 'Everything within the state, nothing outside the state, nothing against the state.'

> **Exam tip**
>
> Although Hitler's Nazi Germany is the prime example of aggressive and racist nationalism, avoid citing him as a political thinker. Instead, briefly cite him as an example of this idea being put into practice.

Racialism

+ Racialism believes in fixed, scientific categories for distinguishing between races, despite the scientific evidence, inaccurately equating nation with race.
+ This splits the world into 'us' versus 'them' on the basis of race, seeing some races as superior to others and all races pitted into competition against each other in a war of survival.
+ Racialism is exclusive as you cannot 'opt in' to a race. The 'purity' of one's race must be defended at all costs against 'corruption' by races regarded to be lesser. This form of racialism found its expression in Nazi Germany under Hitler.

> **Key thinker**
>
> ### Charles Maurras (1868–1952)
>
> Charles Maurras was an extremely controversial French writer and critic, who led the Action Française movement in the early twentieth century in France and described his form of nationalism as integral nationalism.
> + Maurras believed that France had lost its greatness and saw the start of the decline as the French Revolution and its principles. He rejected the revolution and democracy.
>   + Political liberty had destroyed the citizen's respect for the laws of the state as well as the natural and spiritual laws that govern humanity.
>   + Equality, in the shape of democracy, had handed over power to the many; the 'most inferior elements of the nation'.
>   + Fraternity had turned France against itself, as anyone who failed to share the same principles was a monster and a villain.
> + Maurras saw Jewish people, Protestants, Freemasons and immigrants as guilty of the French Revolution and as permanent threats to the nation. In his view, they were 'anti-France' and so they should be excluded from the nation.
> + He harked back to France's glorious past and proposed a return to the principles of a hereditary monarchy and the Catholic Church to maintain social order and to promote nationalism rather than individualism.
> + For Maurras, nationalism was integral since 'a true nationalist places his country above everything'.
> + Maurras contributed the idea that the individual is a servant of the nation and that the nation is the highest level of collective identity.

> **Exam tip**
>
> In any essay, emphasise that Maurras is a controversial thinker. For example, in 2018, on the 150th anniversary of his birth, the French government was forced by public outcry to recall all copies of its National Commemoration book. They were reprinted without mention of Maurras due to his anti-Semitic views.

Responses to recent challenges

In recent times, nationalism has faced a series of challenges that potentially threaten its the importance but can also be seen to be revitalising it. The main challenges are summarised in Table 4.1.

Table 4.1 Main challenges to nationalism

Globalisation	The world has become increasingly interconnected, especially in terms of the economy, and this limits the ability of the state to control economic activity within its borders. This is seen as weakening national autonomy.
Cosmopolitanism	The world can increasingly be seen as one society, where people have human rights and obligations to others that extend beyond any national, cultural, religious or ethnic differences. This offers a threat to ideas of national unity and identity by creating a global identity.
Supranationalism	A threat to nationalism is the growth of supranational bodies that are higher than nation-states and can impose laws and decisions on them. The EU is a clear example of this. This removes national autonomy.
Immigration	Immigration increases levels of diversity within societies of different groups with different identities and cultures. This is seen as a threat to national identity and unity.

Check your understanding and progress at www.hoddereducation.co.uk/myrevisionnotes

- Liberal nationalism supports the liberal internationalism of globalisation, accepts the importance of international law and human rights, proposes multiculturalism as a way of creating unity from diversity, and sees supranationalism as enhancing the power of the state through pooled sovereignty.
- These challenges have led to a revival of pan-Africanism to oppose the neo-colonialism seen as being at the heart of globalisation and free trade.
- In recent times, a more regressive, right-wing form of nationalism has arisen which is identified by its opposition to these changes in the world, seeing them as a real threat to either cultural or ethnic identities. This includes:
  - hard-line Eurosceptics in the Conservative Party and (before Brexit) UKIP
  - the impact of Donald Trump's 'America First' and 'Make America Great Again' campaigns (see p. 62)
  - nationalist parties across Europe, including the AFD in Germany, the Freedom Party in Austria and the Law and Justice Party in Poland

Making links
An effective synoptic link can be made between modern nationalist ideas and the policies of many right-wing parties in both Europe and the USA. The Eurosceptic call to 'Take back control' and Trump's pledge to put American interests first, are two examples of this.

Revision activity
Create a spider diagram showing all the synoptic links that you can think of between nationalism and other areas of the course that you have studied. This might include links to democracy, electoral behaviour, interest groups, the media, party policies and programmes, and political agendas.

Summary of key types of nationalism

As you should have grasped, nationalism is much more diverse than the other political ideas you have studied. It can be right-wing or liberal, imperialist or anti-imperialist, aggressive or peaceful, expansionist or self-contained. Figure 4.1 summarises the main variants.

Liberal nationalism
Key thinker: Rousseau
Key ideas: freedom for all nations and for all their citizens; civic nationalism and social contract
Origins: mid-eighteenth century, reaction against absolutism
Impact: influenced both French and American revolutions

Cultural nationalism
Key thinker: Von Herder
Key ideas: focus on shared culture, language and 'national spirit'
Origins: late eighteenth century, reaction to empires and absolutism, but with less focus on creating a political state
Impact: partially influenced Bismarck's German nationalism and unification in 1871

Romantic nationalism
Key thinker: Mazzini and 'Young Italy' movement
Key ideas: embraces aspects of both liberal and cultural nationalism; sees political independence/self-determination as linked with shared history and culture
Origins: mid-nineteenth century, reaction against both foreign and monarchical rule
Impact: influenced Italian unification

Expansionist/chauvinistic nationalism
Key thinker: Maurras
Key ideas: superiority of some nations/races over others; desire to unite all peoples of same language/culture under one empire; rejection of self-determination; supports wars of expansion where necessary
Origins: early twentieth century, reaction against liberalism, democracy and individualism
Impact: influenced Russia and pan-Slavism, Nazi Germany

Anti-colonial/postcolonial nationalism
Key thinker: Garvey
Key ideas: liberation of African colonies from European rule; black nationalism; unity based on common ancestry across state boundaries
Origins: mid-twentieth century, reaction against European empires/racial discrimination and segregation in USA
Impact: major influence on African independence struggles after 1945 and wider black civil rights movement

Figure 4.1 Types of nationalism

Core ideas of nationalism

Human nature

- Nationality is a form of consciousness whereby the individual identifies themselves with a nation based on a common identity that is distinct from other nations.
- Nations are cultural entities, where people are bound together by common ties. However, the difficulty is that there is no clear set of objective factors for a nation; rather a nation is defined by a degree of consciousness among the people that they constitute a nation. There are certain potential options:
    - Language – as argued by von Herder, such as the German language. However, it is notable that states like Belgium and Switzerland have more than one official language.
    - Religion – in particular in recent times, Islam has been important in the formation of national consciousness across the Middle East and North Africa. However, many nations have diverse religions within them, such as the UK.
    - Ethnicity – a distinctive population, territorial area or cultural group provides the national identity. In terms of ethnic identity, this can be seen in the ideas of Maurras and the French nation.
- Cultural nationalism can be expressed as minority nationalism in the cases of Scots or Catalans, where it is progressive and liberal. It can also be seen in the ideas of Garvey, black nationalism and pan-Africanism based on the common ancestry of all Africans, where it is progressive and anti-colonial. However, cultural nationalism can also be exclusive and reactionary, as in the case of Maurras, whereas racialism is both completely exclusive and aggressive.
- There is also the idea of the political nation rather than the cultural nation. The community is defined by its own shared values and ideals rather than its culture or history, as in the sense of the civic nationalism advocated by Rousseau.

The state

- The idea of self-determination arose from the thinking of Rousseau and helped shaped the new map of Europe during the nineteenth century. It was seen as rational and progressive in its opposition to absolute monarchies and imperial domination.
- 'Respect for the principle of equal rights and self-determination of peoples' is a key principle of the UN Charter.
- The nation-state brings together the concept of the nation and the state so that the nation is harmonised with the state, although the nation-state is more of an ideal than a reality.
- Nationalism can also be found among minority groups who wish to establish a state or at least some form of devolution to provide the autonomy to protect their cultural identity.
- For liberal nationalists, the role of the state is to build and maintain the shared values and ideals necessary for the state to realise its goals.
- For conservative nationalists, the state is about preserving order and the organic nation, or changing policies to take the state back to its golden era of times past:
    - For Mazzini, it was the ultimate expression of the unity of the people.
    - For von Herder, it should be based on a people with a common linguistic and cultural heritage.
- For Maurras, the people should be fully subservient to the state and willing to sacrifice everything for it.
- For Garvey, the only important state was the free United States of Africa, which rejects the traditional Western concept of the state.

Check your understanding and progress at www.hoddereducation.co.uk/myrevisionnotes

Society

+ Society can be based on the ideas of civic nationalism in line with Rousseau's thinking:
  + In civic nationalism, cultural identity is not as important as a shared culture.
  + This form of civic nationalism can be one way of building nationalism where there are different cultures within the territory or where there is large-scale immigration.
  + The newcomer to the state can sign up to the language, values and political institutions and can be a fully-fledged member of the nation.
+ Mazzini would argue that all societies should be free and equal communities, based on representative democracy.
+ Von Herder saw society as a cultural concept that emerges from the language, arts and history of each community, and so each society is unique and like a family.
+ Maurras saw society as based on ethnicity and believed that society must be ordered and geared to serve the nation. He argued that society should be protected by excluding other ethnic groups from the territory and that some societies are superior to others.
+ Garvey saw African society as emerging from African culture by throwing off the chains of white views of Africa and black Africans, and by educating Africans about their roots.

The economy

+ Liberal internationalists see free trade between nations as developing interdependence and improving the chances of global peace by increasing the material costs to societies of war.
+ Civic nationalism allows the state to achieve its political goals, which may include economic policies such as welfare and taxation.
+ These types of policy rely on the sense that individuals see themselves as part of the wider community.
+ Conservative nationalism argues that the state should adopt economic policies in defence of the national interest. These polices can be either free trade (as under Margaret Thatcher) or protectionist (as under Donald Trump).
+ Anti/postcolonialism had a strain of thought based on socialist internationalism, which argued that capitalism and globalisation had turned the nations of the South into the world's working class, exploited to pay for the luxuries of the Western world.
+ Garvey saw economic self-sufficiency as vital to black nationalism in the USA, arguing that black Africans should develop their own economic systems and projects for their own benefit.

> **Revision activity**
>
> Create a set of flashcards for all the key terms in this chapter.

Key debates within nationalism

Areas of broad agreement

+ The nation-state should be the central unit of political organisation, representing the only community which is of significance. It should command the allegiance of all its citizens (though pan-Africanism is something of an exception here).
+ The state should either reflect or generate some common shared values that bind people together. These can be both general and broad-based, embracing cosmopolitism (e.g. the USA), or can be narrow and more tightly defined (e.g. around a certain religion or ethnicity). There is also an acceptance that nations will differ in terms of culture, language, race, etc.

Rational versus romantic
+ The most rational way of dividing up the world is into natural political communities that are self-governing: nation-states and nations are modern constructions. Nation-states are states where the nation serves the interests of the state, not the state serving the interest of the nation.
+ Romantic nationalism sees the nation as a historical entity with roots in pre-modern times that is held together by a common culture and language that are distinct. The job of the state is then to serve the nation, protecting its culture and ensuring its future.

Progressive versus regressive
+ Progressive nationalism is based on the idea that it can help the nation achieve political, social and economic progress. This can be achieved by freeing the nation from foreign or supranational domination (e.g. by the EU) so that it can rule itself.
+ Regressive nationalism intends to return society to a previous golden era that is based on a romantic view of traditional culture, institutions and values. It is worth noting that conservative nationalists seek to achieve a return to a previous society, which paradoxically they would consider as progress: Eurosceptics view Brexit in this manner.

Inclusive versus exclusive
+ Inclusive nationalism does not see culture, race and religion as reasons to exclude people from the state. As long as individuals sign up to the values of society and its language, they are welcomed into the state, allowing for a diverse society. In the UK, this involves passing the citizenship test and learning English; in the USA, it means taking the naturalisation test in English and learning about US history and government.
+ Exclusive forms of nationalism see culture as defining the nation – newcomers must adopt the dominant culture.
+ Integral nationalists believe that newcomers cannot become part of an ethnic group as they lack the shared culture.
+ Racialist variants equate nationality with race, which is exclusive by birth.

Expansionism versus self-determination
+ Historically, expansionism has expressed itself through imperialism and colonialism, movements like pan-Slavism, or fascist expansionist policies. In the modern world, there is a sense that states like the USA are involved in neo-colonialism where their power over other states is economic, political and cultural and so does not require conquest. There is also the re-emergence of pan-Slavism in the Russian state.
+ Self-determination remains a powerful ideal, enshrined in the UN Charter and at the heart of independence movements across the globe. Kurds, Catalans and Scots are examples of nations seeking their own state.

Liberal versus conservative
+ Liberal nationalism is concerned with the freedom of all nations and the freedom of all individuals within those nations. This involves nations freeing themselves from state nationalism or oppression by foreign states. However, this desire to be free can lead to violence and conflict, as seen in the civil war in Sri Lanka between the majority Sinhalese and the minority Tamils, who desire a separate Tamil state.
+ Conservative nationalism tends to develop in well-established states, such as France and the UK, and focuses more on maintaining the organic society than the freedom of the individuals within the nation. It is generally seen as wanting to keep society as it is or returning it to a previous golden era, so is viewed as regressive, whereas liberal nationalism's attachment to freedom is seen as progressive.

> **Exam tip**
>
> Don't just explain the differences and similarities within nationalism. Answers should also look to evaluate the significance of those differences and similarities.

> **Revision activity**
>
> Investigate the party manifestos of three of the following: Plaid Cymru, the SNP, the Conservative Party and UKIP. Identify any nationalist policies to use as examples in your answers.

Check your understanding and progress at www.hoddereducation.co.uk/myrevisionnotes

Now test yourself

TESTED

8. Why is nationalism distinct from racialism?
9. Why does liberal internationalism see the nation-state as the cornerstone of a peaceful world?
10. Why can nationalism be seen as an incredibly flexible ideology?
11. Copy and complete the following table with the main ideas of the key thinkers.

Thinker	Human nature	The state	Society	The economy
Jean-Jacques Rousseau				These thinkers had very little to say specifically on the links between nationalism and the economy.
Giuseppe Mazzini				
Johann Gottfried von Herder				
Marcus Garvey				
Charles Maurras				

Exam practice

1. 'Nationalism is aggressive and expansionist.' Analyse and evaluate this statement with reference to the nationalist thinkers that you have studied. In your answer, you should draw on material from across the whole range of your course of study in politics. [25]

2. 'Nationalism is not a single doctrine.' Analyse and evaluate this statement with reference to the nationalist thinkers that you have studied. In your answer, you should draw on material from across the whole range of your course of study in politics. [25]

Summary

You should now have an understanding of:
+ debates about the nature of nationalism
+ types of nationalism and the extent to which they vary
+ the impact of recent developments on nationalism
+ the contributions of the five key thinkers (Rousseau, Mazzini, von Herder, Garvey and Maurras) to nationalism in the areas of human nature, the state, society and the economy

My Revision Notes: AQA A-level Politics: Political Ideas Second Edition

5 Feminism

Feminism is a complex ideology with a diversity of strands. It covers a range of beliefs and interests that are different from and sometimes even incompatible with each other. However, it has two key principles: first, that women historically have had a role in society which is inferior, and so suffer both injustices and institutionalised disadvantages; and secondly, that this forced subservience of women is neither inevitable nor desirable, so it can, should and will be changed through awareness and, above all, by action.

Origins of feminism

+ The two key texts at the heart of the emergence of liberal feminism are Mary Wollstonecraft's *A Vindication of the Rights of Woman* (1792) and Harriet Taylor's *Enfranchisement of Women* (1851).
+ The main thrust of this era was that there were societal customs and legal constraints that stopped women from entering the public sphere or made their success in it impossible.
+ Women were deemed not to be rational, intellectual or physically capable enough, so were denied a place in politics, the economic marketplace and academic/professional life.
+ The main aim initially was to achieve basic rights and formal equality for women to make sure that the rules of the game were fair and all could compete free from discrimination.
+ There are three main waves of feminism, which are reliant on and reactions to the waves that come before them. The first wave is liberal feminism, the second is Marxist, radical and socialist feminism, and the third is postmodern feminism. These waves should be understood by the main themes that bind each wave together rather than chronologically.

Public sphere Typically seen as the world of politics, culture and industry, where public values, ideals and goals of society are formed.

Exam tip

As feminism has such a diversity of ideas, there is a tendency to focus on the differences between the different strands and to neglect the common ground between them. Make sure you identify areas of agreement.

Main waves of feminism

First wave: liberal feminism

Liberal feminism had the following characteristics:
+ **Classical liberalism.** Liberal feminism in its earliest form utilises classical liberalism's ideas about human nature, freedom and the individual to create a feminist theory that liberates women.
+ **Rational.** Wollstonecraft's argument started with the premise that women are human. All humans have the same capacity for rationality, so women have the same capacity as men.
+ **Education.** Wollstonecraft demanded real education (the same as men's education) for women on the basis of their capacity for reason. This would have two benefits:
  + Rational and independent women would bring benefits to wider society.
  + It would allow rational and independent women to be autonomous, making their own choices about their life, which for Wollstonecraft was the basis for being fully human.
+ **Gender justice.** Discrimination against women could be found in the lack of rights and equal opportunities for women. In line with the liberal idea that all have equal moral worth, there should be equality of treatment in the following areas:
  + the intellectual sphere – all have an equal right to education

- civic life – all should have the right to vote, and women should play a role and have a say in the making of the law
- economic life – equal opportunities to access all jobs and equal pay for the same work; the idea of economic independence for women was crucial to Charlotte Perkins Gilman
- **Reformism**. Crucial to achieving gender justice was winning the right to vote. Once women could influence the making of laws, these could be shaped to tackle discrimination against them and ensure equality of treatment.

> **Making links**
>
> In addition to the key thinkers that you learn about in feminism, you can link back to both Mary Wollstonecraft and Betty Friedan in liberalism (see Chapter 1), as both made key contributions to liberal feminism.

Contemporary directions in liberal feminism

Originally, liberal feminists thought that equal rights and anti-discrimination laws would be enough to achieve their aims, but in recent times liberal feminists have realised that more needs to be done to counteract years of gender discrimination. This can involve affirmative action to ensure that women are recruited over *equally qualified* men into jobs or into higher education. Two examples of positive discrimination in practice are:

- The use of all-women shortlists by political parties, such as the Labour Party, to tackle the gender imbalance in Parliament. Following the 2019 election, 51% of all Labour MPs were women.
- Affirmative action in the USA – when introduced by President Kennedy in 1961, this was based on 'race, creed, colour or national origin', but in 1967 President Johnson added gender to that list.

> **Key thinker**
>
> **Charlotte Perkins Gilman (1860–1935)**
>
> In her work *Women and Economics* (1898), Charlotte Perkins Gilman was in tune with liberal feminism as she saw clear economic hurdles blocking women's progress However, her writing did not fit comfortably with any particular strand of feminism and her idea of gender as socially constructed was well ahead of its time.
>
> - Humanity was the only species where 'the female depends on the male for food' and 'sex-relations is also an economic relation' and this had limited social progress and evolution.
> - As a woman lacks economic independence, she was assigned a 'social role that locked her into her home' and this role was culturally created, not based on biological difference.
> - This male domination can also be found in an **androcentric** culture, with male domination in the arts, humanities, fashion and health reinforcing the domestic role of women as wife, mother and housekeeper.
> - Women have 'the same human energies and human desires and ambition within', but their culturally defined roles have 'kept them back from their share in progress'.
> - As a **reform Darwinist**, Gilman believed that humanity could direct and control evolution through its own actions.
> - Her proposed solution was economic independence for women, centralised nurseries and co-operative kitchens to create true freedom for women to think and judge for themselves.
> - This freedom for women, and equality between men and women, would allow for a more natural growth of the qualities and virtues that would bring true and lasting progress to society.

> **Exam tip**
>
> You can use the Civil Rights Act (1964), in the USA, and the Equality Act (2010), in the UK, as examples of legislation formulated to ban discrimination in the workplace on the basis of sex. You might also discuss the UN's 17 Sustainable Development Goals, which include Goal 5; 'Achieve gender equality and empower all women and girls'. In 2019, globally women accounted for 39% of total employment, but in 2020 women accounted for 45% of global employment losses, highlighting that there is still much work to be done.

Affirmative action Policies to improve opportunities for historically excluded or under-represented groups in education through admissions and employment policies.

Androcentric Placing men or the masculine view at the centre of perspectives on the world.

Reform Darwinism The concept that humans are not helpless in the face of evolution; through their actions, they can shape and control it.

Second wave: Marxist, radical and socialist feminism

Marxist feminism

- Although liberals claimed that discrimination was the root cause of the oppression of women, Marxist feminists saw capitalism as the problem.
- Friedrich Engels, in *The Origin of the Family, Private Property and the State* (1884), made the point that class oppression is the most universal form of oppression and the cause of all other forms of oppression.
- The starting point was the move away from families being matrilineal (where family is traced through the female line of descent) to where 'the man took command in the home'. This move was brought about by the advent of private property and capitalism.
- Marriage was an institution built on exploitation, with the man as the property-owning bourgeois and the woman as the property-less proletarian.
- The property-less woman was degraded and reduced to servitude in her own home as a slave to male lust and an instrument to produce children – the working classes of the future.
- Marxist feminists built on the work of Engels to argue that reproductive labour should either be recognised as productive and fairly paid or be socialised (carried out by wider society) so that women can take their place in the workforce.
- The solution is the abolition of private property, capitalism and the family as an economic unit. This would mean all adults would work and therefore marriage and the family would no longer be based on economic relations as men and women would be equal.

> **Making links**
>
> In discussing Marxist feminism, you can draw on the political ideas of Marx and Engels (see Chapter 3).

Radical feminism

- Although Marxist feminists blame capitalism and private property as the cause of the oppression of women, radical feminists argue that patriarchy is the root cause of oppression.
- Kate Millett's *Sexual Politics* (1970) (see p. 78) was integral to the radical feminist approach, with its focus on patriarchy and how the family and wider culture are used to support masculine authority in all areas of life and, outside the home, permit women no authority at all.
- Patriarchy (see p. 77) is the most universal and the most damaging form of oppression and historically the first form of oppression. This means that tackling discrimination or overthrowing capitalism cannot eradicate the oppression of women.
- Radical feminism is a broad collection of different ideas and there are three key elements worth considering here: 'the personal is the political', sex and gender, and patriarchy.

'The personal is the political'

- Radical feminists argue that patriarchy is a pervasive relationship that dominates both the public sphere and the private sphere.
- The personal includes the experiences of women related to the female body (e.g. menstruation, child birth and pregnancy) and the experiences of women in the home and in the workplace (e.g. sexual harassment, domestic labour and sexual violence).
- By bringing these issues out into the light, the understanding of oppression was greatly deepened. The home and the female body were now added to the political and the social as sites of oppression.

> **Exam tip**
>
> As examples of liberal feminism in action, you can use the suffragettes and suffragists in the UK and the National American Woman Suffrage Association in the USA, who all campaigned for women's voting rights. The National Organization for Women (NOW) was founded in 1966 to promote feminist ideals, lead societal change, eliminate discrimination, and achieve and protect the equal rights of all women and girls in all aspects of social, political and economic life. Betty Friedan was one of its original founders.

> **Reproductive labour** Unpaid labour performed by women in the home, such as cooking, washing clothes and bearing/raising children. This unpaid labour produces the workers of the future and ensures the current workers are fit and able to work.
>
> **Patriarchy** A whole network of systems of control, which systematically allow men to dominate and exploit women.

> **Private sphere** The opposite of the public sphere; the family, the home and the body where individuals have freedom largely unregulated by the state.

Check your understanding and progress at www.hoddereducation.co.uk/myrevisionnotes

Sex and gender

- There is a theoretical distinction between sex (a biological distinction) and gender (a socially defined distinction known as 'masculinity' or 'femininity'). This is the issue raised by Simone de Beauvoir when she stated that 'One is not born, but rather becomes, a woman' (*The Second Sex*, 1949).
- Radical feminists do not deny that there are biological sex differences, such as the differences in sexual reproductive organs. However, they see humans as androgynous.
- Biology is not oppressive, but the way men have constructed gender to control women as child bearers and child carers is.
- Gender is a social construct, as femininity has changed over time and varies between different cultures.
- Femininity is constructed and then imposed on women, laying out expectations, rules and restrictions on their behaviour.
- The division into 'masculine' and 'feminine' genders is not a division into two equal parts.
- Masculine traits like competitiveness, assertiveness and courage are seen as superior to feminine traits like passivity, submissiveness and emotion, and these are used to justify the dominance of man over woman.
- These traits are socialised in childhood, with the family and wider culture teaching children the social rules and expectations that they are expected to follow.

> **Androgynous** The characteristics of male and female in the same person, revealing that differences between men and women are so slight that they should have no impact on their political, social or economic role.
>
> **Existentialism** Humans have no nature, or essence, and use their freedom to make themselves through their own actions.

> **Exam tip**
>
> You can illustrate the idea of gender as a social construct using American anthropologist Margaret Mead's *Sex and Temperament in Three Primitive Societies* (1935), which showed clear differences in the social roles and personality traits that were seen as desirable and normal across three different cultures in Papua New Guinea.

Key thinker

Simone de Beauvoir (1908–86)

Simone de Beauvoir in her book, *The Second Sex* (1949), used existentialism to pose the question: 'What is a woman?' In answering this question, she argued that the oppression of women is unique and without a historical starting point.

- In looking for the sources of oppression, Simone de Beauvoir considered biological, psychological and socialist analysis, finding that all only partially answer the question, so she looked for an explanation in women's being or existence.
  - Men are like women in that they are free but are subject to nature, with natural bodies that are neither predictable nor fully controllable.
  - Desiring to be a free being and to create their own meaning in the world, men see themselves as the Self or the norm, and nature is seen as the Other and a threat and a danger.
  - As women are tied to their bodies through the reproductive process, with menstruation a constant reminder of that, they are seen by men as part of nature and so the Other.
  - The Self must control the Other, so men must subordinate women.
- Men create the feminine myth/mystery (about what it is to be a woman, motherhood and female sexuality) to make women the embodiment of nature.
- The essence of femininity has to be a myth as human beings have no nature or essence.
- Women are socialised into this role through childhood experiences and cultural and marital expectations based on socially constructed standards of beauty, behaviour and sexuality. 'One is not born but becomes woman.'
- Women have taken on board this alien point of view of the Self and the Other, and so are complicit in their own oppression.
- De Beauvoir offers four strategies for freedom to create a future where men and women are true equals:
  - Women must go out to work.
  - Women must become intellectuals.
  - Women must exercise their sexuality as they see fit.
  - Women must seek economic justice and independence by changing society into a socialist society.

Patriarchy

Patriarchy is a whole system of control and dominance by men over women and their bodies. It cannot be reformed; it can only be rooted out through revolution. Sylvia Walby in *Theorizing Patriarchy* (1990) identifies six different structures that form this system of control:

+ The state – the legal and political structures that prevent or limit representation for women within the state.
+ The household – housework is a woman's most fulfilling role; even if a married woman works, housework remains her domain.
+ Culture – women are expected to want children and to sacrifice their careers when they have children in order to bring them up. Perhaps the most pervasive and damaging current myth is the 'beauty myth'.
+ Sexuality – women should be virgins until marriage, practise monogamy in marriage and subordinate their sexual needs to those of their husband.
+ Work – where women have sought work, this is in the part-time sector or lower-paid roles that are associated with 'feminine' traits, such as teaching, nursing and caring.
+ Violence – high levels of domestic abuse have historically been kept off the public agenda as the home is seen as 'personal'.

The solutions to patriarchy proposed by radical feminists are radical and involve a sexual revolution to eradicate it. However, these solutions reveal an incompatible divide within radical feminism between equality feminists and difference feminists, as shown in Table 5.1.

> **Exam tip**
>
> You can use Naomi Wolf's *The Beauty Myth* (1990) to illustrate how, as the social power and prestige of women has grown, so has the pressure to adhere to unrealistic standards through the role of the mass media.

Equality feminists Those who believe that the goal of feminism is to achieve equality between the sexes by freeing women from difference. Liberal, radical, socialist and postmodern feminists all have different visions of how this will be achieved.

Difference feminists Those who believe that women are essentially different from men biologically and psychologically. These differences matter.

> **Exam tip**
>
> It is important to show that patriarchy is not the same as gender inequality or discrimination; it is far more than that. It is a system of control that is rooted in all the main societal institutions and ensures the male domination of women.

Table 5.1 The divisions between equality and difference feminists

	Equality feminists	Difference feminists
Explanation	+ Equality feminism sees patriarchy as a male-imposed construction and imposition of difference. + Patriarchy must be removed by freeing women from 'difference' so that there is sexual equality. + Sexual equality is equality in family and personal life. + This is based on the idea that biological differences between men and women are of little importance and their human nature is basically the same.	+ There are clear biological and psychological differences between men and women, and these differences matter. + By seeking liberation through equality, women are seeking to be like men rather than having their own woman-centred approach. + The idea of androgyny is entirely misplaced as it ignores the significance of these biological differences. + Carol Gilligan's *In a Different Voice* (1982) showed that men and women had a different approach to moral dilemmas.

Potential solutions	+ Shulamith Firestone argued in *The Dialectic of Sex: The Case for Feminist Revolution* (1970) that if women are to be liberated, they must have control over their own bodies. This is the ability to choose when and if to use technology to control reproduction (contraception) and to aid in reproduction (*in vitro* fertilisation or even artificial gestation outside the womb).
	+ Women should be released from the domestic responsibility of bringing up children by the creation of socialised child care.
		+ Women should create a women-centred culture (cultural feminism) because:
		  + gender is male-defined, so women should throw off the male definition of gender and define their own femininity in a way that it is entirely unrelated to men or masculinity, *or*
		  + patriarchy has imposed a false nature on women, which they must throw off to discover their true identity – the true feminine self

- Women should be free to explore and experiment with their sexuality as they wish, to learn and understand their own desires so they can be sexually fulfilled. Women should take back control of their own bodies and enjoy their bodies as they are.
- Every individual should be given the freedom to be androgynous and to choose from the various masculine and feminine traits that are beneficial to both sexes.
- Equality feminists see the ideas of **cultural feminism** as rolling back the gains of feminism by focusing on female traits. They argue that **separatist feminism** replaces sexual freedom with sex as a political statement.

- Either way, the feminine self will be based on the values of women that are different from men.
- Some difference feminists go further, arguing that sex differences are natural and patriarchy is a direct expression of male human nature.
- The solution is female separatism as all male–female relations are oppressive.
- So women must escape the male-defined concept of sexuality (heterosexuality) and define their own form of sexuality through autoeroticism, lesbianism or celibacy.

Cultural feminism A new form of culture could be developed based on feminine traits that women possess, but which are devalued by patriarchy. Strong cultural feminism argues that women have essential traits that are peaceful, nurturing and intuitive.

Separatist feminism Believes that political and sexual inequalities between men and women cannot be resolved and so opposes heterosexual relationships of any kind. It focuses on women working together, living together and engaging in relationships with each other to achieve their goals.

Exam tip

There is a tendency to focus just on contrasting the views of equality and difference feminism rather than focusing on how difference feminism has developed a critique of equality feminism based on the idea that it encourages women to be like men.

Key thinker

Kate Millett (1934–2017)

Kate Millett was a radical feminist who argued for 'sexual politics', as politics refers to any power-structured relationship like the relationship between men and women. In 1970, Kate Millett's *Sexual Politics* was published, highlighting the subjugation of women in great literature and art, and showing the value of a feminist critique in all areas of life.

- The roots of the oppression of women can be found in patriarchy's sex/gender system.
- Patriarchy is pervasive; it is found in every sphere of life including education, work, family life, religion and sex.
- In the patriarchal family, the man has priority, with marriage being the exchange of female domestic service and sex in return for financial support.
- The key institution of patriarchy is the family – it acts as 'a patriarchal unit in a patriarchal whole'. It is within the family that children are socialised into patriarchy-prescribed gender roles. This socialisation is reinforced by peers, education and the wider culture to create a uniformity of attitudes.
- All systems of oppression that operate in society – racial, political and economic – cannot be overturned unless the fundamental form of oppression – patriarchy – is overturned. To overturn patriarchy, it is necessary to overturn gender as constructed by patriarchy. This sexual revolution would involve:
  - the end of sexual inhibitions and taboos to create sexual freedom.
  - the end of the ideology of patriarchy and its means of socialisation – the family unit.
  - the undermining of the traditional family unit through the abolition of the sex role for women, full economic independence for women and the socialisation of care of the young.
  - a re-examination of the masculine and feminine traits of gender, selecting those traits which are desirable to both sexes.

> **Now test yourself** TESTED
>
> 1. What are the key differences between liberal and radical feminists?
> 2. What is the distinction between sex and gender?
> 3. How did Kate Millett make a case for the idea that 'the personal is the political' in her demand for sexual politics?
> 4. What is the difference between the public and private spheres?

Socialist feminism

Socialist feminism is closely associated with Sheila Rowbotham and emerged in the 1970s, looking to blend the ideas of radical feminism with Marxist feminism.

+ Women act as a reserve army of labour, working for low pay when needed, keeping wages low and then returning to their family when there is unemployment.
+ Labour in the home is unrecognised, certainly in terms of pay, and is used to suggest that women are unreliable and often absent from the workplace, so need to be kept out of better jobs.
+ The propaganda around femininity is to make the subordination of women to men appear as 'natural'.
+ Reform will never be enough as it not possible for women to be free within patriarchy or capitalism.
+ Socialist feminism recognises patriarchy and capitalism as forms of oppression that are separate but linked, so both must be tackled separately as well as collaboratively by a revolution if women are to be liberated.

> **Key thinker**
>
> **Sheila Rowbotham (1943–)**
>
> Sheila Rowbotham offered a revolutionary challenge to capitalism and patriarchy in her work, *Woman's Consciousness, Man's World* (1973).
>
> + The issue of being born a woman in capitalism is specific and not an issue that affects all of humankind.
> + Patriarchy predates capitalism and is embedded in the sexual division of labour and the possession of women by men. It comes from a pre-industrial period when it was common for some humans to be owned by others.
> + Under capitalism, the boss controls the labour power of the workers but does not own the workers. This undermines the patriarchal idea that men own women.
> + At the same time, women are allowed into the workplace but not to be exploited equally with men. They are limited to low-paid roles, still responsible for childbearing and rearing, and so continue to need the economic support of men to survive.
> + Women are badly paid and underprivileged in the workforce, yet handy for capitalism as a reserve army of labour that allows men to 'console themselves for their lack of control at work with the right to be master in their own home'.
> + An effective movement for the liberation of women must be one in which working-class women are in the majority.

Third wave: postmodern feminism

+ Postmodernism, which emerged towards the end of the twentieth century, rejects the idea that there are grand narratives that offer one all-encompassing theory that explains everything. As a result, postmodern feminism is more of a collection of different ideas.
+ There is no one single explanation for the oppression of women and there is no singular or uniting experience of oppression for women.
+ Different women, in different locations and at different times, all experience oppression in different ways.
+ The theory therefore focuses more on the differences between women rather than between men and women.
+ One key criticism levelled by bell hooks at all the preceding forms of feminism is that they represented the interests of white, middle-class women who sought sisterhood within their experiences. This side-lined the experiences of black women in the USA and meant their voice was not being heard.

> **Exam tip**
>
> As an example of postmodern feminism in action, Kimberlé Crenshaw co-founded the African American Policy Forum, one of the USA's leading social justice think tanks. In 2015, it created the hashtag #SayHerName, which in its own words was to highlight 'awareness to the often invisible names and stories of Black women and girls who have been victimized by racist police violence, and provides support to their families'.

Check your understanding and progress at www.hoddereducation.co.uk/myrevisionnotes

- Gender should be understood via intersectionality. In 1989, Kimberlé Crenshaw coined this term to detail how systems of oppression overlap and create unique experiences for people based on their multiple identity categories.
- She describes this in her famous quote: 'The experience of being a black woman cannot be understood in terms of being black and of being a woman considered independently, but must include interactions, which frequently reinforce each other.'
- Postmodern feminism also focuses on the idea that there is no single way of understanding feminism, and each new generation of women has to define feminism for themselves in the light of their own experiences.

> **Intersectionality** The idea that women experience oppression in varying configurations and in varying degrees of intensity based on the intersection between different forms of oppression such as race, gender and class.

Key thinker

bell hooks (1952–2021)

bell hooks was a contemporary feminist who dealt with the issues of gender, race, class and sexual oppression in her book, *Ain't I a Woman: Black Women and Feminism* (1981).
- hooks describes feminism as the 'the struggle to end sexist oppression'.
- hooks refused to accept that gender defines everything about who a female person is. There is a need to consider other elements such as class and race.
- hooks wrote a withering critique of Betty Friedan's *The Feminine Mystique*, arguing that 'the problem that has no name' is not the condition of women in society. It is 'the plight of a select group of college-educated, middle- and upper-class, married white women' who wanted more than their husband, children or house – they wanted careers.
- hooks argued that the feminist movement gave a voice to this group and drowned out the voices of women without men, without children, without homes, poor white women and all non-white women.
- This led bell hooks to talk about the interlocking systems of 'imperialist white supremacist capitalist patriarchy', which shape the dominator culture in the USA and work to promote injustice, exploitation and oppression.
- Of these interlocking systems, patriarchy is the system that exploits the family to teach these dominator values, socialising both men and women to believe men are inherently dominating, superior to the weak, especially women, and have 'the right to dominate and rule over the weak and to maintain that dominance through various forms of psychological terrorism and violence'. These systems of oppression have left black women as the most marginalised group in society.
- The answer is to acknowledge that patriarchy is the problem and to work together, between genders, classes and races, to end it and all other forms of oppression. By doing this, the feminist movement can have more impact and can be more diverse and inclusive.

> **Exam tip**
>
> In the exam, it is important to show how intersectionality has impacted on feminism. There is now a debate that a fourth wave of feminism is here, which is both intersectional and inclusive. It is fuelled by the battles of the previous waves to shatter the glass ceiling and for reproductive rights alongside new issues such as sexual harassment, workplace discrimination and violence against women, and is empowered by the connectivity of the internet and the power of social media activism. A good example of this is the #MeToo global movement.

Post-feminism

- Post-feminism sees many of the objectives of the feminist movement as having been achieved – in women's employment, financial independence, political power, and increasing control over their bodies through reproductive technology and increased choice in sexual relationships and partnerships.
- As a result, it is time to move on from feminism. Now, women should focus on female accomplishments and female power. Some have gone further, arguing that women should claim the power to dominate and manipulate using their sexualised bodies. Many feminists do not see post-feminism as a form of feminism at all but rather as a form of anti-feminism.

> **Exam tip**
>
> Don't confuse postmodern feminism, which is based on diversity and difference, with post-feminism, which argues that it is now time to move on from feminism as it has largely achieved its goals.

> **Revision activity**
>
> Create a spider diagram detailing key quotes from Gilman, de Beauvoir, Millett, Rowbotham and hooks. Write your explanations of what the quotes mean underneath.

> **Now test yourself** TESTED
>
> 5 What is bell hooks' criticism of earlier forms of feminism?
> 6 About what do radical, socialist and postmodern feminists agree?
> 7 Explain how capitalism and patriarchy are linked for socialist feminists.

> **Key thinkers in context**
>
> **Charlotte Perkins Gilman**
> Charlotte Perkins Gilman in her collection of essays, *Women and Economics* (1898) details her ideas on the liberation of women. Key to her approach was that marriage was a sexual economic bargain, where men provided financially while women had to look after the home and meet their husband's needs. Women were prepared for this role as wives and mothers through a culturally created social role that locked women into their homes. Her answer was a radical call for economic independence for women.
>
> **Simone de Beauvoir**
> Simone de Beauvoir considered herself to be an author but is now regarded as a philosopher and key theorist and activist. *The Second Sex* (1949) details the ways in which the sciences, literature and social, political, and religious traditions have produced and reinforced a world view of women's inferiority to justify patriarchy. The most famous line 'One is not born, but rather becomes, a woman' is seen as the critical starting point for the sex–gender distinction.
>
> **Kate Millett**
> Kate Millett was the author of the ground-breaking bestseller *Sexual Politics* (1970) and developed the idea that for women the personal is political. Millett's critique of patriarchy positions sexual dominion 'as perhaps the most pervasive ideology of our culture and provides its most fundamental concept of power', arguing that 'every avenue of power within the society, including the coercive force of the police, is entirely in male hands'.
>
> **Sheila Rowbotham**
> Sheila Rowbotham is a historian of feminism and radical social movements as well one of the UK's most important feminist thinkers. In her work *Women, Resistance and Revolution* (1972), Marxism and feminism 'cohabit in the same space somewhat unequally' and the connection between the oppression of women and the class exploitation of work will emerge out of a movement of working-class women and their lived experience. The revolution will have to fundamentally transform the organisation and control of production as well as 'the production undertaken by women in the family and the production of self through sexuality'.
>
> **bell hooks**
> bell hooks' key work *Ain't I a Woman* was first published in 1981 and examines how black women, from the seventeenth century to the present day, were and are oppressed by both white men and black men, and by white women. She insisted that struggles to end racism and sexism were fundamentally connected. bell hooks wanted to redefine feminism and argued that to be feminist 'in any authentic sense of the term is to want for all people, female and male, liberation from sexist role patterns, domination and oppression'.

Core ideas of feminism

REVISED

Human nature

Areas of agreement

+ The main issue in regard to human nature for feminists is sex and gender.
+ For most feminists, sex or biological differences are inconsequential and not relevant to the way in which women should be treated by the state and society, or in the economy.
+ Gender is seen as a cultural not a biological construct, based on the artificial creation of 'masculine' and 'feminine'. In reality, most feminists would argue that humans are androgynous.
+ Gender and fixed and inherited gender roles are rejected by most feminists.

Areas of tension

Liberal feminists

+ Mary Wollstonecraft and Charlotte Perkins Gilman focused on human nature being the same for men and women. Wollstonecraft saw humans as rational, self-seeking, independent individuals who wish to be autonomous and pursue their own version of the good life.
+ Liberal feminists are equality feminists, seeing all humans as being of equal moral value and so entitled to formal equality and equality of opportunity.

Marxist/socialist feminists
+ Engels saw gender roles as part of the construct of capitalism to ensure that women fulfil the role of reproductive labour that is essential to the functioning of capitalism.
+ Marxist feminists are equality feminists, focusing on economic equality between men and women.
+ Sheila Rowbotham blended the Marxist and radical critiques of gender, arguing that gender is a construct of both capitalism and patriarchy to ensure that women are subordinate. Hence equality is required in an economic sense, as well as in the family and personal life.

Radical feminists
+ Simone de Beauvoir and Kate Millett saw gender roles and traits as artificially constructed and imposed on women to secure the dominance of men through patriarchy. Women are socialised into seeing gender roles as 'natural' when they clearly are not.
+ Most radical feminists reject equality feminism, arguing that equality in the family and personal life is central to equality between men and women.
+ However, some radical feminists (difference feminists) see biological differences as essential to understanding the differences between men and women, and the quest for equality as dangerous because it is a quest to be like men.

Postmodern feminists
+ Postmodern feminists see gender roles as forced on women by society. However, gender is not the only influence on identity; it coincides with class and race, creating different experiences for different women.
+ Postmodern feminists are also equality feminists, seeing different experiences for different women as a way to understand how all are oppressed under patriarchy.

The state

Areas of agreement
+ All feminists recognise that the state has the potential to serve a useful purpose for women.
+ Most feminists agree that – historically, currently or both – the state is complicit in women being subordinate to men.
+ Feminists believe that the state could be used more to enhance women's position in society.

Areas of tension
Liberal feminism
+ Wollstonecraft and Friedan pointed to the failure of the state to tackle the problem of discrimination against women, so perpetuating women's subordinate role.
+ The state is also the source for ending this discrimination through the granting of formal equality for women, as campaigned for by Mary Wollstonecraft and Harriet Taylor.
+ The state can ensure access to education and the world of work for women to secure economic independence, as Perkins argued.
+ The state can pass laws to guarantee the equality of women. It can:
  + ban discrimination, as with the Civil Rights Act (1964) in the USA
  + impose gender justice in the public sphere, as with the Equality Act (2010) in the UK
  + impose laws and measures to protect equal pay, as with the Lilly Ledbetter Fair Pay Act (2009) in the USA, and the Equal Pay Act (1970) in the UK, superseded by the Equality Act (2010)

- impose laws and policies to tackle domestic violence and rape in marriage, as with the 'Call to End Violence Against Women and Girls' strategy launched by the Coalition government in 2010 and renewed by the Conservative government in 2016
+ Friedan would go further, arguing that affirmative action policies should be used by the state to tackle past injustices and promote equality.

Radical feminism and socialist feminism
+ Second- and third-wave feminists might agree that such measures and laws are useful, but don't do anywhere near enough to tackle the systemic oppression of women.
+ Kate Millett identified the state as part of the problem, as it promotes and sustains patriarchy, while Sheila Rowbotham argued that it serves both patriarchy and capitalism in their oppression of women.
+ The state could use the law more effectively to prevent oppression – for example, by banning pornography, which for Kate Millett associated power, cruelty and dominance with the masculine and victimhood with the feminine.
+ Sheila Rowbotham argued that equal pay is a start but that it is impossible to see the equality of men and women under capitalism. In fact, it is even impossible to see the equal exploitation of women and men under capitalism, given the division of labour in the workplace and at home.
+ bell hooks saw the state as part of the interlocking system of 'imperialist white supremacist capitalist patriarchy', promoting injustice, exploitation and oppression.

Society

Area of agreement
Society and societal attitudes have placed women in a subordinate role to men, so they suffer injustices and institutionalised disadvantages.

Areas of tension
+ The most significant tension is between the difference and equality feminists within the radical feminist movement.
+ Some difference feminists argue for a cultural feminism based on a woman-centric culture and lifestyle focused on female values, through women either discovering their lost feminine nature or formulating a new nature without reference to men.
+ Others argue for a form of separatist feminism because the desire for men to dominate is part of their basic nature, so women need to formulate a society separate from men to realise their true nature.

Liberal feminism
+ Wollstonecraft saw women as being discriminated against as society fails to accept the full humanity of women and their rationality.
+ Friedan saw women as discriminated against by society through their lack of access to education and to the world of work. In particular, she identified the 'problem that has no name', where women were supposed to find satisfaction in the roles of wife and mother but this left them miserable and empty.
+ Discrimination could be tackled by changes in the law, which would lead to changes in attitudes and behaviours over time. With women taking a full part in society, public values and social institutions would gradually change to end bias and discrimination. This is a process of societal reform, not societal revolution.
+ Liberal feminists are interested in what happens in the public sphere, while the private sphere is the place for personal choice and freedom where the state should not intervene. The personal is *not* the political.

Second- and third-wave feminism
+ Women's subordinate role is caused by discrimination and bias. It has a much deeper foundation in the system of patriarchy and sees oppression as stretching across the public and private spheres. The personal is the political.
+ The answer for radical feminists and postmodern feminists is a revolution to challenge and overthrow patriarchy, whereas for socialist feminists there needs to be an economic and social revolution to create equality politically, legally, economically, sexually and in family life.

Radical feminism
+ Millett argued that patriarchy is pervasive across society in religion, culture, the arts, the media, education, the family and sexual life, with the patriarchal family unit as the key body that reinforces the subordination of women.
+ De Beauvoir saw women as moulded into their gender roles to such a degree that they feel their gender roles are natural. They have become complicit in their own oppression by viewing themselves as the Other and man as the norm.

Socialist feminism
+ Rowbotham saw capitalism and patriarchy as interlinked systems of oppression that teach women to be feminine based on myths made by men. These myths make women subordinate in the home and subordinate in the workplace.

Postmodern feminism
+ bell hooks saw patriarchy as the most important of the wider systems of oppression, such as class and race, and was critical of previous forms of feminism for their narrow focus on white, middle-class women.
+ Patriarchy socialises men to be dominators and women to see themselves as subordinate. Ending patriarchy will free women and remove 'the single most life-threatening social disease assaulting the male body and spirit in our nation' (hooks, *The Will to Change*, 2004).

The economy
Areas of agreement
+ Feminists agree that women have been subordinated to men in the economic sphere in multiple ways, such as the gender pay gap, which is the percentage difference between average hourly earnings for men and women. This pay gap is a result of:
    + women doing the vast majority of reproductive labour, forcing them into temporary, part-time, low-paid work with fewer opportunities for promotion
    + a divided labour market, where women are more likely to be employed in professions that are seen as feminine and so are paid less
    + most senior roles in firms being held by men
+ Feminists agree that women should be economically independent.

Areas of tension
+ Gilman argued that, given the nature of work in modern industrial societies, biological differences were of no consequence.
+ Gilman, Wollstonecraft and Friedan all agreed that women should have access to work and that there should be equality of opportunity in the labour market.
+ Friedan argued that the state had a responsibility to intervene so that there were no obstacles to women competing fairly with men in the labour market.

- Rowbotham saw women as oppressed in the capitalist marketplace, as they are seen as a cheap source of labour used in low-paid, precarious jobs and are quickly discarded in times of economic downturn. At the same time, they are exploited in the home through unpaid reproductive labour.
- For Rowbotham, the overthrow of capitalism and patriarchy is necessary to achieve economic equality and sexual equality, as well as equality within the family.
- De Beauvoir saw patriarchy as the main issue, but argued that socialistic economic equality was part of the social revolution.
- bell hooks argued that capitalism, imperialism and white supremacy combined with patriarchy to create oppression for all women, but that oppression was different for different women depending on how race and class intersected with their gender.
- hooks also argued that when Friedan called for women to have careers, she failed to 'tell readers whether it was more fulfilling to be a maid, a babysitter, a factory worker, a clerk, or a prostitute than to be a leisure-class housewife'.

> **Exam tip**
>
> In your answers it is worth considering the gender pay gap, which measures the difference between average (median) hourly earnings of men and women, usually shown by the percentage that men earn more than women. The Office for National Statistics reported that the UK median hourly pay for full time employees was 8.3% less for women than for men in April 2022.

Key debates within feminism

Public versus private

- Liberal feminists see discrimination and bias in the public sphere as placing women in a subordinate role. However, they do not wish challenge the traditional family and marriage roles, as the private sphere is seen as the realm of personal freedom where the state should not tread.
- In contrast, radical feminists see the personal as political, as the family is the base unit of patriarchy with unequal relations between the sexes in the home passed on from generation to generation as the norm for the relations between sexes.
- Postmodern feminists also see the family as the key patriarchal unit, passing on dominator values based on not just gender but also race and class.
- Marxist feminists also reject the private/public split, seeing sexual inequality rooted in the public sphere of the economy spreading into the home and family unit.

Difference versus equality

- Most of the main strands of feminism subscribe to androgyny and the idea that personhood is difference-blind. They also agree that there is a distinction between sex and gender, and that gender is a socially constructed idea that men and women are conditioned from birth to internalise. However, difference feminists (a strand of radical feminism) disagree, rejecting androgyny for the belief that there are clear, permanent biological differences between men and women. As biology matters, difference feminism argues that women should not desire to be like men; they should reject gender equality and celebrate womanhood.
- Separatist feminists argue that male oppression and dominance is rooted in the male essence, so women cannot live in harmony and equality with men.

Reform or revolution?

- Liberal feminism is rooted in individualism and the idea that formal equality should be granted to all. Discrimination against women in the public sphere is brought about by bias, ignorance and the socialisation of gender roles, and is not rooted in a pervasive system of patriarchy.
- For liberal feminists, social reform can achieve equal access for all to the public realm by making the rules of the game fair and stopping any of the players from being systematically disadvantaged by discrimination. This

will allow the individual to be autonomous, achieve full personhood and follow their version of the good life. However, radical feminism sees the basis of oppression as patriarchy, rooted in the patriarchal family unit, which creates a collective identity for women, or sisterhood, which they can use to advance the revolution. This collective action will bring about a cultural, social and sexual revolution.

+ Postmodern feminism sees oppression as rooted in gender as well as in class and race, and this must be recognised. The revolution must tackle all these interlocking systems of oppression through an approach based on solidarity across the different groups, who all have their own voice expressing their own experience of oppression.
+ Socialist feminism is also about collective action and revolution, arguing for an economic and social/sexual revolution to liberate women from patriarchy and everyone from capitalism.

Is feminism a single doctrine?

Feminism starts from the point that women are people, which was once a radical idea but is now widely accepted. Feminism has two fundamental beliefs that unite it:

+ Women have a subordinate role in the state, society and the economy, suffering persistent injustices and systemic discrimination on the basis of their sex.
+ The subordination of women is not desirable or permanent, and women's role in the state, society and the economy can and should be changed via political action.

Beyond that, there is limited agreement between feminists. There are fundamental clashes between difference and equality feminism; post-feminism suggests that feminism has achieved its goals; and there are the key differences between the main strands, as shown in Table 5.2.

Table 5.2 The key ideas of the four main strands of feminist thinking

Liberal	Radical	Socialist	Postmodern
Reformist.	A social and sexual revolution.	Socialist revolution alongside a social and sexual revolution.	A revolution that overthrows the interlocking systems of oppression.
Discrimination in the public sphere can happen via changes in the law. The increased role of women in the public sphere will whittle away bias and prejudice.	Patriarchy is the oldest, most pervasive and most damaging form of oppression. It has been conditioned into human consciousness.	Patriarchy and capitalist domination work together to oppress women by making them unequal in the workplace and unequal in the home.	The imperialist, white supremacist, capitalist patriarchy promotes injustice, exploitation and oppression that is different for different groups.
Formal equality and economic equality will liberate women as individuals.	The root and branch removal of patriarchy is needed to create sexual equality.	The removal of capitalism, private property and the patriarchal family is central to the liberation of women.	The recognition of different identities and the bringing together of the different voices to challenge oppression are the key to liberation.
Women should have equality in the public sphere and freedom to pursue their own version of the good life in their private lives.	A radical transformation is needed in all spheres of life including a woman's control over her own body, sexual freedom and equality and freedom in terms of reproductive labour.	Women cannot be free unless they achieve freedom from patriarchy and freedom from economic exploitation.	It is essential to counter all the interlocking systems of oppressions, such as class, race and gender.

> **Revision activity**
> Create a set of flashcards for all the key terms in this chapter.

Now test yourself

TESTED

8 What is the difference between equal pay and the gender pay gap?

9 Copy and complete the following table with the main ideas of the key thinkers.

Thinker	Human nature	The state	Society	The economy
Charlotte Perkins Gilman				
Simone de Beauvoir				
Kate Millett				
Sheila Rowbotham				
bell hooks				

Exam practice

1 'Feminism is not a single doctrine.' Analyse and evaluate this statement with reference to the feminist thinkers that you have studied. In your answer, you should draw on material from across the whole range of your course of study in politics. [25]

2 'Feminism aims for equality.' Analyse and evaluate this statement with reference to the feminist thinkers that you have studied. In your answer, you should draw on material from across the whole range of your course of study in politics. [25]

Summary

You should now have an understanding of:
+ debates about the nature of feminism
+ core feminist views and values concerning equality of treatment, recognition of gender differences and affirmative action
+ liberal feminism and radical feminism, and more recent developments such as difference feminism and post-feminism
+ the contributions of the five key thinkers (Gilman, de Beauvoir, Millett, Rowbotham, hooks) to the development of feminism
+ the tensions and agreements within feminism between the different traditions, and within them
+ the extent to which feminism is a single coherent idea

Check your understanding and progress at www.hoddereducation.co.uk/myrevisionnotes

6 Multiculturalism

Multiculturalism is an idea that tries to find a balance between the legitimate competing demands of diversity and unity. Its aim is to achieve a society where there is a shared citizenship and national identity while also recognising the differences between groups within society, so that there is unity without uniformity. Multiculturalism is expressed through a state-led set of policies that look to create a 'community of citizens and a community of communities' (*The Future of Multi-Ethnic Britain: The Parekh Report*, 2000).

Origins of multiculturalism

REVISED

- Multiculturalism emerged in the 1960s and 1970s in response to new social movements that were organised around issues of ethnicity, race, gender, sexuality and nationality. Multiculturalism was developed as an idea that supported diversity and pluralism, in order to protect the characteristics and contributions to society of a range of cultural and minority groups.
- There was a large increase of immigration into European countries in the second half of the twentieth century. This period was marked by immigration from non-European countries, so there was a sense that the new migrants were culturally different and assimilation was no longer the correct approach. The new migrants should be allowed to maintain their distinctive culture while they adapted to working and living in their new countries.
- Diversity can give rise to potentially divisive questions that cause minorities and majorities to clash – one example is what should be contained within a national educational curriculum.
- Multiculturalism emerged in liberal democracies and, although it emerged from liberalism, it argues that the focus on traditional human rights is not enough as they are unable to resolve some of the most pressing questions relating to cultural minorities. For instance, the right to freedom of speech has nothing to say about what an appropriate language policy is for a government to adopt. What languages should be used in Parliament, in the courts, in paperwork and education?
- Multiculturalism also has its roots in the emergence of identity politics in the 1960s and 1970s, marked by social movements such as gay rights, women's rights and black rights.

> **Assimilation** The process where immigrant groups become as much like the majority as possible, by adopting the lifestyles, values and beliefs of the majority culture. This approach is seen as problematic by multiculturalism.
>
> **Identity politics** A form of politics that embraces and celebrates a positive sense of collective identity (e.g. race, religion, culture or gender) and seeks public recognition of that identity.

Exam tip

A good example of identity politics in action is Black Lives Matter (BLM). In 2018 BLM issued a statement to identify themselves: 'We are unapologetically Black in our positioning. In affirming that Black Lives Matter, we need not qualify our position.'

Making links

Multiculturalism both engages with and challenges liberalism, so make sure you have thoroughly revised liberalism so that you can make these connections effectively in your answers.

Debates around the nature of multiculturalism

Assimilation

- In societies where minority communities receive unfavourable treatment from the majority, society needs a process of integration. One such process for dealing with immigrant communities is assimilation. This sees individuals and groups as marked by difference (e.g. differences of race, culture or religion) and views difference in society as provoking discrimination and conflict. In response, assimilation proposes a one-way process where minorities are encouraged to conform to the lifestyles, ideas and beliefs of the dominant culture. This involves the least change for the majority culture and the main institutions of the state and their policies.
- This one-way process is seen as flattening cultural differences to create a strong, homogeneous national identity which is the basis for a stable society. Assimilation has been successful when the new members of society become indistinguishable from the majority. There is a strong belief among those favouring assimilation that unity cannot be achieved while there is diversity.
- The process of assimilation is opposed by multiculturalism as promoting the marginalisation, disadvantage and oppression of minority groups within society. For multiculturalists, assimilation is a recipe for discord and simply fails to recognise the importance of cultural belonging.

> **Exam tip**
>
> In an exam answer, as an example of assimilation you could use the 'Americanisation' policies of the USA in response to European immigrants in the early twentieth century. Since the 1960s, these policies have been seen as impractical and illiberal.

The importance of cultural belonging

Multiculturalism sees identity and culture as inextricably linked. This idea is built on the communitarian critique of liberal individualism:

- Liberal individualism places belief in the individual above the collective within political thought and argues that the individual existed prior to society and has certain fixed traits (e.g. they are rational or self-seeking).
- In contrast, communitarians argue that human nature cannot be understood outside of society or be said to have an innate nature.
- Humans are culturally embedded and so are fundamentally shaped by the values, lifestyles and belief systems of the cultures that they grow up in and see the world through.
- Liberalism sees social goods (like diversity, language and culture) as only valuable in terms of their benefits to individuals, whereas communitarians see them as valuable in their own right and therefore worth protecting.

> **Identity** A person's sense of who they are and what is important about them as a human.
>
> **Communitarian** This relates to an idea which stresses the connection between the individual and the community.

Culture and identity

- In liberal democracies like the USA and the UK, the dominant culture is white, male, heterosexual and able-bodied.
- As a result of their difference, minority cultures and minority groups find themselves marginalised through the creation of stereotypes, which are uniformly applied to all people from that minority group. These stereotypes can promote discrimination in society and the economy, and even lead to group-based violence. They can also create cultural marginalisation and oppression by promoting a sense of inferiority or even shame in individuals from minority cultures, leading them to become further alienated and marginalised from society and increasing the chances of social conflict.
- Although culture can be seen as a means of oppression, it can also be seen as a positive force to challenge oppression. Minorities can take control of their identities and shape them, by creating positive images, changing language and building up a sense of pride in their culture.
- By throwing off inauthentic and demeaning stereotypes, minority cultures can assert themselves politically, socially and economically in an act of

liberation. The Black Power movement in the USA in the 1960s and 1970s emphasised black racial identity, pride and self-determination. It was hugely influential in shaping everything from education through to politics and popular culture.

The politics of recognition

+ The politics of recognition, closely associated with Charles Taylor, takes the debate on culture and identity further.
+ Humans understand themselves through a dialogue with the world and how others see them. As culture is so important to an individual's sense of identity and self-worth, how the wider community views minority cultures has consequences for the individuals concerned.
+ Non-recognition or misrecognition can saddle the 'victims with a crippling self-hatred, denying their desire for self-esteem and stifling a sense of their own authenticity' (Taylor, *Multiculturalism and the Politics of Recognition*, 1994). This cuts individuals from minority cultures off from society and is more likely to breed tension and conflict. As a result, Taylor argued that recognition is a vital human need and so *all* people deserve to have their identity recognised.
+ The answer is the politics of recognition, which can be achieved through a two-step process:
    1 **Equal dignity**. All humans are alike and so all deserve equal treatment. This is achieved by granting equal political and legal rights to everyone and banning all forms of discrimination, so that there are no second-class citizens. However, those who have equal dignity may feel they are second-class citizens as they are culturally marginalised through non-recognition or misrecognition.
    2 **Equal recognition**. Everyone is different, so everyone has the equal right to be recognised. As an individual's identity can only be understood in the context of their culture, this requires that individual cultures are protected and encouraged to flourish.

> **Key thinker**
>
> **Charles Taylor (1931–)**
>
> Charles Taylor's *Multiculturalism and the Politics of Recognition* (1994) laid out the indispensable role of culture in the forming of human nature and the politics of recognition.
> + Taylor started from the basis that identity is 'a person's understanding of who they are, of their fundamental characteristics as a human being'. This understanding is developed in 'dialogue with, sometimes struggle against, the things our significant others [family members, friends, teachers and colleagues] want to see in us'.
> + Non-recognition or misrecognition from society can significantly damage a person or a group of people by mirroring back to them a 'confining or demeaning or contemptible picture of themselves'.
> + The principle of the equal dignity of human life, which is difference-blind in granting rights to all, creates uniform rights and recognises only individuals, not groups or collective goals.
> + The principle of equal recognition is difference-friendly and based on the idea that everyone has an identity. So equal dignity is universal to all and emphasises collective goals like the protection of a culture or language. Equal recognition provides the rationale for states to grant certain rights to specific groups but not to others in order to 'maintain and cherish distinctness, not just now but forever'. This can be seen as a benevolent formula for national existence.
> + A key example used by Taylor is the survival of the culture and language of the French Québécois in Canada:
>   + The French language has been granted official status in Quebec and there are laws in place to ensure that all children of French heritage study the language in school.
>   + This not only preserves French culture but also actively seeks to promote it.

> **Exam tip**
>
> A good example of this type of stereotyping was given by Dame Louise Casey in 2016: 'Every time there's a terrorist attack people automatically blame a person that's called a Muslim. That's wrong. Muslims are no more responsible for terrorist attacks than I am for the IRA.'

> **Non-recognition** The failure to recognise the existence of a culture or cultural identity.
>
> **Misrecognition** Stereotyping, racism or stigmatisation.

> **Exam tip**
>
> For an example of the effect of stereotyping, you could use the words of the founder of the National Association for the Advancement of Colored People (NAACP), W.E.B. Du Bois, who wrote about being African American in the first half of the twentieth century: 'It is a peculiar sensation, this double-consciousness, this sense of always looking at one's self through the eyes of others, of measuring one's soul by the tape of a world that looks on in amused contempt and pity.'

> **Exam tip**
>
> It is worth noting that Charles Taylor has plenty to say about the banning of the wearing of the burqa and niqab in public in France. He argues that the French policy of *laïcité*, which keeps the practice of faith behind locked doors, is unjust, unnecessary and poisonous for social relations. It is about saying your culture is not all right but our culture is, and that is no way to integrate people.

My Revision Notes: AQA A-level Politics: Political Ideas Second Edition

> **Now test yourself** TESTED
>
> 1 How are communitarianism and multiculturalism linked?
> 2 What is assimilation and why is it criticised by multiculturalists?

The liberal state and diversity

There are three key aspects of liberal democracies which can be seen to support cultural diversity within society: the neutrality of the state, toleration and liberal democracy.

The neutrality of the state

+ The liberal state is seen to be neutral between different conceptions of the good life and between different cultures. Its most basic commitment is to the freedom and equality of individual citizens.
+ The purpose of the state is to provide equal rights, anti-discrimination law and equality of opportunity to promote civic nationalism in the public sphere. In this sense, the law is colour-blind.
+ Civic nationalism is based on the idea that if you choose to sign up to the values of the political community, you are welcomed, and this is not restricted by any identity criteria, such as race or religion.
+ The wider political community is united around its political values, not its culture, race or religion.
+ The private sphere is where the individual has autonomy and so is free to celebrate their cultural identity and difference.

Toleration

+ The recipe for toleration can be found in the writings of the key liberal thinker John Stuart Mill (see p. 13). He argued that autonomy is important for individuals, and individuals know what is good for them.
+ There is a clear distinction between self-regarding and other-regarding actions, so there should be toleration of an individual's choice of beliefs, value systems and versions of the good life.

> **Anti-discrimination law** Any law concerning the right of people to be treated equally, such as the UK's Equality Act (2010).
>
> **Civic nationalism** The nation is seen as a community of equal, rights-bearing citizens, united in their attachment to a shared set of political practices and values (e.g. democracy, rights and justice).
>
> **Autonomy** A combination of freedom and responsibility, where the individual is free to make their own choices and is responsible for those choices.

> **Exam tip**
>
> Don't confuse toleration with indifference to or dislike of a particular opinion or action. It is worth noting that toleration is an act of principle about opinions or actions where there is real disagreement over something morally important. This raises the question: why should one tolerate the intolerant?

Liberal democracy

Democracy is the only type of state which can support diversity due to its commitments to democratic values such as freedom, autonomy, formal equality and the consent of the governed. As a result, many liberal states have practised a form of individualist integration.

Individualist integration

+ Minority individuals are free to choose to assimilate (but are not forced to) or to enjoy their cultural identities in the private sphere, but they are discouraged from seeing themselves as part of a minority group in the public sphere, where they are individual citizens.
+ The main policy aim is to end all forms of discrimination and provide equality of opportunity. In this case, everyone is treated equally by the state and society, and in their economic role.
+ This allows individuals to be autonomous and to practise a form of civic nationalism. However, this practice is not seen by multiculturalism as understanding the importance of cultural belonging.

Check your understanding and progress at www.hoddereducation.co.uk/myrevisionnotes

> **Exam tip**
>
> The Equality Act (2010) merged together 116 other Acts to create a new discrimination law and is a key example of liberalism focused on upholding the rights of all citizens. The Act protects individuals from unfair treatment and promotes a fair and more equal society by preventing discrimination based on protected characteristics such as race and religion.

Main strands of multiculturalism

REVISED

Liberal multiculturalism

Liberal multiculturalism is most closely associated with the work of Will Kymlicka and looks to develop a form of multiculturalism derived from liberalism. While liberalism has traditionally focused on the primacy of the individual and the commitment to freedom and equality, liberal multiculturalism argues that 'group-differentiated rights' are justifiable in a liberal framework.

If traditional liberalism is all about the individual and equality, it is worth raising the question: how can liberals accept group-differentiated rights for minorities? Why should members of certain groups have certain rights that are not available to other groups? If rights belong to the individual, how do we justify giving them to members of groups? Liberal multiculturalism aims to answer these questions.

It takes the three key strands of liberalism discussed above (the neutrality of the state, toleration and liberal democracy) and adds two new arguments (autonomy and justice), as shown in Table 6.1.

Table 6.1 The justifications for liberal multiculturalism

Autonomy	Justice
+ Individuals are autonomous. + Individuals should have the freedom to live their lives in line with their own beliefs and values. + Individuals should be able to challenge, revise and change their values throughout their life. + Kymlicka argued that culture provides the 'context of choice' for individuals to make decisions about their values and beliefs so that they can choose their own version of the good life. + The state *has* to move beyond equality and anti-discrimination laws to grant minority rights.	+ The liberal state is seen within liberalism as neutral, but Kymlicka believed this idea was not supportable in practice. + The state, society and its institutions have been developed over time by the majority culture. + The choice of official language, official holidays and the curriculum are all shaped by the majority. + The state and the public sphere are not neutral and this acts to marginalise and oppress minority groups who are forced to conform. + In order to fit with the liberal principle of justice, minority groups should be granted recognition and minority rights.

Minority rights

+ Minority rights are a clear break from traditional liberalism as they are collective rather than individual rights, but they can be justified using liberal multiculturalist arguments.
+ Minority rights are given to specific groups but not others as certain rights will only have meaning for one particular group – for example, the right of Sikhs in the UK to wear the Kirpan (a ceremonial knife) for religious reasons.
+ Minority rights need to be granted by the state in order to promote and protect cultures. This commitment of the state to minority cultures should ensure that minority cultures are committed to the state in return for creating a sense of unity.
+ Kymlicka terms minority rights 'group-differentiated rights'. These are explained in Table 6.2.

> **Exam tip**
>
> Some good examples to use to explain how the public sphere is not neutral include what languages are used in schools and on official documents. California effectively banned bilingual education between 1998 and 2016, and in 2010 France banned the wearing of the burqa or niqab in public places.

Table 6.2 Group-differentiated rights

Rights	Explanation	In practice
Self-government rights	Applied to national minority groups who have been historically oppressed by the majority culture and who are territorially concentrated; the groups as a whole desire political autonomy.	There are 25 self-government agreements across Canada involving 43 Indigenous communities.
Polyethnic rights	Rights applied to immigrant groups who wish to maintain their cultures but are expected to engage in the public sphere. These rights enable individuals from minority cultures to integrate better into society.	Anti-racism laws (e.g. the US Civil Rights Act 1964), legal exemptions (e.g. for the Jewish *shechita* method of animal slaughter) and curriculum changes (e.g. Black History Month in the UK).
Representation rights	Rights given to minorities to tackle the past injustice of exclusion from the public sphere. Measures to ensure that individuals from minority cultures are represented in all spheres of public life, especially politics, ensuring that the state and its institutions reflect the diversity of society. This can only increase the commitment of minority groups to the state. These rights are often defended as a temporary measure on the path to a society where the need for representation rights no longer exists.	In the USA, the use of affirmative action in federal-hiring policies and university admissions. In the UK, this is known as positive action. It involves encouraging particular groups to apply through job advertisements or the treatment of a minority candidate more favourably than another candidate if both are equally qualified.

> **Key thinker**
>
> **Will Kymlicka (1962–)**
>
> Will Kymlicka's *Multicultural Citizenship* (1995) offered a definite statement of liberal multiculturalism. He sought to show that multiculturalism can be derived from the ideas of liberalism.
> + Culture provides the 'context of choice' for individuals to frame, revise and pursue their goals. Without this context, individuals would struggle to make sense of the choices in front of them.
> + Culture is important for personal development, as it provides an anchor for self-identification and gives the individual the confidence that they belong. This needs the liberal state to support different cultures to provide the basis for autonomy and personal development.
> + Kymlicka outlined a detailed defence of group-differentiated rights, as this would ensure higher levels of political and civic participation and lead to the effective integration of all cultures into society.
> + He argued for toleration between different groups, but this is linked directly to the autonomy of the individual within the group to question and revise their goals. This theory is inhospitable to illiberal minority groups that infringe the autonomy of their members and Kymlicka believed that there is a clear responsibility to liberalise such groups, but not by coercion.

> **Exam tip**
>
> It is worth noting that affirmative action has traditionally been supported by liberals as a temporary measure to remedy past discrimination and move to a colour-blind society, while others have criticised the policy as making the problem it tries to solve worse by ensuring people are even more aware of group differences. What multiculturalism argues is that group-differentiated rights should in fact be permanent, as their main aim is to accommodate cultural differences in society, not just remedy past wrongs.

Toleration in liberal multiculturalism

+ Liberal multiculturalism promotes diversity in society, but argues that diversity must exist within the framework of liberal democracy and liberal values. This means that liberal multiculturalism endorses shallow diversity as it cannot tolerate illiberal cultural practices on the grounds that they are an infringement of autonomy and justice.
+ Liberal multiculturalism places two fundamental limitations on minority rights:
  + Minority rights will not justify the demand by minority cultures to restrict the basic civil or political freedoms of their members. Examples here might include patriarchal and/or theocratic cultures where women's rights are sometimes restricted and criticism of the culture and its interpretation of religious text is sometimes forbidden.

+ Liberal justice cannot support any rights which allow one group to exploit or oppress another group – as in the case of the apartheid era in South Africa when the minority group claimed special protections from the majority group in society in order to create a social system which severely disadvantaged and brutally oppressed the majority of the population.

Multiculturalist integration

+ In addition to rights and equality of opportunity, the state should put in place different measures for different groups to enable groups and individuals to maintain their cultural identity.
+ This is a two-way process where the state commits to individuals from minority groups in return for their commitment to the state.

Pluralist multiculturalism

+ Pluralist multiculturalism goes beyond liberal multiculturalism as it values diversity as good in its own right, irrespective of its use to individuals. Minority rights and the politics of recognition are tools to ensure that diversity is maintained.
+ Pluralist multiculturalists endorse deep diversity, which argues from the starting position that all cultures have some worth and so are due our respect. The key difference with liberal multiculturalism is that this applies to all cultures, not just those based on liberal principles.
+ Support for this view comes from two different positions: value pluralism and the value of diversity.

Value pluralism

+ Value pluralism is an idea that is closely associated with the liberal philosopher Isaiah Berlin. It sees a world full of absolute values like justice, freedom, equality and co-operation, so conflict between these principles is inevitable.
+ The issue is that there is no single method for effectively resolving these conflicts, so the liberal state should not decide that any particular value is more valid than another to reduce conflict.
+ When picked up by multiculturalists, this idea was applied to cultures. It is used to argue that the state must recognise different cultures as it is not in a position to decide if one culture and its values are more valid than any other.

> **Key thinker**
>
> **Isaiah Berlin (1909–97)**
>
> Isaiah Berlin was one of the most important philosophers of the twentieth century for his contributions to liberalism through the concepts of positive and negative freedom (see pp. 11, 14–15). His connection to multiculturalism emerges from his principle of value pluralism, which first emerged in his book *Two Concepts of Liberty* (1958) and was continually refined by Berlin throughout the rest of his life.
>
> + Positive freedom is the presence of something (e.g. authentic identity), whereas negative freedom is the absence of something (e.g. legal or social restrictions) in relation to the ability of a group or individual to act autonomously.
> + Human nature generates certain values that are absolute, ultimate and sacred to people. The issue is that there is no 'possibility of establishing an objective hierarchical relation among them'. Therefore, it is impossible to say if autonomy is more important than human solidarity.
> + These values are bound to come into conflict with each other and there is no way for the state to resolve these conflicts fairly. Therefore, to stop the increasing tension and antagonism between absolutes, the state and society should practise value pluralism by allowing different values to exist.
> + The only type of society that can provide the framework for value pluralism is a liberal one. Berlin saw liberty as the primary goal, as it allows individuals to choose which absolutes are sacred and ultimate for them.

The value of diversity

+ The most thorough articulation of the pluralist multiculturalist case is made by Bhikhu Parekh, who believed it offers three central insights on the world, as shown in Table 6.3. These ideas led Parekh to attack the ideas of liberal universalism.
+ Liberal universalism assumes that its great values like equality, autonomy and liberty are universal and absolute: they apply to all cultures, irrespective of difference. However, liberalism is embedded in culture as it represents one view of the good life, so its understanding of the world can only be partial and narrow.
+ Parekh argued that liberal universalism should be rejected in favour of deep diversity, where the starting point is that all cultures must have some worth. Deep diversity will allow an ongoing conversation within cultures and between cultures that is necessary for the enrichment, development and deepening of each culture, and this will benefit society as a whole.
+ At the same time, the state and society's commitment to all cultures means that individuals from minority cultures will feel that the wider community belongs to them and they to it.

> **Liberal universalism** The idea that liberal values apply to all individuals, societies and cultures, irrespective of the differences between them.

Table 6.3 Parekh's justification for pluralist multiculturalism

Culturally embedded	Difference	Internally plural
+ Human beings are culturally embedded. + They grow up and live in a culturally structured world that gives meaning and value to their lives. + Individuals can critically evaluate their culture and can overcome some but not all of its ideas, but they ultimately view the world from within that culture.	+ Different cultures have different value systems and views of the good life. + Each culture is necessarily limited and can only grasp part of the full richness of human life. + So cultures need each other to understand themselves better, but also to grow, develop and learn. + No culture is perfect so no culture should impose on others, and no culture is worthless so all cultures deserve respect.	+ All cultures are internally plural and are in constant dialogue with themselves. + A culture must be able to discuss its own internal differences and be at ease with them. + Then it can be at ease with differences with other cultures and engage in debate with them. + This debate creates a shared public commitment to the wider political community, creating unity without uniformity.

Key thinker

Bhikhu Parekh (1935–)

Bhikhu Parekh wrote *Rethinking Multiculturalism* (2000), which is a book that looks to redefine the role of the state in light of pluralist multiculturalism and the value of diversity.

+ Multiculturalism should allow the conversation within cultures and between cultures to take place, as this will promote co-operation and toleration of difference. This ongoing conversation will enrich the cultural development of each culture and enrich the individuals from those cultures, creating a 'community of communities and individuals'.
+ Parekh did not just oppose liberal attempts to impose their will on others; he was similarly critical of conservatism, socialism and nationalism, as all are embedded in a particular culture.
+ He also argued that a multicultural society relied on a 'common sense of belonging' among its citizens. This cannot be based on race, religion, nationality, culture or other characteristics, as society is too diverse. It needs to be based on a shared commitment to the political community and support for its wellbeing, even where citizens are critical of it.
+ This can be achieved if the political community accepts each citizen as fully part of society; then each citizen will commit to the community. Consequently, Parekh favoured 'such measures as group-differentiated rights, culturally differentiated applications of laws and policies, state support for minority institutions [funding faith schools] and a judicious programme of affirmative action'.

Multicultural integration
+ Pluralist multiculturalists also support multicultural integration.
+ The state and society 'value and cherish [cultures] all equally and reflect this in its structure, policies, conduct of public affairs, self-understanding and self-definition' (Parekh).
+ This will create a sense of belonging among individuals from minority cultures to the wider political community.

The national story
+ The national story is the story that is told about what it means to belong to a particular nation and helps create a sense of national identity and unity.
+ Multiculturalism is not just about difference; it also has to be related to the things that people hold in common. This is about creating a form of citizenship that moves beyond legal rights, passports and the right to vote, although all of these are important.
+ It is about the importance of a national identity, which is an idea closely associated with the writings of Tariq Modood. He made the argument that it is both possible and necessary to decouple ideas of national identity from nationalism, especially where that nationalism has in the past been linked to the cultural oppression of minorities. This needs to be an open and inclusive national identity, created through an ongoing discussion between all cultures to develop an identity that all want to integrate into.
+ In line with the Parekh Report (2000), it is felt that for multiculturalism to work, all individuals within a nation need to feel 'that their own flourishing as individuals is intimately linked with the flourishing of public institutions and public service'.

> **Exam tip**
>
> The response to the Parekh Report was critical in some elements of the press and you can use this to illustrate some of the criticisms of multiculturalism. For example, 'Ministers welcome report which says "British" is racist and all our history must be rewritten' (*The Sun*, 11 October 2000).

> **Key thinker**
>
> **Tariq Modood (1952–)**
>
> Tariq Modood, in his 2007 book *Multiculturalism*, is particularly concerned with multiculturalism in the twenty-first century, arguing that the rise of Islamist terrorism has not discredited or lessened the importance of multiculturalism. In fact, it may have made its ideas and demands for social cohesion all the more relevant.
>
> + Modood sought unity through diversity by developing a form of multiculturalism that sees strong multicultural identities as a good thing, but they must be balanced with a national identity that creates a sense of belonging to one's country.
> + He raised the important question that if there is no strong national narrative for individuals from minority cultures to integrate to, then why bother with integration at all? This means that the state has to advance multiculturalism through preventing discrimination and inequality, and recognising difference and minority rights, but it must also create a 'framework of vibrant, national narratives … to give expression to a national identity'.
> + Multiculturalist integration stretches beyond individuals to include groups and recognises that these groups themselves are a 'multi', with some identifying themselves by colour, others by national origin and others by religious identity. As a result, there is no single method of integration that fits all groups. Some may wish to assimilate, others may seek to adopt cosmopolitan identities and others may wish for individualist integration. Some minority groups may want different strategies in different areas, such as equality before the law (individualist) but group representation rights in politics (multicultural).
> + The key is that no model of integration is imposed and individuals from within communities can choose from any of the integration models. This gives society the widest possible chance of integrating the greatest possible number. Modood points to success here in terms of the fact that members of minority ethnic communities are now much more likely to identify as British than other people in England.

> **Now test yourself** — TESTED
>
> 3 What are group-differentiated rights and how did Will Kymlicka justify them from within liberalism?
> 4 Why are minority rights and the politics of recognition a challenge to liberalism?
> 5 How far should toleration extend according to Kymlicka?

Cosmopolitan multiculturalism

Cosmopolitan multiculturalists such as Jeremy Waldron endorse diversity, as it increases the freedom of the individual to make choices about their identity. They celebrate difference but at the same time provide a clear critique of groups and propose that they should be dissolved. This is to be achieved through a process of cosmopolitan integration.

Cosmopolitan integration

+ Individuals should not be confined to one culture or 'pigeonholed' into one culture as that both restricts choice and divides society into antagonistic groups. Individuals should be free to 'pick and mix' from different cultures to create new identities for themselves. Cosmopolitan multiculturalism positively embraces this concept of hybridisation.
+ Individuals can develop multiple, fluid identities that change over time by selecting different elements from various cultures. As a result, they themselves will become a multiculture – enjoying Thai food, being a practising atheist, meditating, enjoying reggae music, etc. As this happens, they will become tolerant and aware of their shared interests with others across the globe rather than identifying only with their own culture or nation, creating global, cosmopolitan citizens. The job of the state is therefore to protect the diversity of society to give individuals this freedom of choice. For this reason, cosmopolitan multiculturalists have supported minority rights and diversity as a transitional stage to a new global, cosmopolitan identity.
+ Other strands of multiculturalism have been critical of this approach, arguing that multiple identities and cultural mixing will undermine and weaken any authentic sense of cultural belonging. They argue that cultural mixing can lead to hybridisation, which in the end will undermine the individual's sense of cultural belonging as they lose touch with their original culture, which is so crucial to their identity. Hybridisation will also lead to the dissolving of groups that provide the contexts of choice for individuals to make their decisions and will undermine diversity.

> **Hybridisation** The process of social and cultural mixing that creates multiple, fluid identities.

> **Revision activity**
>
> Draw a table with the four possible forms of integration (assimilation, individualist integration, multicultural integration and cosmopolitan integration) and detail their approach to the issue of diversity. What are the key differences between them?

The critical view of multiculturalism

REVISED

Multiculturalism has come under increasing attack from across the political spectrum, with David Cameron in 2011 arguing: 'Under the doctrine of state multiculturalism, we have encouraged different cultures to live separate lives, apart from each other and apart from the mainstream. We have failed to provide a vision of society to which they feel they want to belong.' In 2010, Angela Merkel, the German chancellor, also attacked multiculturalism, arguing that the multicultural approach had failed.

One of Boris Johnson's key advisers, Munira Mirza, stated that while she fully supported a multi-ethnic society, she was against the idea that differences should define us or determine policy, and that people should be treated differently because of their cultural differences. She argued that these ideas can be very divisive and lead the country into dead ends. Criticism of multiculturalism can be split into different camps, as shown in Table 6.4.

Table 6.4 The main criticisms of multiculturalism

It creates tension and conflict	<ul><li>This idea is most closely associated with conservatism.</li><li>Human nature is imperfect and insecure, so humans need a common cultural identity for security and stability.</li><li>All stable and secure societies are built on shared values, beliefs and lifestyles.</li><li>Multiculturalism undermines both common identity and shared values, creating tension and conflict.</li><li>In particular, minority rights, the politics of recognition and rewriting the national story are seen as unfairly identifying the majority culture with discrimination and oppression.</li><li>Positive or affirmative action also provokes further resentment by favouring the minority over the majority. This only promotes awareness of differences between groups.</li></ul>
Minority rights are discriminatory	<ul><li>Multiculturalism is associated with promoting minority rights and the politics of recognition to cultures that hold distinctly illiberal values.</li><li>In particular, it has been argued that some minority cultures are discriminatory in their practices towards women as they are very conservative and patriarchal.</li><li>This has raised issues such as women's dress codes and forced marriages.</li></ul>
It has led to segregation	<ul><li>Multiculturalism has led to segregation, where groups in society have withdrawn into their own societies, leading to mistrust, suspicion and hostility on all sides.</li><li>In particular, the politics of recognition and the politics of identity lead minority groups to seek authentic cultures which are defined by their difference.</li><li>This makes the difference more visible, both to the majority and to minority cultures.</li><li>This issue seems particularly heightened where minority cultures are defined by a more conservative or traditional interpretation of religious texts, and beliefs are held up as sacred and beyond any form of challenge.</li></ul>

Key thinkers in context

Charles Taylor
- Taylor is an academic, politician and political philosopher who developed the idea of the politics of recognition as a key plank of multiculturalism in his book *Multiculturalism and the Politics of Recognition* (1994). Taylor is particularly focused on how we form our conceptions of our own identity and what it means to be human.
- His 2007 Consultation Commission on Accommodation Practices Related to Cultural Differences, co-chaired with Gerard Bouchard, was pivotal in shaping the Quebec government's policy on cultural diversity.

Will Kymlicka
- A leading theorist of liberal multiculturalism, Kymlicka's book *Multicultural Citizenship* (1995) argued that culture, and, in particular, language, could not be a private matter as liberals assumed.
- By establishing one language for schooling, politics and public services, this naturally gives members of the dominant group a political and economic advantage while also symbolising that language or culture as superior to others. So anti-discrimination laws are not enough – the state must support group-differentiated rights.

Isaiah Berlin
- A liberal philosopher whose most famous work was *Four Essays on Liberty* (1969). He developed the idea of value pluralism when thinking about multiculturalism.
- He argued that fundamental human values are universal, plural and conflicting, and there is no method for measuring these values against each other. Berlin argued that there may be situations where we just cannot make reasoned choices between conflicting values.

Bhikhu Parekh
- An academic, political philosopher and member of the House of Lords. His most relevant work, *Rethinking Multiculturalism: Cultural Diversity and Political Theory* (2005), rejected liberal universalism and built a powerful defence of cultural diversity from a pluralist multiculturalist perspective.
- His work is defined by three key views: human beings are deeply shaped by culture but not determined by it; no culture is totally worthless or totally perfect, so dialogue between cultures is good; and a culture can only have dialogue with other cultures where it is open to internal dialogue within its own culture.

Tariq Modood
- An influential political theorist and sociologist who has written extensively on multiculturalism. In his book *Multiculturalism* (2007), Modood argues that multiculturalism is crucial to successful integration.
- Society is not just about individuals, and integration involves bringing communities, not individuals, into relationships of equal respect. This critically involves challenging racism and Islamophobia, developing positive group identities, adapting customs and institutions to help in that process, and remaking the national story so that everyone can recognise themselves in it.

Core ideas of multiculturalism

Human nature

Areas of agreement
- It is not possible to define the innate qualities of human nature, as the individual does not exist before or outside of society.
- The identity of humans is bound up in their culture.

Areas of tension

Charles Taylor
- Taylor's communitarian critique of the liberal view of human nature argued that humans cannot be understood outside of the communities that they are shaped by.
- Social recognition is central to the individual's identity and self-worth, and misrecognition can gravely damage both.
- Identity is formed dialogically through both struggle and conversation with significant others, so our sense of self is bound up with how the world sees our culture. This provides the basis for the politics of recognition.

Will Kymlicka
- Culture is the 'context of choice' within which individuals can use their autonomy to 'frame, revise and pursue their goals'.
- Without the sense of security and identity created by culture, individuals will be unable to make effective choices, limiting their autonomy and potential for development.
- Culture has value for what it brings to the individual and this provides the basis for group-differentiated rights.

Bhikhu Parekh
- Humans are 'culturally embedded' and deeply shaped by their culture, inevitably seeing the world from within that culture.
- Human life is so rich and textured that there is no way one culture could capture it, so no culture can impose its views on others and no culture is without worth.
- Diversity is good; it provides the basis for an ongoing conversation between and within cultures that creates a more mature, critical and tolerant society.

Cosmopolitan multiculturalists
- Individuals are not culturally embedded. Culture is something that increases individual choice.
- Picking and mixing between different cultures creates global citizens with bonds of trust and affection that go beyond their original culture or nation.

The state

Areas of agreement
- The state promotes cultural diversity and provides a form of multiculturalist integration.
- There is a strong rejection of assimilation, as it ignores the importance of cultural belonging, alienating groups and individuals from society, which is a recipe for tension and conflict.
- Although individualist integration has its place, it is not enough because it is difference-blind. There needs to be state and societal recognition of difference through particular polices for specific groups to create the sense that the state is committed to minority groups.
- Multiculturalism includes formal equality and anti-discrimination legislation, but it is far more than that.

Areas of tension
+ Taylor endorsed a state policy platform based on the politics of recognition, which involves policies to protect and promote cultures, such as have been seen in Canada.
+ Kymlicka argues for group-differentiated rights on the basis of the liberal ideals of autonomy and justice. These will ease the process of integration for immigrant communities while protecting their cultures.
+ Berlin argued that states should practise value pluralism.
+ Parekh goes further, arguing that all functions of the state (e.g. the police service, the wider criminal justice system, political representation, education and our attitudes to asylum seekers) have to be reimagined through multiculturalism.
+ Modood complements Parekh's position by arguing for the creation of a new national story that is inclusive and open, in order to create a sense of belonging (unity) to balance against strong cultural identities (diversity).

Society
Areas of agreement
+ Multiculturalists agree about the benefits of a diverse society. Diversity is far more than a fact of life in the modern world.
+ Diversity guarantees cultural recognition and therefore counters marginalisation and oppression by allowing individuals to integrate into their new society while maintaining their identity.
+ Diversity means that cultural groups can celebrate their identity and benefit from public recognition and respect for their culture, so that they feel part of the wider community.
+ Diversity brings vigour and vibrancy to society, advancing understanding of the world and promoting cross-cultural toleration and understanding.

> **Making links**
>
> Draw links between multiculturalism and other areas of the course that you have studied, such as liberalism, and debates about rights in the UK Constitution and civil rights in the USA, to enrich your analysis and evaluation.

Areas of tension
+ Liberal multiculturalists cannot extend toleration to:
    + values of beliefs that are themselves intolerant or oppressive (e.g. minority cultures that promote forced marriage, female genital mutilation and enforced dress codes), as these conflict with basic rights and autonomy
    + cultures that oppose liberal democracy and wish to replace it with another form of government, such as a theocracy or dictatorship
+ Berlin was clear that multiculturalism and diversity can only exist in a society that is based on freedom.
+ Kymlicka supports diversity due to the benefits it brings to individuals. Diversity is seen to enhance autonomy by giving individuals the context of choice from which they can confidently make decisions about their life.
+ Taylor saw cultures as a collective good that should be protected irrespective of the benefits for the individual today, such as the French language in Quebec.
+ Parekh goes further by arguing for diversity as good in itself. It is absolutely vital as no culture has grasped the full richness of human life. This means that cultures need other cultures to understand themselves better, develop their moral and intellectual horizons as well as their imagination, and not get locked into seeing their values as absolute.
+ Modood focuses on the idea that society is multicultural and that all cultures are internally plural, so individuals from minorities should be able to choose whatever forms of integration best suit them in each situation. No one form of integration should be forced on the individual, as integration is about choice.

> **Exam tip**
>
> There is a tendency to focus only on explaining the differences and the similarities between different thinkers or strands of multiculturalism. However, it is important to evaluate how significant those differences or similarities are.

The economy

+ There is a view that the failure of integration is costly to the state. In 2014, the Social Integration Commission reported that the lack of effective integration was costing the UK up to £6 billion per year and was leading to an increasingly fractured society. This leads multiculturalists to argue that a decent standard of living needs to be provided to all. In addition, there must be fairness and equality in the economic sector to limit the impacts of discrimination.
+ In 2021, the Commission on Race and Ethnic Disparities reported that it did not believe 'that the UK is yet a post-racial society which has completed the long journey to equality of opportunity'. But the report also argued that 'The country has come a long way in 50 years and the success of much of the ethnic minority population in education and, to a lesser extent, the economy, should be regarded as a model for other white-majority countries.'
+ Parekh and Modood are committed to the idea that successful integration requires the state to tackle thoroughly the social and economic inequalities in society.
+ Kymlicka opposes the New Right view of the economy (see p. 31) and argues that undeserved economic differences have significant impacts on people's capacity for choices, agency and dignity.

Key debates within multiculturalism

REVISED

The benefits of cultural mixing to society and the individual are a source of much debate, as shown in Table 6.5. A second major debate emerges around whether multiculturalism is the cause of or the solution to tension and conflict within society, as shown in Table 6.6.

Table 6.5 Potential benefits of cultural mixing

Cultural	+ Cultures are likely to be richer if they also enjoy access to other cultures. It allows all cultures to grow, develop and remain fresh and current. + Cultures are best changed from within through a process of discussion and debate rather than attempts to force change, which can be alienating.
Real dialogue	+ In deep diversity, there are real, deep and clear differences in values, so you end up with lots of talking but no listening. + A case in point is the Salman Rushdie affair in 1988 over the publication of *The Satanic Verses*. Some Muslim groups wanted the book banned, as it was seen as blasphemous, whereas liberals defended it under freedom of speech.
Harmony	+ Cross-cultural dialogue promotes understanding and toleration. + This is vital as it promotes a common sense of belonging and a willingness to respect and cherish deep cultural differences of other groups rather than show suspicion or hostility. + This common sense of belonging and a reciprocal belief that cultures have a right to exist means diverse cultures can live side by side in peace and harmony.
Oppression	+ The majority culture is in an unequal relationship of power to minority cultures, which raises the question of whether minority cultures need to be protected during cultural mixing. + This again raises the issue of whether minority cultures have the right to be protected against deep offence by the majority culture's public criticism, ridicule or insults. + The Salman Rushdie affair in the UK exposed this issue.
Individual freedom	+ Most people are born into and/or are conditioned into a culture during their formative years. + Cultural dialogue and mixing opens up the opportunities for individuals to choose to stay within their culture, revise their culture or reject their culture and adopt another.
Hybridisation	+ 'Pick and mix' multiculturalism will see the dissolution of cultures. + By picking and mixing, individuals move away from their authentic identity, which provides their real sense of identity and rootedness in society. + Given that individuals are culturally embedded, the idea of adopting another culture seems unlikely.

Table 6.6 Is multiculturalism the cause of tension in society or the solution?

A cause of tension	The solution
+ Strong and stable societies are built on a common culture and shared values. By introducing different values, beliefs and cultures, multiculturalism undermines this base for society. It breeds discrimination, hostility and conflict between groups. + Minority rights, the politics of recognition and rewriting the national story are seen as unfairly identifying the majority culture with discrimination and oppression, creating further tension as well as serving to identify difference rather than promote unity. + Multiculturalism is based on the principle of toleration, but this has led societies to tolerate values that go against their way of life. There is particular concern that certain cultures hold misogynist and homophobic views which are oppressive to certain members of society, denying them their basic rights. + Multiculturalism has spawned segregation, not integration. Minority cultures emphasise difference and are inward-looking and suspicious of other groups. This leads to the majority culture viewing such groups as either unwilling or unable to integrate. + This has led to increased support for immigration controls in countries like the USA and the UK, and the return to assimilation and individualist integration. In France, the wearing of the burqa and niqab has been banned in public places. This process has been worsened by the global financial crisis and austerity, as well as the rise of international terrorism, which has increased tensions between cultures.	+ Assimilation is a denial of minority rights and a refusal to recognise cultural difference. As cultural belonging is so central to identity, this can only be a cause of conflict and tension. + Individualist integration, while tackling discrimination and equality, does not go far enough. It still does not recognise difference in the public sphere. + Liberal multiculturalists balance diversity and unity by recognising difference in the public sphere through minority rights. This ensures justice and autonomy for individuals, creating a commitment to the wider political community. + Pluralist multiculturalists embrace deep diversity, seeing diversity as good. The restructuring of the state around the politics of recognition and minority rights ensures that individuals feel a real sense of belonging, creating unity without uniformity. There is a feeling that some of the tensions between cultures are not caused by too much multiculturalism but by too little.

> **Exam tip**
>
> In the UK, David Cameron asked Dame Louise Casey to lead a Review into Opportunity and Integration, which reported back in 2016. Its main findings included worrying levels of segregation, examples of homophobia and misogyny in certain cultures, and a growth in far-right and 'Islamist' extremists promoting hate in the most segregated and deprived communities. It is worth considering whether multiculturalism is the problem or whether multiculturalism is the only answer to tackling these issues.

> **Revision activity**
>
> 1 Create a set of flashcards for all the key terms in this chapter.
> 2 Write a paragraph explaining the differences between:
>   a) liberalism and liberal multiculturalism
>   b) liberal multiculturalism and pluralist multiculturalism.

Now test yourself

6. How can cosmopolitan multiculturalism be seen to lead to cultural hybridisation and why is that an issue?
7. How have recent events, especially the global crash and the rise of terrorism, contributed to current views of multiculturalism?
8. Copy and complete the following table with the main ideas of the key thinkers.

Thinker	Human nature	The state	Society	The economy
Charles Taylor				
Will Kymlicka				
Isaiah Berlin				
Bhikhu Parekh				
Tariq Modood				

Exam practice

1. 'Cultural mixing is beneficial for society.' Analyse and evaluate this statement with reference to the multiculturalist thinkers that you have studied. In your answer, you should draw on material from across the whole range of your course of study in politics. [25]
2. 'Multiculturalism is a source of tension and conflict in society.' Analyse and evaluate this statement with reference to the multiculturalist thinkers that you have studied. In your answer, you should draw on material from across the whole range of your course of study in politics. [25]

Summary

You should now have an understanding of:
+ debates about the nature of multiculturalism
+ core ideas and values of multiculturalism concerning equality of opportunity, anti-discrimination, assimilation, integration and segregation
+ the contributions of the five key thinkers (Taylor, Kymlicka, Berlin, Parekh and Modood) to the development of multiculturalism
+ the tensions and agreements within multiculturalism between the different traditions, and within them
+ the criticism of multiculturalism

7 Anarchism

Anarchism is an ideology with many different traditions, but it is united in its rejection of the state, its opposition to coercive relationships and its belief that society without the state is both possible and desirable. This society should enable everyone to have the widest possible range of individual choices. This chapter will look at the origins, core ideas and strands of anarchism before summarising the areas of tension and agreement.

> **Exam tip**
>
> When studying anarchism, be careful not to interpret 'anarchy' in its modern sense, as chaos due to the collapse of law and order, leaving humanity to run wild. According to its original definition, 'anarchy' simply means 'without a leader/ruler' and describes a society without a state. Anarchists believe that an anarchist society would actually lead to greater order and less conflict. This is shown in the common anarchist symbol below, where the O represents order and unity.

Origins of anarchism

REVISED

- Anarchism draws on both liberalism and socialism for many of its ideas: liberalism for its emphasis on individualism and freedom; and socialism for its traditional critique of capitalism as exploitative, and for its emphasis on communalism and co-operation.
- The roots of anarchism as a coherent political idea can be found in the late eighteenth century, drawing on the growing sense of individualism and the desire for social progress.
- The key catalysts for anarchism were the emergence of the modern state, nationalism, capitalism and the Industrial Revolution. It set itself in direct opposition to the oppression of capital, the state and the Church.
- The nineteenth century saw the emergence of the most influential anarchist thinkers and the arrival of the anarchist movement:
  - Max Stirner offered a stark and brutal form of individualism which rejected the state, society and all forms of coercion and restriction.
  - Pierre-Joseph Proudhon insisted that only a society without a government could bring peace, order and stability, framed in his famous phrase 'Anarchy is order.'

Individualism The individual is of the utmost importance and is placed above the collective.

Capitalism A system whereby wealth in the form of money or assets, such as the means of production, is owned privately by an individual or corporation.

The state Anarchists accept Max Weber's definition of the state as a body which claims the monopoly over the legitimate use of a force within a given territory.

- Mikhail Bakunin pushed Proudhon's ideas to the limits, arguing passionately for revolution to overthrow capitalism, the state and the Church, and to build an ordered society on the twin concepts of freedom and solidarity.
- Peter Kropotkin aimed to ground anarchism in scientific principles and developed an anarchism more closely based on the Marxist principle 'from each according to his ability, to each according to his needs'.
- Emma Goldman looked to balance individualism with the interests of the collective (collectivism) and introduced a critical feminist dimension. Most anarchists, though not anarcho-capitalists, support collective or group ownership of property and industry, rejecting capitalism and exploitative individualism. While anarchists place individualism at the centre of their beliefs, they reject the idea that one individual is free to coerce or exploit/employ another.

> **Solidarity** Bakunin described the single law of solidarity as 'No person can recognise or realise his or her own humanity except by recognising it in others and so co-operating for its realisation by each and all.'
>
> **Collectivism** The idea that the collective rather than the individual is the main economic, social and political unit.

Main beliefs of anarchism

REVISED

The autonomy of the individual

Central to anarchism is the idea that the individual should rule themselves and refuse to be ruled by others. The crucial point for anarchists is that people *are* capable of governing themselves. The argument for autonomy is made in a four-step process:

1. In moral philosophy, all individuals are responsible for their own actions.
2. This assumes that all individuals are 'free' to make their own choices about how they act.
3. As the individual is rational, they should use that reason to reflect on what they ought to do, so that they can set their own laws for themselves about how to act.
4. In this way, individuals are free to act in line with the moral laws that they have decided for themselves.

This makes freedom the central theme of anarchism and the point of society is to give individuals the widest possible range of individual choices. A critical debate within anarchism is what freedom means, with tensions between different thinkers (see Table 7.1).

There is a sliding scale within anarchism from individualism to collectivism. Even Stirner, as the arch individualist, recognises the need for communal life, arguing that relations with others must be free, voluntary, always subject to cancellation and in 'my own personal interest'. For example, if the individual writes books, the individual requires others to read them.

> **Freedom** For anarchists, this means being free from restraint to do as one likes and to fulfil one's dreams and potential. This freedom is only real when it is real for all.
>
> **Egoistical** Humans are self-interested and self-reliant.

Table 7.1 The meaning of freedom according to different anarchist thinkers

Max Stirner	Each individual is unique and egoistical. There can be no restriction on freedom: 'Whether I am in the right or not there is no judge but myself' (*The Ego and Its Own*, 1844). He feared that freedom of the individual would be limited by social duty to the interests of the collective.
Proudhon and Goldman	Both Proudhon and Goldman sought a balance between the interests of the individual and the collective. Proudhon feared the tyranny of the collective, while Goldman feared the oppression of 'uniformity'. However, they argued that the natural complement to the individual is working with others to solve common problems.
Kropotkin and Bakunin	Kropotkin and Bakunin endorsed the widest possible freedom. However, their definition of individual freedom is that it can only be achieved in the company of others. Bakunin argued that 'the isolated individual cannot possibly become conscious of his freedom' (*Man, Society, and Freedom*, 1871).

Check your understanding and progress at www.hoddereducation.co.uk/myrevisionnotes

Opposition to the state

+ **The state**. Anarchists see the traditional nation-state as an artificial construct, separate from society, which acts as a tool of oppression and the cause of social conflict and unrest. Perhaps more accurately, this should be termed a 'compulsory association'.
+ **Authority**. The state claims authority: that is, the right to command and the right to be obeyed.
+ **Command**. This command by the state to obey the law restricts the autonomy of the individual. It strips them of responsibility for their actions, removing both their freedom and their rationality.
+ **Power**. The power of the state is visible in its laws and in the institutions that enforce those laws: the police, the courts and the military. It is also visible in the more hidden forces of control: ideology, in particular nationalism/patriotism, as well as education, formal organised religion, the traditional family unit and institutions such as marriage.
+ **Coercion**. The power of the state means its relationship to the individual is one of coercion: it forces the individual to comply, removing their ability to think for themselves and express their individual judgement. This leads Stirner to argue that 'I am free in no state' (*The Ego and Its Own*, 1844).
+ **Corrupting**. Power, in any form, is corrupting:
  + Bakunin argued that power corrupts the human nature of those in power, who will develop contempt for the masses and an over-estimation of their own ability.
  + Power brutalises the people, turning them into unthinking masses who meekly accept their position, becoming anti-social, aggressive and competitive in fighting for the scraps that fall from the table of the rich and powerful.
+ **Rejection of the state**. All anarchists reject the formal state in all its forms, whether it is a liberal democracy, a Marxist state, a nation-state or a capitalist state (Table 7.2). It is (just) conceivable to envisage an anarchist state, where citizenship is entirely voluntary, and any rules or guidelines are only followed by mutual consent and after full collective agreement. Any individual could of course withdraw from this state/community at any time and without any negative consequences. Individual autonomy is paramount.

> **Making links**
>
> The anarchist view of freedom can be contrasted with the liberal view. For anarchists, freedom can only be achieved without the state, whereas liberals have argued that the state is necessary to protect individual liberty.

Authority The right to exercise power.

Power The ability of one person to influence the actions of others, where that action goes against their own judgement.

Table 7.2 The arguments used by anarchists to reject the traditional state in all its forms

Liberal democracy	The social contract does not exist. No state can have power over anyone who rejects the contract and it is illogical to expect an individual to consent individually to each and every law. Government by consent (by election) is nonsense; if the people are truly sovereign, they will not hand over their autonomy to the state and there will be no government and no governed. As Emma Goldman observed, 'If voting changed anything, they'd make it illegal.' There are echoes here of liberal thinker John Stuart Mill's reference to the 'tyranny of the majority'.
Marxist state	Marxists and anarchists appear to have a great deal in common in terms of the end goal, as Marxists argue that the state will wither away. However, anarchists split from Marxists over the dictatorship of the proletariat, seeing this 'red' state as corrupting, with Bakunin arguing that 'socialism without freedom is slavery and brutality'. The march towards dictatorship in the Soviet Union confirmed for anarchists this view of any utopian socialist state.
Nation-state	Rudolf Rocker argued that 'the state created the nation, and not the nation the state'. Goldman saw nationalism and patriotism as ideological weapons to cultivate unthinking obedience to the state. They constituted a principal cause of division between people to undermine social harmony and solidarity. They also increased the coercive powers of the state to protect or control the masses.
Capitalist state	Collectivist anarchism (see p. 109): the state is a relatively new creation that developed with the emergence of economic inequality, private property and class relations. The state is unjust as it is an expression of social conflict, managed by the few to protect their wealth and private property while keeping the masses in abject poverty.
	Anarcho-capitalism (see p. 109): the state is unjust as it is a parasite that is set up to rob individuals of their property via taxation backed up by threat of the law, police and jail.

> **Making links**
>
> Emma Goldman's view that if voting changed anything they would make it illegal could be used to offer insights into low levels of voter turnout in the USA and the UK, potentially reflecting the views of some people that voting is a waste of time.

Opposition to and abolition of coercive relationships

+ **Coercive relationships**. Anarchists not only oppose the formal state and all forms of government operated by it, they also oppose all forms of coercive relationships within society, as they limit the choices of the individual. This has also led some anarchists to reject conventional marriage, which they view as inherently patriarchal in nature.
+ **Authority**. Coercive relationships in society are based on the idea that certain individuals and ideas have authority, so the people should do as they are told. A clear example would be the authority of church or business leaders, or indeed teachers.
+ **Revolt**. Anarchism is a revolt against existing society and those who guard it to allow the individual to be free:
  + Proudhon rejected all 'official persons', such as the philosopher, the priest, the academic, the politician and the journalist, who see people as 'a monster to be fought, muzzled and chained down'.
  + Stirner offered the most radical critique, arguing that the individual has to throw out 'the vagabonds of the intellect', by which he is referring to religion and existing morality – including existing sexual morality and the morality programmed into children by their parents and teachers. Only then is the individual free and autonomous.

> **Exam tip**
>
> You could use Bakunin's quote, 'the idea of God implies the abdication of human reason and justice; it is the most decisive negation of human liberty' (*God and the State*, 1882), to illustrate the idea that the Church's relationship to its believers is one of coercion and control.

Society without the state

Anarchists believe that, without the interference of the state and other coercive relationships based on models of authority, a harmony of interests will emerge among humans. This harmony is a spontaneous order, as humans are capable of creating social order far more effectively than one imposed by authority.

For individualist anarchists (see p. 108), order emerges through the meeting of individual interests:
+ Individuals are egoistical; they have self-ownership, autonomy and the freedom to determine their own identity.
+ Individuals come together in free, voluntary contracts that work in their own interest and can be revoked at any time.
+ Individuals, by coming together, increase their own strength and fulfil themselves more completely than they could in isolation.

For collectivist anarchists (see p. 109), order emerges when the state and authority are overthrown and humanity's natural tendencies are allowed to grow:
+ Proudhon believed the individual holds within them 'the principles of a moral code that goes beyond the individual', which allows for voluntary co-operation to solve common problems.
+ Bakunin believed that the conscience and reason of humans would lead them all to choose to work collectively.
+ Kropotkin found in nature the concept of mutual aid, where the most successful species work together. Humanity has natural tendencies to sociability and co-operation.

> **Making links**
>
> The importance of anarchism's opposition to coercive relationships can be seen in the waves of direct action by pressure groups including militant feminism, black and LGBTQIA+ liberation movements, radical environmental groups and the anti-capitalist and globalisation movements – the most famous being the Mexican Zapatistas and the Occupy movement.

> **Exam tip**
>
> You could illustrate the idea that harmony is a spontaneous order by using Proudhon's view that freedom is the mother not the daughter of order.

The idea that society without the state is both possible and desirable has led to anarchism being closely linked with utopianism:

+ Utopianism can be seen as a particular way of political thinking, where the construction of an ideal future society allows us to see the failings of current arrangements and the path to achieving that ideal.
+ In a negative sense, utopianism is seen as unrealistic thinking that provided a vision of the future that is based on false assumptions or not grounded in reality.

> **Utopianism** The belief in the ideal or perfect society, Utopia.

> **Exam tip**
>
> You could use the ongoing Zapatista rebellion in Mexico or the Rojava rebellion in Syria as examples of societies based on anarchist principles which show that anarchism is potentially achievable.

Now test yourself   TESTED

1. Why do anarchists believe that their beliefs will lead to a peaceful and orderly society?
2. What did Stirner mean when he wrote 'I am free in no state'?
3. Why and how has anarchism been linked to utopianism?
4. Outline two ways in which the state can be seen to be unjust by anarchists.

Main strands of anarchism   REVISED

Individualist anarchism

+ People are self-seeking or egoistical.
+ The individual and autonomy are at the centre of this approach.
+ Autonomy should not be restricted in any way, so the existing state, and existing societal and economic relations, must be replaced. There must be the widest possible choice for all individuals.
+ There is a real fear that the individual will be made subject to the desires of the collective. Goldman feared the 'uniformity' of society strangling freedom, whereas Proudhon saw the end of private property leaving the individual at the mercy of the wishes of the majority.
+ A meeting of mutual interests through voluntary contracts will provide a natural and spontaneous order.
+ Individualist anarchism is a broad stream of ideas with two separate, identifiable currents: egoism and anarcho-capitalism (see Table 7.3). It is clear that although both strands put the individual, freedom and autonomy first, there is a clear disagreement over the role of private property and capitalism.

> **Key thinker**
>
> **Max Stirner (1806–56)**
>
> Max Stirner is perhaps the most radical and challenging of all anarchist thinkers in his defence of individualism and freedom for all, not just himself, in *The Ego and Its Own* (1844).
>
> + The state restricts freedom: 'I am my own only when I am master of myself.'
> + Stirner attacked all 'fixed ideals' or 'spooks' which limit our autonomy, arguing that 'God, conscience, duties and laws are all errors which have been stuffed into our minds and hearts.'
> + One of the key ideals that must be overthrown is the concept of private property and the division of labour between the owner and the worker.
> + All should be free, but freedom is not something that someone gives you; it comes from self-liberation. Stirner was focused on the individual rebel, not the revolution.
> + The rebel's personal act of revolt involves clearing out the fixed ideals so that the existing state, society and the economy perish and start to rot.
> + Stirner offered no clear blueprint for the new society but argued that the more people become egoists, the more they will recognise the uniqueness of others, creating natural order.
> + This 'Union of Egoists' is based on equality and freedom, where individuals come together in voluntary agreements in their own interest while sacrificing nothing.

Table 7.3 The main currents within the individualist anarchist tradition

Egoism (associated with Max Stirner)	Anarcho-capitalism (associated with Murray Rothbard)
+ The individual is the ego, which is a concept of self-ownership, autonomy and freedom to determine one's own identity. + There can be no restrictions on the ego, so all 'fixed ideas' about the political, social and economic world must be cleared from our minds. + These 'spooks' of the mind include authority, the state, the church, morality, private property and capitalism. + By throwing out the 'spooks' of the mind, existing ideas will crumble into dust, taking the institutions with them. + This will leave a 'Union of Egoists' where individuals come together in voluntary arrangements that suit their own interests.	+ Individual freedom is the supreme value and an end in itself. Liberty is central to the thriving and flourishing of each person. + The ideal society is stateless, as the state is incompatible with liberty because it has the power to tax and control over the powers of coercion. + The state should be replaced by the market, which is an invisible hand that will allow private interests to coincide to create general good through voluntary and mutually beneficial exchanges. + In this case, all current functions of the state would be replaced by market-based services. + Education, roads, policing, law courts and environmental protection could all be provided more efficiently through the market as it offers both choice and competition.

Ego The concept of the individual based on the idea that life should only be lived in the interest of the self rather than in the interest of others.

Exam tip

You don't need to know more than the five specified thinkers (Stirner, Proudhon, Bakunin, Kropotkin and Goldman), but you can use additional thinkers like anarcho-capitalist Murray Rothbard where relevant. Brief reference to anarcho-capitalists can particularly enhance an essay about how anarchists view the economy, and also when considering whether all anarchists are also socialists.

Making links

It is often argued that individualist anarchism is liberalism pushed to the extremes. However, although anarchists and liberals both endorse the individual and autonomy, anarchists do *not* support the night-watchman state of the classical liberals as it is still a restriction on autonomy and freedom.

Collectivist anarchism

The collectivist anarchist tradition applies to all types of anarchism that hold in common the following ideas:
+ Human nature is essentially social, with altruistic tendencies that lead humans to want to work together rather than compete against each other.
+ At the same time, collectivists recognise that human nature is shaped by the world around us. The domination of the many by the few has created the faults in human nature that we see today.
+ The absence of the state and of relationships based on dominance (like capitalism, which is a relationship between master and wage slave) will allow true human nature to flourish and grow.
+ The collectivist anarchist tradition rejects the private ownership of the means of production and distribution, believing that the individual can only be truly free through equal and free relationships with others.

Collectivist anarchism is a wide river of ideas that breaks down into four main streams – mutualism, collectivism, anarcho-syndicalism and anarcho-communism (see Figure 7.1). The key differences emerge over economic organisation

Altruistic Relating to the part of human nature that leads individuals to care for others and act in others' interests rather than their own.

Figure 7.1 The four streams of collectivist anarchism

> **Exam tip**
> Don't confuse collectivist anarchism with collectivism. Collectivist anarchism is a range of anarchist ideas, of which collectivism is only one.

> **Making links**
> Direct action pressure groups like Occupy (formed on anarchist principles), which have sprung up in opposition to the state and capitalism, are good examples to use as evidence of anarchist principles in action. They also make a synoptic link with both UK and US pressure groups. The Occupy activist and anarchist David Graeber coined the slogan 'We are the 99%', which has helped shape modern political debate about inequality and capitalism. The slogan refers to the idea that 1% of the population has a growing slice of wealth, power and work, while for 99% the fear of losing your job is greater than the prospect of ever finding a fulfilling one.

Mutualism

+ Mutualism is proposed as an alternative to both capitalist and socialist forms of economic organisation.
+ Private property in capitalism is a relationship of domination, where the owner dominates the worker through low wages that do not accurately reflect their labour, high rents and high rates of interest. Private property is to be replaced with possessions. These involve the right to ownership based on use (e.g. the tools you use in your work, the house you live in). This form of property is vital, as under collective ownership of property the individual becomes the servant of the collective and so is oppressed.
+ There would be individual ownership of farmland and small-scale production. Large-scale production would be achieved through co-operatives (voluntary organisations run and owned by the workers). Commodities could be exchanged based on labour notes (listing the number of hours of labour that went into the product), which is equal and fair.
+ The individual would keep the fruits of their labour: from each according to his ability, to each according to his deeds (work).
+ Co-operatives would form together into voluntary federations to support each other, building solidarity and mutual aid.
+ This strategy is reformist, with the idea that the new basis for society can be built within the shell of the existing state, eventually replacing the state and capitalism.

> **Mutualism** A system of voluntary association for the free and fair exchange of goods and services at cost (i.e. without profit).
>
> **Federations** Unions of free, self-governing, spontaneously formed bodies of people on the basis of equality.

Key thinker

Pierre-Joseph Proudhon (1809–65)

Proudhon is regarded as the starting point for anarchism, developing an anarchism that was non-violent, rational and anti-utopian, as it was based on a potential within existing society. He argued for small-scale voluntary socialist associations that would in turn create a network within the existing state that would over time render obsolete both the traditional state and the capitalist economy. His work has inspired both the individualist and the collectivist traditions.

- 'Property is theft' – the concept of property allows owners to exploit users, such as property owners charging a high rent for a flat, or factory owners paying wages that are far lower than the actual value of the labour because they own the factories and tools/machines.
- 'Property is despotism' – property creates social relations based on domination, leading to the exploitation of humans by humans.
- 'Possessors without masters' – the idea of a society where individuals have the right to possess the land, property or tools which they use.
- Workers' associations and co-operatives – co-operative associations where each worker has an equal share in the co-operative, which is managed by the workers and where each worker is rewarded for the work done.
- Federations – workers' associations and co-operatives voluntarily join together in federations for administration purposes.
- A mutual bank – a people's bank would provide free credit to co-operatives, allowing workers to create their own means of production.
- Building the new world – the new world of the people's bank and workers' co-operatives can be built in the shell of the existing world and, over time, replace the existing structures of the state, society and the economy.
- 'Anarchy is order' – the idea that without the power of the state and authoritarian relationships in society, natural order will spontaneously emerge.

Exam tip

You can see mutualism as a balance between individualist and collective anarchist traditions, as it wishes to protect the individual from the collective while opposing capitalism and its version of private property.

Exam tip

Be careful in essays not to misunderstand Proudhon's famous quote 'property is theft', which is often misapplied to present Proudhon as an opponent of all forms of private property. In reality, he was a strong supporter of possessions, based on use rights.

Collectivism

- Collectivism, like mutualism, is a sub-strand of the collectivist anarchist tradition, and it is most closely associated with Mikhail Bakunin.
- It differs from mutualism in arguing that all private property should be collectivised into common ownership that is self-managed by the workers. Workers would keep the products of their labour, as in mutualism, so the main principle would be 'from each according to his ability, to each according to his work'.
- Society would be ordered from the bottom up through voluntary collectives into a great federation to administer the production and distribution of all goods.
- Collectivism is revolutionary, arguing that the masses need to rise up to destroy the existing political, social and economic structures.

Key thinker

Mikhail Bakunin (1814–76)

Bakunin was a revolutionary activist and thinker who saw himself as a fanatical lover of liberty and who shaped collectivist anarchism, most famously in his unfinished work, *God and the State* (1882).

- He rejected the individualism of liberalism, arguing that true freedom is only possible when economic and social equality exists.
- Freedom is not a product of being isolated and independent, but is realised through connections with others.
- Bakunin rejected all forms of authority, hierarchy and the state, as they all assume that the masses are incapable of governing themselves. Only by returning power to the collective – the masses – and through self-management by the workers in their collectives can freedom exist.
- He opposed the church and religion, arguing that 'if God is, man is a slave'.
- He opposed the capitalist state as 'the organised authority, domination and power of the possessing classes over the masses'.
- The socialist state would simply replace one oppressive master with another, where the individual would be forced to submit to the collective interests of the 'Red bureaucracy'; this warning was an accurate prediction of the Soviet state under Stalin.

- He opposed capitalism, seeing labour as a 'sort of voluntary and transitory serfdom' and private property as the right to live 'by exploiting the work of someone else'.
- Bakunin believed in the power of the masses to rise up and overthrow the state, and saw a key role for anarchists in inspiring the collective struggle.
- He saw revolution as necessary, probably initially needing to use violence to create the conditions for the new society, as 'the passion for destruction is a creative passion, too'.
- The general strike was a key method for the revolution, as it would create the 'great cataclysm which forces society to shed its old skin'.

Anarcho-syndicalism

- Anarcho-syndicalism merges the currents of syndicalism and anarchism, drawing its inspiration from Mikhail Bakunin.
- Mass meetings, factory committees and workers' councils should be established, as they will create, in Bakunin's words, 'not only the ideas but also the facts of the future' because these bodies will form the basis of the new society.
- The unions should fight for improved conditions, using direct action such as strikes, occupations and sabotage of the factory by workers, and so become the 'elementary school of socialism', in the words of Rudolf Rocker.
- The new world order can only be created by revolution, not reform, and this would involve 'taking over of the management of all plants by the producers themselves' (Rocker).

Syndicalism The practice of workers organising into unions to fight for their interests by taking direct action.

Communes Associations where the members own everything in common, including the fruits of the individual's labour.

Anarcho-communism

- Private property and capital must be abolished and replaced by common ownership.
- Anarcho-communists extend common ownership to the fruits of an individual's labour. This does not mean that people will be sharing hairbrushes, but that all products are 'at the disposal of all, leaving to each the liberty to consume them as he pleases in his own home' (Kropotkin, *The Place of Anarchism in Socialistic Evolution*, 1884).
- Anarcho-communism is based on the principle 'from each according to his ability, to each according to his needs'.
- Society will be based on small, localised communes that are self-managing, with all the wealth under common ownership.
- Membership of communes is voluntary and communes will voluntarily enter into federations to work together at local, regional and international level, but with the key decisions always lying with the individual communes.

Exam tip

You can use the Confederación Nacional del Trabajo (CNT) as an example of anarcho-syndicalist principles in action during the Spanish Civil War from 1936. Free collectives successfully organised both industrial production and agriculture in Catalonia until the experiment was smashed by the nationalist forces under General Franco.

Key thinker

Peter Kropotkin (1842–1921)

Peter Kropotkin was the key exponent of anarcho-communism and through his book, *Mutual Aid* (1902), he attempted to provide a scientific basis for anarchist theory.

- Kropotkin aimed to give a philosophical basis to anarchism through his study of the natural world.
- In *Mutual Aid*, he argued that the view of nature as being based, like capitalism, on competition between individuals was not accurate.
- The struggle for survival is best achieved by mutual aid among the members of a species and so it is the best route for individuals to take.
- Kropotkin applied this to humanity to show that mutual aid is crucial both for humanity's survival and for its ongoing evolution. Society is natural and voluntary co-operation is natural.
- The removal of coercive institutions will allow natural society to flourish and it will be one of spontaneous order which will nourish humanity's social and co-operative nature.
- Kropotkin used this evidence to make a case for anarcho-communism based on the following ideas:
  - private property to be replaced by common ownership.
  - free communism – the commune is a voluntary organisation where people freely share the products of their labour and common resources with others, as this is in their best interest.
  - a free federation of communes that work together in the spirt of mutual aid and solidarity.
  - communes are based on mass participation by their members to build new societies around the ideas of liberty, equality and solidarity.

> **Now test yourself** TESTED
>
> 5 Outline the three different ways the state and coercive relationships will be abolished according to Stirner, Proudhon and Bakunin.
> 6 How did Bakunin differ from Marx as regards the bringing about of a stateless society?
> 7 Why does Proudhon consider property to be theft?
> 8 How do mutualism, collectivism and anarcho-communism differ in their approach to private property?

> **Revision activity**
>
> Create a table to show the main areas of agreement and difference between mutualism, collectivism, anarcho-syndicalism and anarcho-communism.

Core ideas of anarchism   REVISED

Human nature

Areas of agreement

- Human nature – or at the very least the potential of human nature – should be seen optimistically.
- Social order can arise naturally from human nature and does not require the presence of rules imposed from above by the state or other coercive institutions.
- Human nature is 'plastic' and moulded by the social, political and economic environment. The traits of envy, greed and resentment are created by the coercive institutions of the modern society and state.

Areas of tension

Individualist anarchism

- Human nature is egoistical as all individuals are self-seeking and desire to be autonomous and shape their own unique identity.
- Individualists support the end of the state and all coercive institutions so that the individual can be free to express their true nature.
- Anarcho-capitalists argue that the market provides the mechanism to allow the full expression of the individual.
- Stirner favoured a Union of Egoists, where relationships between egos are voluntary and always in the self-interest of the individual in line with their human nature.

Collectivist anarchism

- Human nature is essentially social and co-operative.
- Kropotkin, Bakunin and Proudhon all had a complex view of human nature that saw within it the potential for goodness and for corruption.
- The political, social and economic environment shapes human nature.
- Kropotkin found evidence for the sociability of humanity in how mutual aid benefits individuals within a species in nature.
- Both Proudhon and Bakunin saw within humanity a natural sense of justice that would inform our relations with others in a society without a state.

The state

Areas of agreement

- The traditional state or 'compulsory association' should be rejected in any form, as it is unjust, controlling, coercive and corrupting.
- A society without a compulsory state will be a society of natural order and harmony.
- The rejection of the state is necessary to create liberty.
- The rejection of the state means that any attempt to capture it through either the ballot box or the revolutionary dictatorship of the proletariat (see p. 43) is doomed to failure. This has real implications for anarchist strategies to bring about a society without government.

> **Making links**
>
> The rejection of democracy and of achieving power via traditional political parties links in with the topics of political participation and political parties in both Papers 1 and 2. Unlike the followers of all other political ideas, anarchists have no wish to contest elections and thereby participate in government.

Areas of tension

Individualist anarchism

- Individualists see the state as coercive and controlling, limiting the autonomy of the individual.
- Stirner was opposed to the state in all forms, as it claims to be sovereign but only the ego can be sovereign over itself. He argued for self-liberation, where the individual rebel stops believing in fixed ideals and authority. This form of individual rebellion will see the ideas that support the state and coercive relationships crumble away to create the Union of Egoists.
- Anarcho-capitalists like Rothbard see the state as a predatory body that does not produce anything but steals from those who do. It seizes wealth through taxation, backed by coercion; 'the threat of the jailhouse and the bayonet' (Rothbard, *Anatomy of the State*, 1974).
- For Rothbard, the state must be removed, leaving the free market to be a place of free exchange between individuals for their own benefit. This free exchange means everyone benefits and the living standard flourishes.

Collectivist anarchism

- The state develops a body to protect private property and the inequalities between the few and the many. It is coercive, controlling and unjust.
- The power of the state is always corrupting of human nature for both the governing classes and the governed.
- Bakunin saw the capitalist state as guaranteeing the power and right of the few to exploit the many. At the same time, he saw the dictatorship of the proletariat leading to 'slavery and brutality' as it was socialism without freedom.
- Proudhon argued that the overthrow of the state would be evolutionary and non-violent. He believed the building of co-operatives and a people's bank in the shell of the old society would sow the seeds for the growth of the new society.
- Kropotkin, Goldman and Bakunin saw direct action such as strikes, occupations, industrial sabotage and non-payment of taxes as actions that teach people about the true nature of the state. This creates a spirit of revolt which, when tied to increasing misery and oppression by capitalism and the state, will lead to a revolution. This revolution will inevitably require some elements of violence to destroy the state and existing institutions such as private property.
- Anarcho-syndicalists see trade unions as the key associations that will bring down the state through the mass strike, and form the basis of the new society.

> **Key thinker**
>
> ### Emma Goldman (1869–1940)
>
> Emma Goldman was a revolutionary and anarchist thinker who made major contributions to anarchism, particularly with the incorporation of sexual politics. Her thoughts are best summarised in her collection, *Anarchism and Other Essays* (1910).
>
> - Goldman was associated early in her career with the tactical use of violence in the revolutionary struggle. Such acts were used as an example to inspire revolt and were based on the idea that the ends justify the means.
> - Later, following her experience in Russia during the revolutionary period of 1919–21, Goldman revised her views, seeing violence as a necessary evil in the process of social transformation.
> - Violence was a justifiable act of defence by the revolution, but 'it is quite another thing to make a principle of terrorism, to institutionalise it, to assign it the most vital place in the social struggle'.
> - Goldman argued that only an anarchist revolution, not the ballot box, would free women from the unequal and repressive relations between sexes.
> - Women should free themselves by being personalities, not sexual objects, refuse the right to anyone over their body, only bear children if and when they want to, and refuse to be a servant to a husband, family, society, the church or the state.
> - Women must free themselves from the straitjacket of public opinion in acts of self-expression, so that they can achieve freedom.

Society

Areas of agreement

+ Society without the state will lead to natural, spontaneous harmony; natural order. This emerges from the anarchist view of human nature.
+ Existing society is coercive and existing political, economic and social institutions must be replaced to create freedom for all.
+ Society exists for man, not man for society; society exists to serve the interests of humanity and to allow the individual the widest possible freedom.
+ Freedom and equality are the basis of the new society (except for anarcho-capitalists), but there is no clear blueprint for the anarchist society, as this will develop and evolve naturally.

Areas of tension

Individualist anarchism

+ Individualists fear the power of the collective over the individual.
+ Goldman saw uniformity – through habits, tastes, dress, thoughts and ideas (essentially public opinion) – as a key threat to individuals.
+ Proudhon made the case for possession as a key defence for the individual against the collective.
+ Stirner argued for the removal of all the 'spooks', so that the individual can truly be autonomous.
+ Goldman saw a new social order 'based on the released energies of the individual and the free association of liberated individuals'.
+ Stirner saw the new society as the Union of Egoists.
+ Rothbard saw society without a state, so that society is ordered through the invisible hand of the market.

Collectivist anarchism

+ The state and existing social and economic institutions promote the domination of humans by humans, so they must be removed.
+ Natural order will emerge due to the social nature of humanity, where individuals can only achieve their full liberty through co-operation with others.
+ Bakunin argued, 'I am truly free only when all human beings, men and women, are equally free' (*Man, Society, and Freedom*, 1871).
+ The new society needs to be based on self-managing communes, organised together in voluntary communes in a relationship of mutual aid and co-operation.
+ Society will be ordered from the bottom up, not the top down.
+ This form of organisation will nourish and grow the social aspect of human nature.

The economy

Areas of agreement

+ Economic freedom is central to the freedom of the individual.
+ Private ownership of the means of production is opposed as it creates an exploitative relationship between the few and the many (except for anarcho-capitalists).
+ Inequality is opposed as it is a cause of conflict in society (except for anarcho-capitalists).

Areas of tension

Individualist anarchism

+ Stirner saw private property and capitalism as part of the 'fixed ideals' that limit autonomy, so they should be destroyed.

Check your understanding and progress at www.hoddereducation.co.uk/myrevisionnotes

- For Stirner, when humanity 'reaches the point of losing respect for property, everyone will have property'. So, when all are free, all will be equal and able to enter into voluntary contracts to further their own ends.
- Equality was important to Stirner: 'Can they really be "Egoists" who have banded together when one is a slave or a serf of the other?'
- Proudhon made the case for use rights or possession, so that the individual is not forced to submit to the will of the collective. Possession, rather than capitalist private property, is the basis of freedom.
- Rothbard saw any private property that was legally gained or earned as justified. He argued that the state should be removed from the market, so that free competition becomes the mechanism to create freedom and social order.
- Anarcho-capitalists are unique among anarchists in believing that freedom can exist without equality.

Collectivist anarchism

- Proudhon and the mutualists oppose private property and capitalism. Private property is replaced by possession, with large-scale production organised by workers' associations or co-operatives alongside small-scale producers.
- Workers should keep the fruits of their labour. Exchange is based not on money but on labour notes, which record the value of the labour that went into the produce.
- Co-operatives are organised into voluntary federations that work together to support each other. Collectivists, like Bakunin, go further, taking all property into common ownership. However, they agree with mutualists that the labourer should keep the products of their labour: to each according to his deeds (work).
- Kropotkin pushed this further, advocating all property under common ownership so that all products are at the disposal of the whole community. The basis for this is 'to each according to his needs'.
- Bakunin and Kropotkin saw communes as self-managing but joining together voluntarily into federations on the basis of mutual aid and co-operation.

> **Now test yourself** TESTED
>
> 9 Why do the individualist and collectivist traditions of anarchism view the future anarchist society as one of natural order and peace?
> 10 Why do collectivist anarchists usually support the use of direct action and violence to advance their aims?
> 11 How do mutualism and collectivism differ slightly?

> **Revision activity**
>
> Write brief definitions for anarcho-capitalism, egoism, anarcho-communism, collectivism and mutualism. Use no more than two sentences for each term.

Key debates within anarchism

REVISED

Is anarchism a single doctrine?

- The argument is made that anarchism is too diverse a range of ideas to be considered one single idea, as all that holds it together is a rejection of the state.
- Anarchism is united by its rejection of the traditional state as well as by its rejection of all coercive relationships. Anarchists believe in the autonomy of the individual, the widest possible freedom of choice for all, and that society without the state will be naturally harmonious and ordered.
- The future society will be based on voluntary agreements between individuals and there is no clear blueprint for the organisation of the new world order.
- Anarchism is a wide river with many currents. There are differences between the collectivist and individualist traditions and differences within each tradition.

- The key division between individualist and collectivist anarchism is over the individual and liberty. Individualists fear that the individual will be made a slave to the collective, whereas collectivists see individuals as being truly free only through collective work and links to others.

> **Making links**
>
> **Is anarchism really just ultra-socialism?**
> - Most anarchists, in line with socialism, reject capitalism as a system of class exploitation, reject private property in favour of collective ownership, and have faith in a stateless society where equality and freedom for all will lead to a natural order.
> - Key thinkers from the collectivist tradition, such as Goldman, Kropotkin and Bakunin, agree with Marxism that a revolution is needed to bring about change.
> - The anarchist tradition sees attempts to capture the state by revolution or the ballot box in order to deliver socialism from above as doomed to fail because the state is corrupting of human nature.
> - For anarchists, socialism can never be achieved by the state; it can only emerge from free association and co-operation between individuals, workplaces and communities.
>
> **Is anarchism really just ultra-liberalism?**
> - The individualist anarchist tradition, in common with liberalism, has a positive view of human nature, believing individuals who are self-seeking should be autonomous and will use their freedom to positive ends.
> - Anarcho-capitalism is a radical version of classical liberalism's free-market capitalism.
> - Although liberals are suspicious of the state, they see the night-watchman state as protecting liberty, whereas individualist anarchists see the state as incompatible with liberty and autonomy.
> - Most anarchists see capitalism and private property as exploitative, so they wish to overthrow both, believing equality is necessary for liberty. Liberals hold private property as a central principle, support capitalism and see inequality as justifiable.

Is anarchism only achievable through violence and revolution?

Arguments for and against the idea that anarchism requires a revolution are summarised in Table 7.4.

Table 7.4 Anarchism needs a revolution: arguments for and against

Arguments for	Arguments against
The traditional state and other entities with an interest in the existing order (e.g. big business and institutional religion) will automatically fight to preserve their power and control over individuals. Only an armed struggle can overthrow the state.	An anarchist society can emerge peacefully and gradually as small, voluntary associations grow and over time displace the existing coercive political and economic structures.
Many anarchist thinkers have called for violent revolution, most notably perhaps Kropotkin and Goldman. The latter is especially associated with the idea of 'the propaganda of the deed'. To striking workers in 1893 she said, 'Demonstrate before the palaces of the rich; demand work. If they do not give you work, demand bread. If they deny you both, take bread.'	Not all anarchist thinkers have supported violence or revolution to achieve their objective of removing the coercive state. Some, such as Proudhon, briefly a member of the French parliament, have favoured a peaceful transition. Stirner was more focused on egotistical individualism than political activism.
Anarchism is largely aligned with the economic ideas of socialism/communism, which will inevitably lead to a capitalist counter-revolution and reaction.	Not all anarchists embrace a socialist economic system (e.g. anarcho-capitalists).
Where anarchists have tried to seize power and remodel society, they have been violently opposed (e.g. during the Spanish Civil War). Protests such as those by the Occupy movement are routinely broken up forcibly by the authorities.	Anarchist groups and movements can exist peacefully in the shape of small-scale, largely self-sufficient communes or co-operatives.

> **Revision activity**
>
> 1. Create a set of flashcards for all the key terms in this chapter.
> 2. Write a paragraph explaining the links and differences between:
>   a) socialism and the collectivist anarchist tradition
>   b) the individualist anarchist tradition and liberalism.

Check your understanding and progress at www.hoddereducation.co.uk/myrevisionnotes

Now test yourself
TESTED

12 Copy and complete the following table with the main ideas of the key thinkers.

Thinker	Human nature	The state	Society	The economy
Max Stirner				
Pierre-Joseph Proudhon				
Mikhail Bakunin				
Peter Kropotkin				
Emma Goldman				

Exam practice

1 'Anarchism is not a single doctrine.' Analyse and evaluate this statement with reference to the anarchist thinkers that you have studied. In your answer, you should draw on material from across the whole range of your course of study in politics. [25]

2 'All anarchists are socialists.' Analyse and evaluate this statement with reference to the anarchist thinkers that you have studied. In your answer, you should draw on material from across the whole range of your course of study in politics. [25]

Summary

You should now have an understanding of:
+ the core anarchist principles of autonomy of the individual, opposition to and abolition of coercive relationships, opposition to the state and society without the state
+ the contributions of the five key thinkers (Stirner, Proudhon, Bakunin, Kropotkin and Goldman) to the development of anarchism
+ the tensions and agreements between the individualist and collectivist anarchist traditions, and within them
+ the extent to which anarchism is a single coherent idea

My Revision Notes: AQA A-level Politics: Political Ideas Second Edition

8 Ecologism

Ecologism is one of the most modern political ideas. It deals with the relationship between people and the natural world. Ecologism takes the position that the non-human world is worthy of moral consideration and that this should inform social, economic and political systems.

Ecologism is a broad river with many different streams and currents. On the one hand, there is dark green ecologism and social ecology which favour a radical overhaul of society, while on the other there is environmentalism or light green ecologism, which believes that the threats to the planet can be tackled within the existing economic, political and societal framework. As it is such a new political idea, there is much debate and controversy within ecologism between different strands and thinkers.

Origins of ecologism

- The modern politics of ecologism has its roots in the 1960s and 1970s. During this period, there was growing concern that the industrial process of mass production, industrialised agriculture, chemical pollution and an explosion in population were critical threats to human life and the planet.
- In 1962, Rachel Carson published *Silent Spring*, which became a bestseller by exposing the destruction of wildlife through pesticide use and its impact on the human food chain. The book is credited with introducing the wider public to ecology.
- The publication of *The Limits to Growth* by the Club of Rome in 1972 called for a complete rethink of humanity's approach to nature. It outlined the finite limits of the Earth, the terrible consequences of overshooting those limits and the need for a 'fundamental revision of human behaviour, and by implication, of the entire fabric of present-day society'.
- Ecologism tends to view all other political ideas as obsessed with economic growth, and creating the conditions for it, without paying attention to the damage this causes to the natural world. In this way, other mainstream political ideologies are seen as human centred – anthropocentric.

> **Ecology** The scientific study of plants and animals in relation to their environment, with a focus on the interdependence and interrelationships that support different forms of life.

> **Exam tip**
>
> It is worth highlighting the difference between ecologism, the political idea, and ecology, the science. Ecologism is inspired by the science of ecology, as ecology reveals that humans are not masters of nature but part of an intricate, delicate web of interrelationships and interdependencies that support human life.

Main beliefs of ecologism

The intrinsic relationship between humankind and nature

Opposition to anthropocentrism
- Anthropocentrism is the view that humans are above and outside of nature and may exploit it for their own purposes. Anthropocentrism places humanity as the master of nature, which is seen as a resource whose value is measured only by its use to mankind. Nature is said to have instrumental value – value purely as a means to an end. In this way, nature

- is seen as a commodity that can be bought and sold, and is valued as a means to generate wealth.
- During the Enlightenment (see p. 10), science and philosophy developed a mechanistic world view that was reductionist in its approach. The consequence was that nature was seen as existing for humanity's use, while technological solutions could be found to fix or improve on nature.
- Francis Bacon (philosopher and scientist, 1561–1626) wrote that nature is to be 'put in constraint, moulded, and made as it were new by art and the hand of man'.
- The findings of ecology suggested that the relationships and dependencies between all forms of life and their environment sustain life. This intricate web of dependencies and relationships needs to remain in balance. This holistic view argued that humanity is not the master of nature and that, where humanity damages the natural balance through environmental destruction, it threatens the very ecosystems that make life possible. This makes holism and the lessons of ecology the central guiding principles of *all* forms of ecologism.

Enlightened anthropocentrism

- Enlightened anthropocentrism is the light green view (see p. 126) that nature should be protected so that it continues to sustain human life.
- This limited holistic view places humankind not as the master of nature but as its steward. This is the protection of nature for practical, self-interested reasons, as nature has value as a means to sustain human life rather than purely as a commodity.
- This creates a new ethical principle that extends moral obligations to those yet to be born based on the principle of intergenerational equity. This is critical as environmental issues like climate change will have a bigger impact on future than on current generations.
- The concept of intergenerational equity became part of mainstream political debate when in 1987 the Brundtland Report, sponsored by the UN, defined sustainability as 'development that meets the needs of the present without compromising the ability of future generations to meet their own needs'. This ideal underpins the UN's 17 Sustainable Development Goals, adopted in 2015, which set targets to be achieved by 2030.

Ecocentrism

- Ecocentrism is the dark green view (see p. 124) that nature has intrinsic value or value in its own right, which is entirely separate from its value to humanity. The priority is ecological balance, not human ends.
- It opposes the mechanistic world and argues for a radical holism, where nature is seen as a system of relationships rather a collection of separate particles and fragments.
- This radical holistic view places humanity as living within the intricate web of human nature rather than acting as its master or steward. In essence, humans are plain members and citizens of nature.
- Natural systems, such as the sea, the land and ultimately the Earth, are seen as having value in their own right, as they are greater than their individual parts.
- There is a strong ethical imperative to protect nature, which emerges from a deep moral concern for the planet and all living things.
- The ecocentric approach involves dismantling existing moral frameworks and replacing them with something radically different.

> **Mechanistic world view** This redefines nature as a machine, composed of independent parts, rather than a living organism.
>
> **Reductionism** Study of the independent parts rather than the whole (e.g. the world is like a clockwork machine that can be understood by taking it apart and looking at its component parts).
>
> **Holism** Nature is a system of relationships and ecosystems and not a collection of particles or fragments that exist in isolation from each other.
>
> **Light green** The view that environmental problems can be managed and solved without fundamental changes in society's values or economic approach.
>
> **Intergenerational equity** The present generation must not compromise the ability of future generations to meet their needs.
>
> **Dark green** The view that there needs to be a radical change in our relationship to non-human nature and in our political, social and economic approaches, in order for humanity to have a rewarding and sustainable existence.

> **Making links**
>
> It is worth highlighting that there is a clear difference between ecologism and other political ideologies which focus only on relations between living people and have no concern for other forms of life (e.g. plants or animals) or wider nature (e.g. the land, water and the atmosphere).

Key thinker

Rachel Carson (1907–64)

Rachel Carson's book, *Silent Spring* (1962), was the basis for the emergence of the environmental movement, as it opened the public's eyes to the damages to nature and humanity caused by the pesticide DDT.

+ The legacy of the book was the idea that 'man is a part of nature, and his war against nature is inevitably a war against himself'.
+ Carson was questioning society's faith in science and technology, government and businesses to deliver progress and prosperity.
+ Science and technology's reductionist and mechanistic world view, alongside the state and businesses worshipping the 'gods of profit and production', were damaging the Earth and human life.
+ Carson proposed a more holistic approach based on the sustainable management of resources. This involves working within the limits of ecology by managing natural resources to protect the sustainability of the Earth.
+ Her ecological vision of the interconnectedness of life inspired the environmental movement, with Friends of the Earth and Greenpeace both tracing their founding to her work.
+ *Silent Spring* also provoked the US government under President Nixon into establishing the Environmental Protection Agency in 1970 to safeguard the environment. The agency regulated the use of pesticides and banned DDT in 1972.

Sustainability The ability of a system, such as the Earth, to maintain its health over time.

Biosphere Made up of all the parts of Earth where life exists: the ground, the air and the water.

Industrialism Large-scale production, faith in technology and a belief in limitless growth to satisfy material needs and consumer desires based on an anthropocentric world view.

Exam tip

It is worth noting that the key division between light greens and dark greens is the question of intrinsic and instrumental value, enlightened anthropocentrism or ecocentrism.

Sustainability

+ In the science of ecology, one of the key concepts is sustainability. The ability of the biosphere to maintain its health over time has become a central concern for green thinking.
+ The Club of Rome report, *The Limits to Growth* (1972), argued that the Earth is limited in terms of its:
    + carrying capacity – the ability to support population growth
    + productive capacity – the supply of natural resources
    + absorbent capacity – the ability of the Earth to absorb pollution
+ Currently, all mainstream ideologies are based on industrialism, which is a kind of meta-ideology accepted by conservatism, liberalism and socialism.
+ In light of *The Limits to Growth* and the centrality of industrialism to modern societies, green thinking has had to tackle the idea that, in order for the biosphere to be sustainable, changes will be needed in the way our societies are ordered:
    + First, the consumption of material goods by individuals will need to be reduced, especially in modern, capitalist economies.
    + Secondly, there needs to be a change of attitude to recognise that human needs are not satisfied by continual economic growth and the purchasing of more and more, newer and newer material goods.
+ Light greens have to tackle these issues through the concept of weak sustainability. This is often defined as sustainable development, which clashes with the strong sustainability view adopted by dark greens and social ecology (see Table 8.1).

Exam tip

It is important to note in your answers that many ecologists argue that, although capitalism has generated great wealth, many people across the planet are living in absolute poverty, while growing wealth in nations like the UK and USA has not led to greater happiness. According to this view, continuing with a pattern of more production and more growth will cause enormous ecological damage and do little to improve the quality of human life.

Sustainable development Development that meets the needs of the present without compromising the ability of future generations to meet their own needs.

Check your understanding and progress at www.hoddereducation.co.uk/myrevisionnotes

Table 8.1 The difference between weak and strong sustainability

Weak sustainability	Strong sustainability
Economic growth at a slower pace – this is more a question of 'greening' economic growth. In essence, it means doing more but with less.	A steady-state economy – a period of de-growth in wealthier economies will be needed to find a human economy that fits with the Earth's ecosystems. At this point, the economy should remain steady, with zero growth.
Smarter growth – a form of technological optimism that believes in using technology to reduce the environmental impact of growth and solve any environmental issues.	Technology can be part of the solution, but it is not *the* solution. The technological fix is not enough as it fails to recognise the finite limits of the Earth and its resources.
Natural capital (e.g. coal, gas and water) can be depleted as long as they are used to build manufactured capital (e.g. infrastructure such as roads) of the equivalent value.	Natural capital should be maintained as it is crucial to the sustainability of the Earth's ecosystems.
Growth should meet the needs of the present generation without compromising the needs of future generations.	Growth is only supportable where the benefits outweigh the costs (i.e. to ensure that people can meet their basic needs). As society will be built on satisfying basic needs, there will have to be a radical alteration in society's materialist attitude.
The consumption of goods is still possible if we move to a green lifestyle based on green consumerism, recycling and environmental awareness. An example might be consumers switching to renewable energy sources.	There is a clear difference between needs and wants. Wants are turned into needs by powerful corporations to sell goods – society should focus on consumption based only on real needs. This new society will be built on looking for a deeper and more profound happiness than that provided by consumerism – a new society that is inwardly rich, but outwardly poor.

Steady-state economy Herman Daly defines this as 'constant stocks of people and physical wealth, maintained at some chosen, desirable level by a low rate of output'.

Materialism Considering material possessions and the social image that they project as more important than spiritual values.

Consumerism The idea that the consumption and acquisition of material goods is the principal goal of human existence. Through material goods we will achieve happiness and social status.

Exam tip

'Sustainability' is one of the most used words when it comes to discussing environmental issues, but it is rarely defined accurately. It raises questions about whether sustainability means de-growth, no growth or smarter, greener growth. Make sure you distinguish between weak and strong sustainability within your answers.

Now test yourself

TESTED

1. a) What are the three limits to growth identified in the Club of Rome report?
   b) How do these limits clash with industrialism?
2. Why do dark greens oppose consumerism and materialism?
3. Outline the differences between anthropocentrism and enlightened anthropocentrism and between enlightened anthropocentrism and ecocentrism.

Main strands of ecologism

REVISED

Dark green ecologism

Dark green thinking is based on the premise of a radical transformation of our relationship with non-human nature and therefore the organisation of the state, society and the economy.

Ecocentrism

Dark green thinking is opposed to the idea that mankind is either the master or the steward of nature. The basis of its ideas is to move beyond human instrumental reasons for protecting the environment and this can happen in two ways:
+ **Biocentric equality.** This is the creation of a new form of ethics that places intrinsic value in nature. Aldo Leopold's 'land ethic' is the most influential example of this approach.

Intrinsic value According to Næss, this is 'the value of non-human life forms' which is 'independent of the usefulness these may have for narrow human purposes'.

- **Environmental consciousness.** This can found in the work of Arne Næss and his deep ecological theory, Ecosophy T, which has two key principles:
  - **Self-realisation.** This means rising above the egotistical view of the self to realise that all life is fundamentally one. Once this spiritual realisation has occurred, harming the natural world will be harming oneself, so no one will do it and there will be no need for any further ethical rules.
  - **Biocentric egalitarianism.** This is the idea that all life forms have an 'equal right to live and blossom'. It means applying the idea of equality across the whole of nature. Humans have no right to reduce the richness and diversity of nature except to satisfy vital needs. This raises questions about what vital needs are and what is justifiable interference in the natural world.

Extending the moral community to include the natural world and building a closer identification with nature is central to deep ecology. It argues that humans can only be free when all parts of nature are free. But it leaves many questions open, such as: do simple organisms like amoeba have the same rights to live and bloom as complex ones like humans and how do we resolve situations where rights clash?

> **Exam tip**
>
> A good way to illustrate intrinsic value is the Robin Attfield thought experiment: if you were the last human left on Earth facing the last tree on Earth, would it be wrong to cut it down, knowing you would die before the tree? If the answer is yes, the tree has intrinsic value.

> **Key thinker**
>
> **Aldo Leopold (1887–1948)**
>
> Aldo Leopold's *A Sand County Almanac* (1949), although it predates the rise of ecologism, is seen now as one of the clearest expressions of ecocentric thinking.
> - Leopold saw traditional economics as unable to solve the problem of wilderness protection and wildlife management. He saw capitalism and all alternatives to capitalism as based on the idea of the 'distribution of more machine-made commodities to more people'.
> - His conclusion was that a 'new kind of people' with a holistic, ecocentric, ethical approach was needed.
> - His 'land ethic' is perhaps the most influential statement on holistic, ecocentric ethics and it came in two parts:
>   - Leopold extended the community that is worthy of moral or ethical consideration 'to include soils, waters, plants, and animals, or collectively: the land'.
> - His moral rule was that 'A thing is right when it tends to preserve the integrity, stability and beauty of the biotic community. It is wrong when it tends otherwise.'
> - This holistic approach extends ethical consideration to the non-human world, including the non-living elements, as Leopold sees the Earth itself as having a certain kind of life.
> - It also provides a guide for action by creating a rule for what can and cannot be done, which acts as a limit on the actions of the state, society and the economy.
> - This form of ethical consideration involves a radical transformation in humanity's understanding of non-human nature. Humanity will move from being 'conqueror of the land-community to a plain member and citizen of it'.

Environmental consciousness and spirituality

Environmental consciousness has a strong spiritual element that connects with New Age thinking. Such thinking formed part of the counter-culture in the 1960s and 1970s and drew its inspiration from Buddhism and Hinduism as well as the attitudes of Indigenous peoples in their strong attachment to their natural environment.

Dark green ecologism is clearly radical in its outlook, yet its method for transforming the world appears to rest on individuals having a personal, spiritual revolution rather than a revolutionary method of overthrowing the existing political, economic and societal structures. This raises questions about the practicality of the dark green approach.

Sustainable societies

These would be based on the principle of a new relationship between humanity and nature, involving:
- Strong sustainability, where natural capital must be preserved and capitalism must be opposed.
- The end of the domination of materialism and consumerism and its replacement with more profound forms of human happiness and fulfilment.

> **Exam tip**
>
> To illustrate the difference between environmental consciousness and biocentric equality, use Warwick Fox's example of the Nez Perce American Indian, Smohalla. When asked why the Nez Perce peoples don't plough the Earth, his answer was not about the intrinsic value of nature but about a state of environmental consciousness: 'Shall I take a knife and tear my mother's breast?'

Check your understanding and progress at www.hoddereducation.co.uk/myrevisionnotes

- A period of de-growth in advanced economies, which are currently based on the consumption of commodities and so are the greatest source of environmental destruction. Countries with high standards of living in general have a high carbon footprint, emitting far greater amounts of carbon dioxide per person.
- The steady-state economy, which is based on zero economic growth and production for needs rather than wants.
- A move away from gigantism to small autonomous economic communities, using local skills, local resources and local knowledge, and in which land and resources are communally owned. This is based on E. F. Schumacher's ideas.
- Spiritually fulfilling and creative work, reconnecting humanity with each other, the land and nature. Wealth will be measured in spiritual, not material, terms.

> **Gigantism** The growth of huge, greedy, global corporations that mass produce goods in vast numbers in huge factories, creating dehumanising work. The term also refers to the growth of massive cities that separate people from each other and nature.

Living democracies

Dark green ecologists believe that the state and society should be built on ecological principles which favour decentralised, interdependent communities modelled on anarchist lines:

- **Bioregionalism**. There are natural regions across the Earth, with their own natural cycles and boundaries. These should provide the basis for organisation rather than the artificial boundaries of the state, allowing for an approach that is connected to the local environment and includes humans alongside plants, animals, water and the land in these democratic communities.
- **Interdependent**. Based on the lessons of ecology, communities would be interdependent in both their political and economic life. This would create a federation of local communities.
- **Communal**. Nature is naturally communal with no centralised control. Societies should be organised on communal lines, with the land communally owned and political decisions taken locally. Local decisions will be more in tune with nature and so will be both ecologically and socially fair.
- **Diversity**. Nature is diverse, so bioregional communities can be diverse but will be based on the concepts of true democracy, freedom, toleration and equality.

Key thinker

E. F. Schumacher (1911–77)

E. F. Schumacher's *Small is Beautiful: A Study of Economics as if People Mattered* (1973) attacked the gigantism of mass production, questioned the importance of economic growth and insisted that human happiness would not be achieved by material wealth.

- Global capitalism is squandering the 'capital represented by living nature'.
- The gigantism of mass production and industrialised agriculture based on modern technology is wreaking havoc on the natural world. It is also causing misery for humanity by creating unemployment, migration from local communities into gigantic cities, and work that is mind numbing and soul destroying.
- This mind-numbing work leads humanity to have a 'greater concern with goods than with people' and to an 'evil lack of compassion'.
- Replacing gigantism should be a move towards 'lots and lots of small autonomous units' which use local resources, skilled labour and appropriate technology, empowering people to produce high-quality products that satisfy 'simplified and reduced' needs, not our 'temptation for luxuries'.
- 'Technology must be the servant of man, not its master' – currently science and technology is used to further economic growth but it should be oriented to 'the organic, the gentle, the non-violent, the elegant and beautiful'.
- Schumacher criticised traditional economics, arguing 'there is more to life than GDP'. The gross domestic product measure sees economic growth as positive and links happiness to consumerism and materialism.
- In its place, Schumacher proposed 'Buddhist economics', which replaces the quantity of goods with quality, wants with simplified needs to make production sustainable, and dehumanised work with employment that is spiritually fulfilling.

Light green ecologism

Light green ecologism draws on the principles of ecology and holism to promote policies and practices that are in line with environmental protection. There are limits to growth, but it is possible within mainstream political ideas and capitalism to promote sustainable development. There are four main principles:

+ **Enlightened anthropocentrism.** This is based on the lessons of ecology that humanity is part of nature; poisoning nature in the end means nature will poison man. Therefore, nature needs to be protected in order to protect human societies.
+ **Weak sustainability.** The principle of getting richer 'slower and smarter'. It is possible to work within modern societies to 'green economic' growth so that it works with nature and not against it.
+ **Intergenerational equity.** This is expressed through the principle of sustainable development.
+ **Technocentric approach.** There is faith in the ability of science and technology both to 'green' economic growth and to resolve environmental issues.

> **Exam tip**
>
> Dark green ecologists tend to see light green ecologism as part of the problem, not part of the solution, as it is a form of denial about the real problems. Only a radical change in humanity's relationship with nature can bring the necessary change to avert ecological catastrophe. This can be used to show in your analysis the depth of the differences between dark and light green ecology.

There are a range of different light green approaches, supported by different elements of the light green movement:

+ **'The private is political'.** Individuals can become ethical consumers, 'green' their lifestyle and focus on non-material happiness. By using their purchasing power ethically, individuals can drive corporations to act in a more environmentally sensitive way.
+ **Green capitalism.** Corporations react to the market and will be forced to respond to ethical consumerism. In addition, the rising cost of natural resources will force corporations to find cheaper, more environmentally responsible alternatives in order to maintain their profits.
+ **Managerialism.** This approach utilises intervention at state and international level in the market to promote environmental regulations:
  + **International treaties** such as the Paris Agreement (2015), where 195 countries entered into a legally binding global deal to limit global warming well below 2°C above pre-industrial levels, with an aspirational target of less than 1.5°C and a long-term goal of net zero emissions, which would phase out fossil fuels.
  + **Individual states** can set their own binding targets. In 2008 the UK passed the Climate Change Act, which committed the UK government by law to reducing greenhouse gas emissions by at least 80% of 1990 levels by 2050.
  + **Policy approaches** include the use of green taxes or cap and trade schemes to reduce pollution or conserve natural resources. Further approaches can include options like plastic carrier bag charges and banning plastic straws.

> **Exam tip**
>
> As examples of the light green approach, you could use environmental pressure groups like Greenpeace and the Sierra Club, which focus on lifestyle choices, technological fixes and the ability of the state to manage the environment through regulation.

> **Exam tip**
>
> It is worth considering in your answers whether traditional economics and its fixation on GDP provide an accurate vision for progress. For greens, this fixation is all about quantity, not quality. It fails to factor in the human misery it has created in term of inequality and poverty, fails to measure the costs of environmental destruction and fails to measure how the benefits of growth are distributed.

> **Exam tip**
>
> As examples of 'the private is political', you can use consumers purchasing goods that have environmental stamps of approval, such as certification by the Rainforest Alliance or the Forest Stewardship Council, and boycotting companies and products that are environmentally damaging.

Green taxes Taxes placed on products or activities that are associated with environmental damage, to make them more expensive so that people buy or do fewer of them.

Cap and trade Large emitters such as power plants, refineries and factories buy permits for the greenhouse gases they release, allowing the government to cap emissions by limiting the number of permits. 'Trade' refers to a market where companies can buy and sell emissions allowances, giving them a strong incentive to cut emissions in order to save money.

Check your understanding and progress at www.hoddereducation.co.uk/myrevisionnotes

> **Exam tip**
>
> It is worth noting that there has been an emergence of green political parties such as Die Grünen in Germany, which has been electorally successful, and the Green Party in the UK, which has had less electoral impact. These parties tend to be based on light green thinking/environmentalism rather than dark green principles. At the same time, mainstream political parties in the UK have added green policies to their manifestos. The rise of green politics within liberal democracy means that many people think enough is already being done, and this limits the space for more radical dark green political ideas to gain a foothold.

Social ecology

+ Social ecology is inspired by the science of ecology and wants to transform the way humans see their place in nature and the relationship between humans and the Earth. It therefore has much in common with dark green ecology. Its prescription for the future society, based on the idea that humanity is one species among many on a changing planet, also has a lot of overlap with the dark green view.
+ However, there is a passionate and deep divide between social ecology and dark green ecology over the root cause of ecological problems. Social ecology has its origins in the idea that the ecological problems that society currently faces arise from deep-seated social problems. Therefore, ecological problems can only be understood and tackled by facing up to the problems within society.
+ Murray Bookchin summed this view up with his view that 'the domination of nature by man stems from the very real domination of human by human' (*The Ecology of Freedom*, 1982).
+ These problems need to be tackled by social movements and collective actions that tackle the source of ecological problems rather than by ethical consumerism and lifestyle choices or some sort of eco-spiritual revolution in terms of environmental consciousness, which is entirely unrealistic. Social ecology is also dismissive of the enlightened anthropocentric approach that still views nature in terms of its instrumental value.
+ Social ecology argues that light greens, by focusing on short-term fixes built on better technology, better planning or better lifestyle choices, ignore the root cause of environmental destruction, which lies in human-to-human relationships.

Social ecology divides into three further sub-strands: eco-anarchism, eco-socialism and eco-feminism.

> **Exam tip**
>
> Murray Bookchin, who shaped social ecology, saw dark green thinking as 'eco-la-la', as it is unrealistic in its expectation of an ethical/spiritual revolution in how people think and also misanthropic in seeing humanity as the problem. He was also critical of light greens, arguing that their enlightened anthropocentrism is just the domination of nature. Murray Bookchin can be used in the exam to show just how deeply he, and social ecology, disagree with both light and dark green thinking.

Eco-anarchism

+ Eco-anarchism argues that the idea that humanity must dominate nature has its origins in the domination of humans by humans. This has led humanity to become separated from its own true nature and from the natural world itself.
+ All forms of hierarchy, such as the domination of the young by the old, women by men, countryside by city and one ethnic group by another, must be challenged and overthrown. The rise of capitalism creates new forms of hierarchy and domination, reinforcing the idea that the only possible relationship between humanity and nature is one of domination.
+ Capitalism must 'grow or die' as its core elements are competition, capital accumulation and limitless growth. It must be replaced by an 'ecological society based on non-hierarchical relationships, decentralised democratic communities, and eco-technologies like solar power, organic agriculture, and humanly scaled industries' (Bookchin, *Remaking Society*, 1989).

> **Key thinker**
>
> **Murray Bookchin (1921–2006)**
>
> Murray Bookchin was a radical thinker who saw the domination of humans by humans as central to the destruction of nature, and who set out many of his ideas in his book, *Post-Scarcity Anarchism* (1971). The move to a democratic, co-operative, ecological society was central to a free society and the survival of humanity.
>
> + Social hierarchy and social domination are central to humans becoming estranged from their own true nature as well as non-human nature.
> + Bookchin developed social ecology, with the aim of replacing capitalism, the nation-state and other forms of domination with a rational, ecological and anarchist commune society based on co-operative and humane relations between humans and between humans and nature.
> + Capitalism's 'grow or die' imperative meant that persuading capitalism to 'green' and to limit growth was no more possible than persuading a human to stop breathing.
> + Modern technology had eliminated the need for 'toil', which would free up people to become 'citizens' who could reconstruct their worlds by participating in democratic self-government.
> + Bookchin developed the idea of 'libertarian municipalism', where self-governing assemblies practise face-to-face democracy based on the ideals taken from Ancient Greece.
> + Citizens' active participation in assembly democracy would lead to a moral and material transformation in human nature and society would become deliberative, rational, ethical and focused on co-operation.
> + Based on the principles of ecology and holism, municipalities would be interdependent, especially economically, and based on **communalism**; a 'commune of communes'.
> + Economic life is also 'municipalised' as it is placed under community ownership in the guise of the citizens' assemblies. Economic policies would be devised in the interests of the community as a whole, with technology used to meet basic needs and free humans from toil and drudgery. This would lead to a moral economy, not a market economy.
> + The ecological principles of limits and balance, rather than the capitalist principles of expansion and competition, would guide communities, with co-operation between people and nature the result.

Communalism A loose confederation of self-governing communes, where the confederation's purpose is administration between communes through committees formed of members from each commune. Decisions must be approved in all communes as power comes from the bottom up.

Eco-socialism

+ The dominant ideology of capitalism includes climate-change deniers and those who acknowledge there is a problem but turn to market or technological fixes. Both positions are really just a defence of the economic arrangements that benefit the few.
+ John Bellamy Foster argues that capitalism is 'a system of unsustainable development' and goes back to the writings of Karl Marx (see p. XX). Land was turned into private property and became seen as merely a means for the accumulation of profit. Capitalism is based on an unquenchable thirst for profit, so systematically exploits 'the original sources of all wealth – the soil and the worker' (Marx, *Das Kapital*, 1867).
+ This creates a growing environmental proletariat, working in inhumane conditions and directly in line to face the worst consequences of the impending ecological disasters, such as rising sea levels. This proletariat, mainly based in the global South, will rise in revolution to overthrow capitalism and existing human–nature relations to create a sustainable, equitable society. This eco-socialist society, according to John Bellamy Foster, will be based on the social use, not ownership, of nature, the satisfaction of communal needs and the regulation of human–nature relations by those who work with nature.

> **Exam tip**
>
> One clear example that you could use in your answers about the impact of social ecology is the Rojava revolution. The ideals of social ecology, and Bookchin in particular, have had a huge influence on the Rojava revolution, which started in 2012 when the Kurdish-inhabited areas of Syria declared their autonomy from the central government. The revolution has been looking to build a grassroots, gender-equal and ecological society in these areas.

Check your understanding and progress at www.hoddereducation.co.uk/myrevisionnotes

> **Exam tip**
>
> It is worth noting that, while everyone on the planet feels the impact of climate change, the impacts are not evenly distributed. Three out of four people living in poverty rely on agriculture and natural resources and are the most vulnerable to the impacts of climate change. In 2022, around one third of Pakistan was underwater after historic floods which caused loss of life, destruction of villages and the loss of huge swathes of agricultural land, leaving the country with an estimated build-back cost of over £10.5 billion.

Eco-feminism

+ Eco-feminism links the exploitation of nature with the oppression of women. It challenges the idea that men are identified with culture, reason and science, and so are superior to women who are identified with nature.
+ The Scientific Revolution is built on the idea that nature is female but should be viewed like a machine, not a living organism, and needs to be interrogated and 'her' secrets extracted. This domination of nature by men of science is also the domination of women (patriarchy).
+ At the same time, women are made inferior as they are closer to nature and so further away from reason. Patriarchy needs to be overthrown and a new relationship with nature put in place, built on partnership and not domination.

> **Key thinker**
>
> **Carolyn Merchant (1936–)**
>
> Carolyn Merchant developed a form of socialist eco-feminism which is clearly articulated in her book, *The Death of Nature* (1980).
>
> + Before the Enlightenment and Scientific Revolution, 'the female earth was central to organic cosmology ... [and] the root metaphor binding together the self, society and the cosmos was that of an organism'. This mothering image of the Earth helped to restrain the destruction of the natural world.
> + During the rise of early capitalism, women were being removed from the sphere of production while at the same time losing control over their own bodies in the sphere of reproduction.
> + Women were forced into the role of the reproduction of labour by birthing the new generation of workers and domestic labour.
> + At the same time, the Scientific Revolution, led by Francis Bacon, was arguing that nature should have 'her' secrets wrested from her 'womb' by science and technology.
> + The domination of man over woman is central to the domination of science, technology and capitalist production over nature.
> + The mechanistic world view of the Scientific Revolution was seen as a marker of progress but is implicated in the creation of ecological crises.
> + The domination of man over woman needs to be overthrown.
> + Nature should no longer be gendered or dominated and there should be 'an ethic of partnership with nature in which nature was no longer symbolised as mother, virgin, or witch but instead as an active partner with humanity'.

> **Revision activities**
>
> 1 Outline what the ecological society looks like to eco-anarchists, eco-socialists and eco-feminists.
> 2 Create a spider diagram detailing key quotes from Carson, Leopold, Schumacher, Bookchin and Merchant. Write your explanation of what the quotes mean underneath.

> **Now test yourself** TESTED
>
> 4 What similarities are apparent between Bookchin and dark green thinking?
> 5 Should Leopold and Carson be considered as informing light or dark green thinking?
> 6 On what grounds does Bookchin criticise dark green thinking?
> 7 Copy and complete the following table to show the differences between dark green and light green thinking.
>
> | Dark green | Light green |
> | --- | --- |
> | Radical holism | |
> | Strong sustainability | |
> | | Intergenerational equity |
> | | Enlightened anthropocentrism |
> | | Moderate and reformist |

> **Key thinkers in context**
>
> **Rachel Carson**
> + Carson's book *Silent Spring* (1962) brought the issue of pesticide use, especially DDT, to a wide audience and popularised modern ecology. It is credited as the inspiration for the environmental movement, with both Greenpeace and Friends of the Earth established within ten years of its publication. The book was a bestseller, caught the attention of President Kennedy and set the groundwork for the establishment of the Environmental Protection Agency in the USA in 1970.
> + On the flip side, the book and Carson attracted widespread criticism from the chemical industry, which was the first sign that the environment would become a deeply contentious political issue.
>
> **Aldo Leopold**
> + Leopold was an American conservationist, forester and wildlife ecologist who was deeply worried about the impact of industrialisation on the land.
> + He believed economists had no meaningful way of conserving the wilderness or the health of the land. He developed the land ethic in his book *The Sand County Almanac* (1949), as a new tool for creating harmony between humanity and the land.
>
> **E. F. Schumacher**
> + Schumacher's book *Small is Beautiful* (1973) was an attack on conventional economic thinking, its fixation with growth and its value system.
> + He wanted to replace this with Buddhist economics that would disarm greed and envy, and replace them with a socially and environmentally just way of living.
>
> **Murray Bookchin**
> + Bookchin was a social ecologist and radical political thinker, who produced three significant books, *Post-Scarcity Anarchism* (1971), *Toward an Ecological Society* (1980) and *Ecology of Freedom* (1982), among others.
> + Bookchin developed a critique of hierarchy and capitalism, as well as a view of what an ecological society would look like.
>
> **Carolyn Merchant**
> + Merchant developed eco-feminist thought in her book *The Death of Nature* (1980). Her critique of the mechanistic world view of the Scientific Revolution showed that the way science and capitalism treats nature is related to their treatment of women.
> + This patriarchal and mechanistic world view needs overthrowing to generate healthier and more just relations between humans and between humans and nature.

Core ideas of ecologism

REVISED

Human nature

Ecologism opposes the anthropocentric view that humans are above and outside of nature and may exploit it for their own purpose. The agreements and tensions between the different strands are shown in Table 8.2.

Table 8.2 Tensions and agreements within ecologism over human nature

Dark greens	Light greens	Social ecology
+ Oppose all forms of anthropocentrism and propose ecocentrism, where nature has value in its own right, independent of its value to humanity. + Ecocentrism presupposes a radical transformation in human nature to identify deeply with non-human nature. + This could be achieved by arriving at an environmental consciousness through self-realisation (Næss) or by radically transforming our ethical outlook to one of biocentric equality, based on the 'land ethic' (Leopold).	+ Using the lessons of ecology, Rachel Carson argued that if humanity destroys nature then nature will end up destroying humanity. + Enlightened anthropocentrism, where humanity changes its view to see itself as part of nature and its role as the steward of nature. + The protection of nature is based on nature's instrumental value to humanity. Protecting nature is about protecting human life now and in the future.	+ Opposes both anthropocentrism and ecocentrism. + Anthropocentrism is the domination of nature, whereas ecocentrism places humanity and the non-human world on the same ethical footing. This misanthropic logic leads to the smallpox virus and humanity being worthy of equal moral consideration (Bookchin). + The end of the domination of humans by humans can lead to a society where humanity can rediscover its true nature and relationship with non-human nature.

The state

The disagreements within ecologism over the role of the state in tackling environmental problems are very marked, as shown in Table 8.3.

Table 8.3 Tensions and agreements within ecologism over the state

Dark greens	Light greens	Social ecology
+ The state is part of the problem, not part of the solution, as it is tied into industrialism and the mechanistic world view. Dark greens therefore offer a radical challenge to the existing territorial state. + Power should be decentralised to local communities based on bioregions, which manage themselves using direct democracy. + Decisions taken within these living democracies will be environmentally and socially just, as they will value both people and nature. + Much of the dark green approach to the future of the state overlaps with social ecology.	+ Light greens take two different approaches to how the state should promote the sustainable management of resources. + Either: the state should play a managerial role by negotiating international agreements to protect the environment and intervening in the market at home to cap and reduce emissions and the depletion of natural resources. + Or: the state should leave environmental protection to the market. Green capitalism will naturally drive an emphasis on environmental behaviour through green consumerism and the rising costs of natural resources. This will lead to corporate responsibility and corporate research and development of green technologies.	+ Social ecology, like dark green thinking, is radically opposed to the existing state, although for different reasons. For social ecology, the existing state is an expression of domination of humans by humans. + Eco-anarchism is perhaps the most closely linked to dark green thinking, with its emphasis on decentralisation. It favours a 'commune of communes', based on the principle of assembly democracy (Bookchin). + Eco-socialism views the state as a committee for the ruling class that needs to be overthrown and replaced by communism (Foster). + Eco-feminism is radically opposed to patriarchy, embedded in both the state and society. The new ordering of the state and society will be based on equality and partnership between humans and between humans and nature (Merchant).

Society

Ecologism is critical of the following key ideological positions held by society, as shown in Table 8.4:

+ Consumerism and materialism, which see the consumption of goods as the end goal of society and which link material wealth to human happiness. This view was strongly criticised by E. F. Schumacher.
+ Reductionism and the mechanistic world view, which view nature as machines with parts that can be studied in isolation, repaired or even replaced. This drives the view that humanity can dominate nature and fix environmental problems in isolation. Both Carson and Merchant provided strong criticisms of this position.
+ Conventional ethics that focus *only* on relations between living people.

> **Exam tip**
>
> It is worth considering whether the Green Party in either the USA or the UK can really advocate a dark green approach, based on de-growth and a steady-state economy, and win votes in national elections.

Table 8.4 Tensions and agreements within ecologism over society

Dark greens	Light greens	Social ecology
+ The lessons of ecology suggest a radical holism, which breaks cleanly with consumerism and materialism, the mechanistic world view and conventional ethics. + A holistic ethic, such as the 'land ethic' (Leopold) and/or a radical transformation to an environmental consciousness (Næss) would form the basis of the new society. + A new society should be created where happiness and fulfilment are found not in material wealth but in creative work, community and closeness to nature (Schumacher). + The method of transformation is based on individuals undergoing a spiritual revolution and an appeal to reason and evidence.	+ The lessons of ecology suggest a form of limited holism that sees the interdependence of nature and that humanity should work within the limits of the Earth (Carson). + This proposes a change in societal attitudes to the idea of getting richer but 'slower and smarter'. + Society must move beyond traditional ethics to the principle of intergenerational equity. + Some green thinkers have proposed a more radical extension of rights to animals. + Peter Singer, in his work *Animal Liberation* (1975), proposes the idea that animals are sentient, so experience both pain and pleasure like humans, and so should be accorded the same rights as humans. + This would make 'speciesism' (discrimination on the basis of species) a form of discrimination in the same way as sexism and racism.	+ Social domination through the creation of hierarchy within society is the root cause of environmental destruction (Bookchin). + Hierarchies based on wealth, gender, age and race promote the domination of humans by humans and the domination of nature by humanity. + The removal of these societal structures is central to create more equitable societies, which will promote a fulfilling life based on partnership between humans and between humans and nature (Merchant). + The method of transformation here is a revolutionary overthrow of all existing hierarchies to allow the new world to be built.

> **Exam tip**
>
> Don't mix up the idea of animal rights, as argued for by Singer, with the less radical concepts of animal protection and animal welfare.

The economy

Ecologism starts from the basis that there are limits to growth, so there need to be changes in patterns of production and consumption, as shown in Table 8.5.

Table 8.5 Tensions and agreements within ecologism over the economy

Dark greens and social ecology	Light greens
+ Dark greens and social ecology are both opposed to capitalism; as the limitless exploitation of resources is impossible, production is also destruction. Total recycling is impossible and increasing GDP does not increase happiness. + Central to this view is the idea of a steady-state economy (Daly). + Underpinning capitalism is the mechanistic world view, which is opposed by dark greens and social ecology: in particular, this criticism is strongly made by Merchant. + Both social ecology and deep greens propose a form of strong sustainability. + Taking the ideas of Schumacher and Bookchin, the economy should be based on small-scale production for use, using local resources and local skills. + All should work fewer hours doing creative, fulfilling work and work should be shared equitably among society. + This will create an emphasis on working with nature and within the limits of local ecosystems. The result will be an existence far richer in spiritual wealth. + Both eco-anarchists and eco-socialists go further by arguing for the abolition of private property and replacing it with common ownership.	+ Weak sustainability; the 'greening' of economic growth to reduce pollution and the depletion of natural resources. + The sustainable management of resources to operate within the limits of ecology (Carson). + This approach is possible within capitalism – the idea of the sustainable management of resources proposed by Carson. + Light greens agree that protecting the environment can be a lifestyle choice and that technology can play a key role in minimising environmental impacts. + However, light greens differ in their approach, with some proposing green capitalism, where the market will 'green' the economy through corporations' desire for profit. Corporations will react to ethical consumerism and the rising price of natural resources to produce goods in a more environmentally friendly way. + Some light greens propose a managerialist approach to the economy, which involves state intervention in the form of green taxes or cap and trade schemes to promote sustainability.

Revision activity

Outline the following different approaches to traditional ethical/moral thinking:
+ intergenerational equity
+ animal rights
+ biocentric equality/the 'land ethic'
+ environmental consciousness.

Key debates within ecologism

REVISED

Ecologism springs from the acceptance of the lessons of ecology, some form of holism and that there are finite limits to natural resources. However, how these lessons are put into practice is the source of much controversy within ecologism.

Radical versus limited holism

Dark greens favour radical holism, which has a deep understanding of the interconnectedness of everything and sees humanity as a plain member and citizen of the natural world. Light greens favour limited holism, where humans recognise the interdependence of the world and the importance of nature to sustaining human life, and where humanity is the steward of nature.

Mechanistic world view versus holism

Dark greens and social ecology both advocate the overthrow of the mechanistic world view and its replacement by holism. Light greens' limited holism and technocentric approach mean they believe that individual ecological problems can be tackled in isolation from each other without a radical overhaul of existing societal views.

Enlightened anthropocentrism versus ecocentrism

+ Dark greens, social ecology and light greens agree that humanity has been cut adrift from nature.
+ Light greens endorse an enlightened anthropocentric approach, whereas dark greens support a radical transformation to ecocentrism, based on either the principle of biocentric equality or a spiritual revolution to achieve environmental consciousness.
+ Social ecology favours neither, seeing the issue as social relations; the domination of humans by humans, which leads to the domination of nature by humanity.

Weak versus strong sustainability

Light greens favour weak sustainability, which can be achieved within capitalism, whereas dark greens and social ecology favour strong sustainability and the overthrow of capitalism.

Radicalism versus reformism

Light greens believe that ecological issues can be solved without a fundamental change in society's present values or patterns of consumption and production. Both dark green thinking and social ecology favour a radical change in our relationship with nature and in our social, political and economic structures.

Technology

Light greens adopt a technocentric approach, whereas social ecology and dark green thinking agree that technology can be a part of the solution but not the whole solution. There needs to be a radical shift in values and social, political and economic structures.

> **Revision activity**
>
> Create a set of flashcards for all the key terms in this chapter.

> **Now test yourself** TESTED
>
> 8 Why can dark green thinking and social ecology be seen as radical and revolutionary?
> 9 Why can light green thinking be seen as moderate and reformist?
> 10 How would dark and light greens approach the depletion of fossil fuels like coal, gas and oil to satisfy growing energy demands?
> 11 Copy and complete the following table with the main ideas of the key thinkers.
>
> | Thinker | Human nature | The state | Society | The economy |
> |---|---|---|---|---|
> | Rachel Carson | | | | |
> | Aldo Leopold | | | | |
> | E. F. Schumacher | | | | |
> | Murray Bookchin | | | | |
> | Carolyn Merchant | | | | |

Exam practice

1 'Anthropocentrism is incompatible with ecologism.' Analyse and evaluate this statement with reference to the ecologist thinkers that you have studied. In your answer, you should draw on material from across the whole range of your course of study in politics. [25]

2 'The protection of the environment cannot be achieved in a capitalist economy.' Analyse and evaluate this statement with reference to the ecologist thinkers that you have studied. In your answer, you should draw on material from across the whole range of your course of study in politics. [25]

Summary

You should now have an understanding of:
+ the debate within ecologism over anthropocentrism and ecocentrism
+ the key divisions within ecologism between the different strands – dark greens, light greens and social ecology – and within the different strands
+ the debate over sustainability between weak and strong sustainability
+ the contributions of the five key thinkers (Carson, Leopold, Schumacher, Bookchin and Merchant) to ecologism in the areas of human nature, the state, society and the economy

Glossary

Term	Definition	Page
Chapter 1: Liberalism		
Absolute monarchy	When the monarch exercises arbitrary (unlimited) power over the people as God's representative on Earth. The concept of the 'divine right of kings' embodies this notion of royal absolutism.	10
Authority	The legitimate right to exercise power.	12
Constitutionalism	The government must be legally limited in its powers by a constitution in order to protect freedom. This links in with the concept of the 'rule of law'.	12
Collectivism	The idea that the collective rather than the individual is the main economic, social and political unit.	18
Difference principle	Economic inequality is permissible if there is equality of opportunity, and the inequalities in society are only justifiable if they are to the greatest benefit of the least well-off.	17
Developmental individualism	Focuses on personal growth and flourishing rather than just self-satisfaction, emphasising what the individual can become rather than what they are.	14
Discrimination	The differential treatment of groups or individuals, such as women, usually without any real justification for doing this based on the differences between them (between men and women).	15
Divine right of kings	The idea that a monarch is not subject to earthly authority but instead gains the right to rule directly from God.	13
Egotistical individualism	Humans naturally seek to advance their own happiness and interests. This selfish approach involves self-restraint and co-operation as the individual wants to have their rights respected, so in turn must respect the rights of others.	11
Enlightenment	An intellectual movement that opposed the medieval politics and philosophy of faith, superstition and religion.	10
Equality of opportunity	The concept that all individuals have equal life chances, so inequalities generated by society must be tackled. If there is equality of opportunity, inequalities which result from differences in ability, creativity and hard work are acceptable.	15
Fiduciary power	The state holds its power in trust and must act in the interests of and for the benefit of the people, otherwise the social contract is invalid.	12
Formal equality	Equality under the law, as well as the principle that every individual is entitled to equal treatment in society.	12
Foundational equality	All humans are born morally equal and so are deserving of equal natural rights, which are enshrined in law as legal and political rights.	17
Harm principle	John Stuart Mill argued that the government can only rightfully extend its power over the individual to prevent actions or beliefs that bring harm to others. It cannot extend its power over the individual in relation to self-regarding actions to protect the individual's own good. For example, it is right to stop person A destroying the property of person B, but wrong to stop person A from destroying their own property.	11
Hedonism	Happiness is the ultimate good and can be measured as pleasure and the absence of pain. This idea is based on the quantity of pleasure rather than the quality.	13
Individualism	The individual is of the utmost importance and is placed above the collective.	12
Individuality	The uniqueness of each individual.	13
Meritocracy	Social position and economic reward are based on talent and hard work. Where there is equality of opportunity, there is an incentive to work hard and realise your talent, ensuring everyone gets what they deserve and that society is led by the most talented.	20
Negative freedom	A concept of liberty or freedom that sees it as meaning an absence of constraint, described by the liberal thinker Isaiah Berlin as 'freedom from' rather than 'freedom to'.	11

Check your understanding and progress at www.hoddereducation.co.uk/myrevisionnotes

Republicanism	A republic is a political system without a monarch and emphasises citizens taking an active role in public and political life.	13
Positive discrimination	State intervention to give preferential treatment to particular groups in society to tackle historical discrimination and inequalities in society. Affirmative action in the USA is an example of positive discrimination.	15
Positive freedom	Isaiah Berlin defined it as 'freedom to' rather than 'freedom from'. The individual is free to develop, flourish and pursue their own version of the good life.	14
Social contract	There is a contract between the individual and the government, where the individual agrees with the state to obey its laws and, in return, the state improves their life. The state is invalid *either* if there is no consent *or* if it fails to improve the individual's situation.	12
State	A body that is sovereign within a defined territorial area, with a legitimate monopoly of the use of force.	10
State of nature	A concept used by political thinkers such as Locke and Hobbes to describe the hypothetical original characteristics of humankind and how people related to each other in a time before states and organised governments.	12
Toleration	The virtue of not using one's power to interfere with another's opinion or action over something morally important and where you morally disapprove of that opinion or action.	20
Tolerant society	A society that is willing to accept a wide range of moral values, lifestyles, faiths and beliefs in society.	10
Tradition	A form of knowledge passed down through the generations as customs and habits that enable us to know what to do in order to achieve a task successfully and so provide security and stability in an uncertain world.	13
Welfare state	The provision of education, health, housing and social security (e.g. pensions and benefits) by the state.	15
Chapter 2: Conservatism		
Anti-permissive	A rejection of permissiveness, which is the liberal belief that people should make their own moral choices (e.g. about abortion, marriage and relationships), stemming from the 1960s. The state should impose social order and public morality by promoting traditional values and tough law and order policies.	32
Atomism	The concept that society, if indeed it exists, is a collection of individuals pursuing their own individual lives and being responsible for themselves. Collective identities, like class, are meaningless.	33
Change to conserve	Conservatives oppose radical social change as they view society as an organic, complex whole. Long-established institutions and practices, such as the monarchy and parliamentary sovereignty, reflect the accumulated wisdom of the past and so are tried and tested. Change should be incremental, building on what works in order to conserve what is valuable.	26
Empiricism	Politics should be based on what works most effectively, not on abstract principles or ideas. This idea emerges from the politics of imperfection, as human are limited in what they are able to know and understand about the world.	29
Hierarchy	Human nature and society are naturally divided by wealth, status and power. For conservatives, there is a natural ruling class with the necessary wealth and authority to govern, while the masses should naturally obey the elite that is governing in their best interest.	26
Objectivism	Rand's philosophy based on the principles of reason, self-interest and capitalism, which she claims will deliver freedom, justice, progress and human happiness. It is set against statism or collectivism, where people's life and work belong to the state, which she argues leads to 'slavery, brute force, stagnant terror and sacrificial furnaces'.	32
Organic society	Society is a natural, complex body like a tree. It develops and grows slowly, needs constant nurturing and pruning to ensure its health, and should not be uprooted and replaced with something new through radical change/revolution.	26
Statism	A political system where the state has a large degree of control over social and economic affairs.	32

Chapter 3: Socialism		
Bourgeoisie	The Marxist term for the class that owns the means of production in capitalism.	42
Class consciousness	Workers first become conscious of sharing common complaints against capitalism (a class 'in itself') and then develop an awareness of themselves as forming a social class, the proletariat (a class 'for itself'), opposed to the bourgeoisie.	43
Collective action	Working together in order to achieve mutual benefit, as co-operation is both more effective than, and morally superior to, individual competition.	41
Common ownership	The means of production are placed in the hands of the workers, so that they can control their working lives and the economy as a whole.	43
Communism	A classless society, with no state and the common ownership of wealth. Production would be for necessary consumption and use, and to satisfy need rather than profit, freeing humans' creative energies and allowing full freedom for all.	43
Democratic socialists	Those who believe that socialism should be pursued by democratic means, where the electorate is persuaded of the moral superiority of socialism in a state with representative institutions.	45
Dictatorship of the proletariat	The transitional phase from capitalism to communism, where the workers' state protects the gains of the revolution and replaces private ownership with common ownership.	43
Evolutionary/reformist socialism	Socialism delivered by the ballot box and legal, piecemeal reforms. It rejects the revolutionary road to socialism.	45
Fraternity	The uniting of all humanity in bonds of affection on the basis of common humanity.	51
Historical materialism	Marx's view of historical change is based on the idea that changes in the way humans work together to produce things then change the way society is organised and the attitude of people in that society.	42
Keynesian economics	The use of taxation and spending policies to create full employment and continuous economic growth.	47
Proletariat	The Marxist term for the class in capitalism that has to sell its labour to the bourgeoisie in order to survive, as it has no ownership over the means of production.	42
Scientific socialism	A scientific analysis of the economic development of society that reveals the division of society into distinct classes locked into struggle with each other. This struggle is the motor of history, meaning it is inevitable that socialism will replace capitalism.	41
Social democrats	Those who believe in philosophical and practical attempts to blend democracy, capitalism and social justice.	47
Social equality	An equal distribution of wealth, income and status within society.	41
Utopian socialists	Those who adhere to the blueprint for an ideal, future socialist society, or Utopia, to illustrate how life will be better under socialism.	41
Utopianism	The belief in the ideal or perfect society, Utopia.	107
Chapter 4: Nationalism		
Chauvinistic nationalism	An irrational dedication to a particular group or community based on the idea that it is superior.	65
Cultural nationalism	This focuses on protecting a nation's unique culture rather than on the importance of self-determination. The state is there to support the nation, not the nation to support the state.	63
Culture	The values, beliefs and customs that are passed down the generations through learning.	59
Ethnic nationalism	Nationalism driven by the idea that there is a loyalty to a distinctive population, territorial area or cultural group where the group is believed (rightly or not) to have common ancestors.	65
Ethnies	Historical entities bound by shared beliefs and commitments, shared memories and the perception that their culture is different from and distinctive to others.	58
General will	Human society is a collective individual and the general will comes from all and applies to all. This ensures liberty and equality while also helping to develop a sense of fraternity.	57
Imperialist	Relating to the extension of power through conquest, to establish political and economic control over another country.	57

Check your understanding and progress at www.hoddereducation.co.uk/myrevisionnotes

Term	Definition	Page
'Melting pot'	A diverse society becoming more homogeneous as the diverse elements 'melt together' into a unified whole with a common culture.	60
Militarism	The idea that a nation-state should keep a strong military capability and be prepared to use it aggressively to defend or promote national interests.	65
Multiculturalism	State-led policies to balance diversity and unity by creating political unity through recognising the rights of different cultural groups to respect and recognition.	62
National autonomy	The right to self-government.	57
National identity	Individuals identify with the distinctive heritage and culture of their community, recognising it as distinct from other nations.	57
Neo-colonialism	Where the state *appears* sovereign, but its economic and political policies are directed from outside by multinational companies and international organisations like the World Bank and Western countries like the USA.	64
Political nationalism	Where the nation is the natural political community and has the right to govern itself.	59
Popular sovereignty	No law or rule can be legitimate unless it comes directly (direct democracy) or indirectly (representative democracy) from the consent of the individuals concerned.	59
Protectionist economic policies	Shielding the domestic industries of a country by imposing taxes on imports.	62
Sovereignty	The principle of unrestricted power.	60
Chapter 5: Feminism		
Affirmative action	Policies to improve opportunities for historically excluded or under-represented groups in education through admissions and employment policies.	73
Androcentric	Placing men or the masculine view at the centre of perspectives on the world.	73
Androgynous	The characteristics of male and female in the same person, revealing that differences between men and women are so slight that they should have no impact on their political, social or economic role.	80
Cultural feminism	A new form of culture could be developed based on feminine traits that women possess, but which are devalued by patriarchy. Strong cultural feminism argues that women have essential traits that are peaceful, nurturing and intuitive.	77
Difference feminists	Those who believe that women are essentially different from men biologically and psychologically. These differences matter.	76
Equality feminists	Those who believe that the goal of feminism is to achieve equality between the sexes by freeing women from difference. Liberal, radical, socialist and postmodern feminists all have different visions of how this will be achieved.	76
Existentialism	Humans have no nature, or essence, and use their freedom to make themselves through their own actions.	75
Intersectionality	The idea that women experience oppression in varying configurations and in varying degrees of intensity based on the intersection between different forms of oppression such as race, gender and class.	79
Patriarchy	A whole network of systems of control, which systematically allow men to dominate and exploit women.	74
Private sphere	The opposite of the public sphere; the family, the home and the body where individuals have freedom largely unregulated by the state.	74
Public sphere	Typically seen as the world of politics, culture and industry, where public values, ideals and goals of society are formed.	72
Reform Darwinism	The concept that humans are not helpless in the face of evolution; through their actions, they can shape and control it.	73
Reproductive labour	Unpaid labour performed by women in the home, such as cooking, washing clothes and bearing/raising children. This unpaid labour produces the workers of the future and ensures the current workers are fit and able to work.	74
Separatist feminism	Believes that political and sexual inequalities between men and women cannot be resolved and so opposes heterosexual relationships of any kind. It focuses on women working together, living together and engaging in relationships with each other to achieve their goals.	77

Glossary

Chapter 6: Multiculturalism		
Anti-discrimination law	Any law concerning the right of people to be treated equally, such as the UK's Equality Act (2010).	90
Assimilation	The process where immigrant groups become as much like the majority as possible, by adopting the lifestyles, values and beliefs of the majority culture. This approach is seen as problematic by multiculturalism.	87
Autonomy	A combination of freedom and responsibility, where the individual is free to make their own choices and is responsible for those choices.	90
Civic nationalism	The nation is seen as a community of equal, rights-bearing citizens, united in their attachment to a shared set of political practices and values (e.g. democracy, rights and justice).	90
Communitarian	This relates to an idea which stresses the connection between the individual and the community.	88
Hybridisation	The process of social and cultural mixing that creates multiple, fluid identities.	96
Identity	A person's sense of who they are and what is important about them as a human.	88
Identity politics	A form of politics that embraces and celebrates a positive sense of collective identity (e.g. race, religion, culture or gender) and seeks public recognition of that identity.	87
Liberal universalism	The idea that liberal values apply to all individuals, societies and cultures, irrespective of the differences between them.	94
Misrecognition	Stereotyping, racism or stigmatisation.	89
Non-recognition	The failure to recognise the existence of a culture or cultural identity.	89
Chapter 7: Anarchy		
Altruistic	Relating to the part of human nature that leads individuals to care for others and act in others' interests rather than their own.	108
Authority	The legitimate right to exercise power.	105
Capitalism	A system whereby wealth in the form of money or assets, such as the means of production, is owned privately by an individual or corporation.	103
Collectivism	The idea that the collective rather than the individual is the main economic, social and political unit.	104
Communes	Associations where the members own everything in common, including the fruits of the individual's labour.	111
Ego	The concept of the individual based on the idea that life should only be lived in the interest of the self rather than in the interest of others.	108
Egoistical	Humans are self-interested and self-reliant.	104
Federations	Unions of free, self-governing, spontaneously formed bodies of people on the basis of equality.	109
Freedom	For anarchists, this means being free from restraint to do as one as one likes and to fulfil one's dreams and potential. This freedom is only real when it is real for all.	104
Individualism	The belief in the importance of the individual over the collective within political thought, which is central to liberalism, and also that the individual exists prior to society.	103
Mutualism	A system of voluntary association for the free and fair exchange of goods and services at cost (i.e. without profit).	109
Utopianism	The belief in the ideal or perfect society, Utopia.	107
Power	The ability of one person to influence the actions of others, where that action goes against their own judgement.	105
The state	Anarchists accept Max Weber's definition of the state as a body which claims the monopoly over the legitimate use of a force within a given territory.	103
Solidarity	Bakunin described the single law of solidarity as 'No person can recognise or realise his or her own humanity except by recognising it in others and so co-operating for its realisation by each and all.'	104
Syndicalism	The practice of workers organising into unions to fight for their interests by taking direct action.	111

Check your understanding and progress at www.hoddereducation.co.uk/myrevisionnotes

	Chapter 8: Ecologism	
Biosphere	Made up of all the parts of Earth where life exists: the ground, the air and the water.	120
Cap and trade	Large emitters such as power plants, refineries and factories buy permits for the greenhouse gases they release, allowing the government to cap emissions by limiting the number of permits. 'Trade' refers to a market where companies can buy and sell emissions allowances, giving them a strong incentive to cut emissions in order to save money.	124
Communalism	A loose confederation of self-governing communes, where the confederation's purpose is administration between communes through committees formed of members from each commune. Decisions must be approved in all communes as power comes from the bottom up.	126
Consumerism	The idea that the consumption and acquisition of material goods is the principal goal of human existence. Through material goods we will achieve happiness and social status.	121
Dark green	The view that there needs to be a radical change in our relationship to non-human nature and in our political, social and economic approaches, in order for humanity to have a rewarding and sustainable existence.	119
Ecology	The scientific study of plants and animals in relation to their environment, with a focus on the interdependence and interrelationships that support different forms of life.	118
Gigantism	The growth of huge, greedy, global corporations that mass produce goods in vast numbers in huge factories, creating dehumanising work. The term also refers to the growth of massive cities that separate people from each other and nature.	123
Green taxes	Taxes placed on products or activities that are associated with environmental damage, to make them more expensive so that people buy or do fewer of them.	124
Holism	Nature is a system of relationships and ecosystems and not a collection of particles or fragments that exist in isolation from each other.	119
Industrialism	Large-scale production, faith in technology and a belief in limitless growth to satisfy material needs and consumer desires based on an anthropocentric world view.	120
Intergenerational equity	The present generation must not compromise the ability of future generations to meet their needs.	119
Intrinsic value	According to Næss, this is 'the value of non-human life forms' which is 'independent on the usefulness these may have for narrow human purposes'.	121
Light green	The view that environmental problems can be managed and solved without fundamental changes in society's values or economic approach.	119
Materialism	Considering material possessions and the social image that they project as more important than spiritual values.	121
Mechanistic world view	This redefines nature as a machine, composed of independent parts, rather than a living organism.	119
Reductionism	Study of the independent parts rather than the whole (e.g. the world is like a clockwork machine that can be understood by taking it apart and looking at its component parts).	119
Steady-state economy	Herman Daly defines this as 'constant stocks of people and physical wealth, maintained at some chosen, desirable level by a low rate of output'.	121
Sustainable development	Development that meets the needs of the present without compromising the ability of future generations to meet their own needs.	120
Sustainability	The ability of a system, such as the Earth, to maintain its health over time.	120

Index

A
absolute monarchy 10
affirmative action 73
altruism 108
American Declaration of
    Independence 1776 10
American Revolution 1775–83 29
anarchism
    collectivist 106, 108–10
    and communism 111
    and the economy 114–15
    and human nature 104, 112
    individualist 107–8
    mutualism 109–10
    origins 103–4
    and society 114
    and the state 105–6, 112–13
anarcho-capitalism 108
anarcho-communism 111
anarcho-syndicalism 111
anarchy 103
androcentric culture 73
anthropocentrism 118–19, 124, 132
anti-colonial nationalism 63–4
anti-permissive society 32
assimilation 87–8
atomism 33
Attfield, R. 122
Attlee, C. 46, 47
authority 12, 105–6
autonomy 90, 91, 104

B
Bacon, F. 119
Bakunin, M. 103–4, 106, 110–15
Berlin, I. 14, 93, 97, 99
biocentric egalitarianism 122
bioregionalism 123
biosphere 120
Black Lives Matter 87
black nationalism 64
Black Power movement 89
Blair, T. 46, 50
Bookchin, M. 125–6, 128–30
bourgeoisie 42–3, 74
Burke, E. 26, 29–30, 34, 35–7

C
Cameron, D. 96, 101
cap and trade schemes 124
capitalism 11, 20, 31, 37, 41–3, 46–8,
    53–4, 103, 125, 127
    see also free-market capitalism
Carson, R. 118, 120, 128, 130–1
Casey, L. 89, 101
chauvinistic nationalism 65
civic nationalism 58, 60, 90

Civil Rights Act (1964) 73, 81
class consciousness 43
classical liberalism 11–13, 72
class structures 42–4, 48
climate change 126–7
climate-change deniers 126
coercion 105–6
collective action 41
collectivism 18, 32, 42, 104, 110
colonialism 63–5
Colston, E. 64
common good 16
common ownership 43, 46–7
communalism 126
communes 111, 126
communism 43, 54, 111
conservatism
    change to conserve 26, 29, 30
    and the economy 31, 34, 37–9
    and human nature 26–7, 30, 33,
        35–6, 38
    ideology 28
    neo-conservatism 32
    New Right 28, 31–3, 37–9
    one-nation 30–1
    origins 26
    and society 30, 32, 36–7, 38
    and the state 32–3, 34, 36, 38
    traditional 28–30, 38–9
Conservative Party 28
constitutionalism 12, 21
consumerism 121
cosmopolitanism 66
Crenshaw, K. 78–9
Crosland, A. 47, 48, 50–4
culture
    androcentric 73
    and feminism 76–7
    and identity 88–9
    and language 89
    and nationalism 59, 63, 68
    politics of recognition 89
    see also multiculturalism

D
dark green ecologism 119, 121–3,
    129–32
Darwin, C. 65
d'Azeglio, M. 60
de Beauvoir, S. 75, 80–1, 83–4
democracy 14, 90, 123
democratic socialists 45
developmental individualism 14
difference feminism 76–7, 84
difference principle 17
direct action 109
discrimination 15, 90
    positive 15, 73
    against women 72–3

Disraeli, B. 30
diversity 90, 94–5, 99, 123
divine right of kings 13

E
eco-anarchism 125
ecocentrism 119, 121–2, 132
eco-feminism 127
ecologism
    dark green 119, 121–3, 129–32
    eco-anarchism 125
    eco-feminism 127
    and the economy 130–1
    eco-socialism 126
    and human nature 128–9
    ideology 118–21
    light green 119, 124–5, 129–32
    origins 118
    social ecology 125, 129–32
    and society 130
    and the state 123, 129
ecology 118
economy
    and anarchism 114–15
    and conservatism 28, 31, 34, 37–9
    and ecologism 130–1
    and feminism 83
    invisible hand 22
    Keynesian economics 47–8, 54
    and liberalism 11, 21–2, 23–4
    and multiculturalism 100
    and nationalism 69
    protectionist economic policies 62
    and socialism 53–4
    steady-state 121
    trickle-down economics 31
    see also capitalism
eco-socialism 126
egalitarianism 42
ego 108
egoism 107–8
egotistical liberalism 11, 19
empiricism 29
enabling state 15
Engels, F. 41, 44–5, 50–4, 74
English Civil Wars 1642–51 27
Enlightenment 10, 19, 26, 41, 119
equality
    formal 12, 21
    foundational 17
    gender 16
    of opportunity 15
    social 41, 48
    wealth 37
Equality Act (2010) 73, 81, 91
equality feminism 76–7, 84
Equal Pay Act (1970) 81
ethnicity 68
ethnic nationalism 65

ethnies 58
existentialism 75

F

Fabian Society 46
fascism 57, 65
federations 109
femininity 75, 78
feminism
 difference versus equality 76–7, 84
 eco-feminism 127
 and the economy 83
 first wave 72–3
 and human nature 80–1
 liberal 72–3, 84–5
 Marxist 74, 84
 origins 72
 post-feminism 79
 postmodern 78–9, 84–5
 radical 74–7, 84, 85
 second wave 74–8
 socialist 78, 85
 and society 82–3
 and the state 81–2
 third wave 78–9
fiduciary power 12
formal equality 12, 21
Foster, J.B. 126, 129
foundational equality 17
Fourier, C. 41
Fox, W. 122
fragmented government 21
fraternity 51
freedom
 and anarchism 104
 and conservatism 29
 and liberalism 10, 12, 19
 negative 11, 13
 positive 14, 16
free-market capitalism 11, 21, 30–1, 33, 34
French Revolution 1789–99 26, 28, 30, 57–8
Friedan, B. 16, 18, 19, 21–2, 74, 82, 84

G

Garvey, M. 64, 68–9
gender 75
gender equality 16
gender pay gap 84
general will 57
Giddens, A. 44, 47, 49–50, 50–4
gigantism 123
Gilman, C.P. 73, 80, 83
globalisation 35, 66
Goldman, E. 104, 106, 113–14
government 13, 20, 34
 limited 20–1
 paternalistic 28–9
Green, T.H. 14, 16, 17, 19–20, 22
Green Party 125
green taxes 124
group-differentiated rights 91–2

H

harm principle 11, 13
Hayek, F.A. 18
hedonism 13
hierarchy 26, 28
historical materialism 42
Hobbes, T. 19, 27, 34, 35–7
holism 119, 131
homosexuality 37
hooks, b. 78–80, 82–4
human nature
 and anarchism 104, 112
 and conservatism 26–7, 30, 33, 35–6, 38
 and ecologism 128–9
 egotistical liberalism 11, 19–20
 and feminism 80–1
 and liberalism 10, 19–20, 22
 and multiculturalism 98
 and nationalism 68
 and socialism 51
hybridisation 96

I

identity 88–9
identity politics 87
immigration 66
imperialism 57, 65
individualism 12, 19, 22, 30, 32–3, 88, 103–4
individualist integration 90
individuality 13
industrialism 120
Industrial Revolution 41
intergenerational equity 119
intersectionality 79

K

Keynes, J.M. 15, 22
Keynesian economics 47–8, 54
Kropotkin, P. 104, 106, 111–13, 115
Kymlicka, W. 91–2, 97–100

L

Labour Party 46, 73
laws 12, 13, 21
Leopold, A. 121–2, 128, 130
liberal feminism 72–3, 84–5
liberal internationalism 60
liberalism
 classical 11–13, 72
 and democracy 14
 and the economy 11, 21–2, 23–4
 and human nature 10, 19, 22
 modern 13–18
 and multiculturalism 88, 90–1
 neo-liberalism 18–21, 23, 32, 49
 origins 10
 social 15
 and society 10, 21, 23
 and the state 10–15, 20–1, 23
liberal universalism 94

liberty 13–14, 19
light green ecologism 119, 124–5, 129–32
Lilly Ledbetter Fair Pay Act (2009) 81
limited government 20–1
'little platoons' 26, 29
Locke, J. 11–12, 17, 19, 20–3
Luxemburg, R. 45–6, 50–3

M

marriage 74
Marx, K. 41, 42–5, 48, 50–4
Marxism 42–3
Marxist feminism 74, 84
masculinity 75
materialism 121
Maurras, C. 66, 68–9
Mazzini, G. 61, 68–9
Mead, M. 75
mechanistic world view 119, 131
'melting pot' 60
Merchant, C. 127, 128–30
meritocracy 20
Merkel, A. 96
militarism 65
Mill, J.S. 11, 13–14, 17, 19, 20–1, 90
Millett, K. 74–7, 77, 80–3
minimal state 33
minority nationalism 59
minority rights 91–2, 97
Mirza, M. 96
misrecognition 89
modern liberalism 13–18
Modood, T. 95, 97, 99–100
monarchy 10, 12, 13, 27
multiculturalism
 assimilation 87–8
 cosmopolitan 96
 and the economy 100
 and human nature 98
 and identity 88–9
 liberal 91–3
 and liberalism 88, 90–1
 and nationalism 62
 origins 87
 pluralist 93–4
 and society 99
 and the state 98–9

N

nationalisation 46
nationalism
 and colonialism 63–5
 conservative 61–3, 70
 and the economy 69
 expansionist 65–7, 70
 and human nature 68
 liberal 59–61, 70
 origins 57
 and society 69
 and the state 68
National Organization for Women (NOW) 74
nations 58

nation-states 58, 61
negative freedom 11, 13
neo-liberalism 18–21, 23, 32, 49
New Age thinking 122
New Labour 50
New Lanark 41
New Right 28, 31–3, 37–8
Nez Perce peoples 122
night-watchman state 11
Nkrumah, K. 63–4
Nozick, R. 31, 33, 34, 36–8

O

Oakeshott, M. 28, 31, 34, 35–8
objectivism 32
one-nation conservatism 30–1
opportunity, equality of 15
organic society 26
Owen, R. 41

P

pan-Africanism 64, 67
pan-nationalism 65
Parekh, B. 94, 97–100
paternalism 28, 30
patriarchy 74, 76–7, 127
politics of recognition 89
positive discrimination 15, 73
positive freedom 14, 16
post-colonial nationalism 63–4
post-feminism 79
postmodern feminism 78–9, 84–5
power 20, 105
    and corruption 105
    fiduciary 12
    sovereign 27
pressure groups 109, 124
private sphere 74, 84
proletariat 42
property 11, 12, 33, 37–8, 43
protectionist economic policies 62
Proudhon, P.J. 103–4, 106, 110, 112–13, 115
public sphere 72, 84

R

racialism 66
radical feminism 74, 84, 85
Rand, A. 31, 32, 34, 36–7, 60
rationalism 30
Rawls, J. 17–18, 20
Reagan, R. 18
reductionism 119
reform Darwinism 73
religion 68, 106
reproductive labour 74
republicanism 13
revisionist socialism 47–50, 55
    see also social democracy
revolution 26, 45, 54, 76, 106, 116
Rothbard, M. 108, 113–15
Rousseau, J.J. 57–8, 68–9
Rowbotham, S. 78, 80–4
rule of law 21

S

Schumacher, E.F. 123, 128, 130
scientific socialism 41
self-determination 59–60, 63, 70
self-interest 31, 32–3
self-ownership 33
self-realisation 121
separatist feminism 77, 84
sex, and gender 75
sexual politics 77
Smith, A. 21
Smith, A.D. 58
social contract theory 12, 20
social democracy 47–8, 52–3, 55
social ecology 125, 129–32
social equality 41, 48
socialism
    common ownership 43, 46–7
    and the economy 53–4
    eco-socialism 126
    evolutionary/reformist 45–6, 52–3
    and human nature 51
    ideology 41–50
    origins 41
    revisionist 47–50, 55
    revolutionary 45, 52–3, 54
    and society 52–3
    and the state 52
    third way 46–7, 48–9, 52–3, 55
socialist feminism 78, 85
social justice 33, 48
social liberalism 15
society
    and anarchism 114
    anti-permissive 32
    and conservatism 30, 31, 36–7, 38
    and ecologism 130
    and feminism 82–3
    and liberalism 10, 21, 23
    and multiculturalism 99
    and nationalism 69
    organic 26
    and socialism 52–3
solidarity 104
sovereign power 27, 59–60
spirituality 122–3
state 10, 103
    and anarchism 105–6, 112–13
    and conservatism 32–3, 34, 36, 38
    and ecologism 123, 129
    enabling state 15
    and feminism 81–2
    and liberalism 10–15, 20–1, 23
    minimal 33
    and multiculturalism 90, 98–9
    and nationalism 68
    nation-states 58, 61
    and power 12
    social contract theory 12, 20
    and socialism 52
state-nationalism 59
state of nature 12, 27
statism 32
steady-state economy 121
stereotyping 89
Stirner, M. 103–4, 106–7, 113–15
strike action 45–6
suffrage 45, 55
suffragettes 74
suffragists 74
Sunak, R. 28
supranationalism 62, 66
sustainability 120–1, 122–3, 132
sustainable development 120
syndicalism 111

T

Taylor, C. 89, 97–9
Thatcher, M. 18, 37
third way 46–7, 48–9, 52–3, 55
tolerant society 10
trade unions 45–6
trickle-down economics 31
Trump, D. 62
Truss, L. 28

U

Ujamaa, J.N. 63
United States
    American Revolution 1775–83 29
    Black Power movement 89
    Civil Rights Act (1964) 73, 81
    Declaration of Independence 1776 10
    nationalism 62, 67
Universal Negro Improvement Association (UNIA) 64
universal suffrage 45, 55
utopianism 107
utopian socialists 41, 51

V

value pluralism 93
von Herder, J.G. 62–3, 68–9

W

Walby, S. 76
Waldron, J. 96
wealth inequality 37
Webb, B. 45, 46, 50–4
Weber, M. 103
welfare state 15, 18
'Wilt Chamberlain' argument 33
Wolf, N. 76
Wollstonecraft, M. 11, 12–13, 17, 19, 21, 72, 80, 82
women
    education 72
    equality and rights 12, 15, 16, 22, 72–3, 113
    see also feminism

Y

Young Italy 61

Notes